Rozelle

Jerry Izenberg

Rozelle

A BIOGRAPHY

Foreword by David Stern

UNIVERSITY OF NEBRASKA PRESS
LINCOLN AND LONDON

Library of Congress Cataloging-in-Publication
Data

Izenberg, Jerry.
Rozelle: a biography / Jerry Izenberg;
foreword by David Stern.
pages cm
Summary: "A biography of Pete Rozelle, the man
who brought the NFL to the forefront of profes-
sional sports"—Provided by publisher.
Includes bibliographical references and index.
ISBN 978-0-8032-5574-6 (hardback)
ISBN 978-0-8032-6697-1 (epub)
ISBN 978-0-8032-6698-8 (mobi)
ISBN 978-0-8032-6699-5 (pdf)
1. Rozelle, Pete. 2. Football commissioners—
United States—Biography. I. Title.
GV939.R695.I94 2014
796.332092—dc23
[B]
2014016577

Set in Janson Text by L. Auten.

For Anne Marie (Rozelle) Bratton, clearly her father's daughter

Contents

Illustrations

Foreword

by David Stern

During my career I have had the great fortune to know and work with many talented and creative sports executives. Pete Rozelle was unique among them. Pete was a passionate and knowledgeable fan, an extraordinary communicator and marketer, and a visionary commissioner. He also had a keen wit and a generosity of spirit that were on display to all who knew him.

Pete was the iconic commissioner for those who came after him, a complete package. He excelled in all key areas of commissionership, including league administration and the relationship between the league and its teams, where his efforts transformed the National Football League (NFL). With his background in public relations (PR), Pete was an extraordinary marketer, becoming the first sports "brand manager," with a broad understanding of all that would entail. Under his guidance, the strength of the NFL brand led to a bond with the American public that has only grown in subsequent years.

And, of course, he was legendary for his negotiations with the television networks over his league's broadcast rights. Before Pete assumed his commissionership, interest in individual NFL teams was local. Recognizing competitive balance was the key to the league's success, Pete convinced the owners that forming a strong partnership was in their best interests, and they started by combining their games into one television package and splitting the revenues equally. Revenue sharing was only one of Pete's innovations. Confident there was an audience for a primetime weeknight game, Pete pitched the idea, and *Monday Night Football* was born. Pete also had a concept for the NFL's championship game.

He turned that vision into the Super Bowl, America's preeminent sporting event and perennially one of the most watched programs on television.

Like any chief executive officer (CEO), Pete had his share of challenges, and there, too, he met them head-on. He was only thirty-three when he became commissioner, but he established his authority quickly, earning the trust and respect of the league's owners and players. Understanding that the NFL's integrity was vital to its reputation, Pete early in his tenure fined the legendary George Halas for abusing officials, and a year later he suspended two of the league's biggest stars, Paul Hornung and Alex Karras, for betting on NFL games. Decades later, Pete led the way in combating the use of steroids and other performance-enhancing drugs. In speaking out publicly on the issue, Pete expressed great concern about the dangers the drugs posed to players who used them.

Pete was also politically savvy, twice petitioning Congress successfully to grant the NFL exemptions to the Sherman Anti-Trust Act. He believed the NFL was strongest when its franchises acted in concert for the best interests of the sport, and the first exemption allowed the teams to sell the television rights to their games collectively. The second, long rumored to have been assisted by the grant of the Saints franchise to Senator Russell Long's beloved Louisiana, allowed the NFL to merge with the American Football League (AFL), a major building block of today's immensely successful NFL. When the teams stopped cooperating, Pete's enthusiasm for his job waned, as the Oakland Raiders sued the league. It bothered Pete terribly that his league was being torn apart by one of his teams—to say nothing of the endless depositions.

That Pete was able to accomplish so much has much to do with his business acumen and vision. But he was also extraordinarily well prepared; few people knew as much about the issues or were as adept at reading people and situations as Pete. When you are in a position of leadership and are able to accrete experience, facts, and knowledge, there comes a time when you know more about the key topics than most everybody else. Simply stated,

there were no questions on any sports-related subject where Pete was not comfortable.

On a personal note, for me Pete was more than simply the archetype of what the modern sports commissioner could and should be. When I became commissioner of the National Basketball Association (NBA) in 1984, Pete was wonderfully helpful. He could not have been more giving of his time, sharing his experiences and expertise, no matter the subject. I was fortunate to get to know him. There was, over our years, a fair amount of tennis played on Sundays—Pete was as competitive on the tennis court as he was in the boardroom. When Pete announced he was stepping down, he and I had lunch together; I wanted to personally thank him for the example he had set and the help he had provided. I also attended his retirement party. It was there that he told a couple of saucy jokes, which I have embraced as my own in later years. That was Pete, though. He was warm. He was genuine. He was funny.

There is nobody better able to tell Pete's story than the acclaimed veteran sports journalist and columnist Jerry Izenberg. Jerry has reported on many of the key sports figures and events of the past sixty years. He is one of only a handful of reporters to have covered every Super Bowl, and few people, if any, are as knowledgeable about the sport of football and the NFL as he.

As one of the most highly respected professionals in his field, Jerry's body of work is extraordinary and his knowledge of the subject unparalleled. Having long been a fan of his writing, I have no doubt readers will find his telling of Pete's story to be complete, insightful, witty, and well written.

Acknowledgments

I am indebted to numerous people for the extraordinary amount of time they gave me during this four-decade search for the many dimensions of Pete Rozelle. There were many, far too numerous to mention here, but the ones to whom I owe a particular debt of gratitude are Pete's daughter, Anne Marie Bratton; former NFL commissioner Paul Tagliabue; Joe Browne; Ernie Accorsi; Art Modell and Wellington Mara, both of whom sadly passed away before this book was finished; Anson Christian; Colleen Smith-Grubb; Aileen and Bob Izenberg; and, finally, my long-suffering agent, Peter Sawyer.

Rozelle

Prologue

It was the year when we all reached the undeniable conclusion that Pete Rozelle had put a golden lariat around all of professional football and brought it peace in our time at last. Al Davis was merged and deceptively (but temporarily) silenced. College All-Americans, once wooed by the NFL and the AFL with money, women, and more money, had been dumped into the new common draft. Now, with the end of the war between the two leagues, the most talented college football players on the planet were lucky if they could get a scout to buy them a cup of coffee.

It was January 1969, and we were in Miami Beach, at the Doral Beach Hotel, the media and league headquarters for Super Bowl III. This would be the Super Bowl of "Joe Willie" Namath and his "guarantee of victory" that rocked America's 100-yard world. It was the game that finally breathed credibility into the notion of one football universe indivisible and bankable under the benevolent dictatorship of one man.

His name was Pete Rozelle.

Subsequent events would stamp him as the man who, above anyone else, gave America a brand-new national game. Nobody— not Kennesaw Mountain Landis (who scrubbed the Black Sox scandal white as snow), not Walter O'Malley (who opened the West Coast to the high-powered business of sports), not David Stern (who saved the NBA from banishment forever as a cable-TV sport), not Avery Brundage (the International Olympic Committee dictator)—had the impact on sports in the twentieth century that Pete Rozelle did.

He never played the game. He never owned a franchise. He

never went to law school. He never even was a serious candidate for the job that would ultimately catapult him into the role of lord high architect of every new artistic and economic advance that made the NFL the trailblazer for all of sports in the second half of the twentieth century.

The men who owned the National Football League didn't even think of him as the combination of George Halas (the football maven), George Preston Marshall (entertainment genius), and Moses (the parter of a sea of red ink) necessary to keep them artistically and economically afloat. At the time they weren't even sure what they wanted. But Rozelle, a reluctant candidate, knew what they needed once he became the commissioner. Time and again he would surprise them, to the point that they eventually rarely questioned his wisdom.

Back on that evening in Miami Beach (Super Bowl III minus three days), I was sitting in the hotel bar with Jim Kensil, who would put in sixteen years in the NFL office under Rozelle before he became president of the Jets in 1977. Rozelle repeatedly referred to him during his tenure as "my offensive and defensive coordinator," and with good reason.

Recruited out of the Associated Press (AP) sports department to serve as Rozelle's director of public relations, he ultimately became the commissioner's sounding board, friend, trusted lieutenant, and point man. His effectiveness was matched only by his loyalty to his boss.

We had each drunk a great deal that evening. Now Kensil—a good friend—was pissed at me because I was reminding him that his boss was simply a czar of 100-yard jocks and not a man for the ages. My belligerence was not his fault. My first marriage was already rocketing toward disaster, and the alcohol was not helping my mood. Ironically, when we talked later, those very circumstances and our shared experiences as "single parents raising children" would give Rozelle and me a common bond.

"You think you know the guy," Kensil, clearly annoyed because I was not yet ready to canonize his boss, insisted, "but you really don't know him. Very few people do. He is capable of anything he sets his mind to. I really think that this is a guy who could find a way to settle the war in Vietnam if he were a diplomat."

"Don't be ridiculous."

Clearly, in that moment we were both tipsy and pissed off.

I began to stagger off toward my room. A long line had formed outside the elevators, and at the rear Pete Rozelle had joined it. "Great," I mumbled to myself. "Don't tell me this freakin' elevator stops at Saigon." And then I waved and he nodded back, and I walked over and said something very pithy like, "You got a minute?"

"From the size of this line, I've got an hour," he said and laughed. So we walked back to the lobby and sat on a low bench, and I thought, hyperbole aside, what if Kensil is right about this guy? What will be his next move?

"It's none of my business," I said, "but what the hell is a nice guy like you doing in a place like this? I mean, why don't you get the hell out of the football business and do something interesting?"

"I thought about that," he said. "A lot of people have talked to me about running for public office, but that's really out of the question. But, yes, I thought about making a change for some of the reasons you said, but then I had to make a much more serious personal decision. I wanted to put together enough investments and things so that my daughter would never have to worry. And then I wanted to get other parts of my own life straight."

Having worked hard to raise his daughter from a previous marriage, he would ultimately remarry. With that possibility in the back of his mind, he added, "I think now I just want to sit back and enjoy life."

The Pete Rozelle I knew and the Pete Rozelle I would discover more than thirty years ago when I first decided to write this book always enjoyed life. But sit back? That would have been like telling the Mississippi River not to roll.

I never did ask him if he planned to go to Vietnam. Kensil being

Kensil, he never would have forgiven me for that. But it was on that night that the notion of this book began to take shape.

Why I didn't begin to write it then was very simple. After the merger I figured he would not occupy as much of my time anymore. In private I had found him to be shrewd, willing to concede a point, inquisitive on his own, and not afraid to tell an anecdote (which was invariably usable). And never after the fact did he append, "Of course, that's off the record."

I thought that our relationship from that point forward would be casual and that I would miss the way it had been. It seemed to me that all he had to do was sit back and let the good times roll. I was wrong. There were more worlds left to conquer for him than either of us knew. There would be more head-knocking with Al Davis . . . major labor troubles . . . and, of course, the United States Football League (USFL) lawsuit. I think the latter wore him down the most.

As a syndicated columnist I had continued to write about the man, the workings of his inner sanctum, and the trials and perils of the NFL. But in 1977 I began to do serious research for a book I knew I would one day write.

That was the year I told Pete what I planned to do, and he said he'd rather I didn't. He wanted to keep his private world private. I reminded him that whether he wanted it or not, somebody would write one, and then, as we sat in his office, I told him, "It's going to happen, but the truth is that nobody who would write one really knows who you are. At the bottom, I sure as hell don't. Give me the names of the people nobody knows . . . the people I should interview beyond the obvious football names . . . the people who shaped you. I want to start with them."

A week later Kensil called me with the message that Pete had thought about it and he would do it. We were to meet in his office. After that meeting I set out to find another Pete Rozelle to fill in the blanks on the public one I already knew.

For openers I got to interview people who have since passed away and without those meetings would never have been on the record about Rozelle. That side of it began as though I were trying to unravel a mystery. The football people I knew were already part of my work. They were easy.

But finding the past that became the prologue that would shape him into the dominant sports administrator of our time was not. The key to understanding that for me was light-years from the Sunday world in which Rozelle was king. I found it in the lush vineyard country of Sonoma, California, from a man named Myron De Long, who shared a critical slice of that past with him.

De Long and Rozelle grew up together in Lynwood, a suburb of Los Angeles. They went to the same schools, played on the same teams, and dated the same girls. They each went off to World War II, met again afterward, founded something called the Compton Junior College (JC) News Bureau, and later finished their educations at the University of San Francisco (USF), where they worked in the Athletic Department.

When De Long became an educator and Rozelle became football's leader with the golden touch, they remained friends. As Rozelle moved from one opportunity to the next—always on an upward path—most saw his growth as the residue of incredible luck. But De Long understood what Branch Rickey meant when he said, "Luck is the residue of design."

All along De Long felt that Rozelle was destined for something special. He explained it to me like this: "I've had a lot of people tell me that all his life Pete happened to be in the right place at the right time. That would seem to indicate that most of which happened to him happened out of sheer luck. That could be true except for one thing. Every time . . . and I mean *every* time it happened . . . he knew exactly what to do. I mean, every time he was ready every step of the way. That wasn't luck. That was Pete." It was the stuff of which giant footprints were made.

David Stern, the commissioner of the National Basketball Association, knew exactly where the quality De Long spoke of led

Rozelle. "Baseball is America's pastime," he told me when discussing Pete. "Basketball is America's game. But Pete Rozelle made football America's passion."

If you doubt that, then find me the president who would dare schedule a national television address to coincide with the kickoff on Super Bowl Sunday.

1

In the Beginning

Just as the twig is bent, the tree's inclined.
—Alexander Pope

Now that I think of it, I can honestly say that we never once discussed his personal goals. He had a lot of friends, but to my knowledge he never had a confidant.
—Myron De Long, longtime boyhood friend

What Pete Rozelle was was the product of a classic, traditional small-town American upbringing. If there hadn't been a Lynwood, California, Norman Rockwell would have invented it. It was virtually an all-white town, an insular place that was home first to hardscrabble farmers and later known as one of America's first suburbs—just nine miles southwest of Los Angeles and home to more than a few workers at the Alcoa plant in nearby Vernon.

Across the line that was Alameda Street lay the crazy-quilt sprawl of Watts, even then an Afro-American enclave. Lives on either side of that line rarely mingled back then.

Looking through the prism of history, Lynwood was not just a dot on the expanding map of California. It was a kind of movie-lot definition of small-town America. The Lynwood of the 1930s and 1940s was Jimmy Stewart in *It's a Wonderful Life* and Mickey Rooney in *Love Finds Andy Hardy*.

And why not? According to Bill Cunningham, a contemporary of Rozelle who served for years on the town's parks and recreation commission, Lynwood "may have been the place where the idea of the drive-in restaurant was born. We had one on Long Beach

Boulevard," he says, and you get the idea that teenage Pete and his buddies went there as much for the carhops as the burgers.

"Growing up in Lynwood was a lot of simple but terrific things," the late Myron De Long once told me. Theirs was a friendship that lasted beyond Lynwood and beyond the University of San Francisco, where they later worked in the sports information department.

De Long was the perfect source to reconstruct the way it was for the two of them and their friends in a Lynwood boyhood. When I met him it was in his home in the Sonoma wine country, where he had become a respected educator.

Remarking on the difference between their Lynwood days and the way it had become for that whole generation, he said, "The kids, they grow up too fast now, get sophisticated too soon. They've got all the answers right away—they think. The world has to be boxed and organized for them. They have never had the pure fun of just being young."

In reaching into the back roads of his mind to re-create the way it was and what they shared during those years, he had the recall of a man who knows who he was and what that did for him and his friends. He did not let the calendar deceive him. Steve Owen, the old New York Football Giants coach, used to say that the more years a player is retired, the faster he thinks he used to run.

But Myron De Long still clearly saw the way it was. I asked him what Lynwood was to him and Pete, and the answer came right on the money.

Lynwood was a man named Bill Schliebaum [years later hired by Pete as an NFL official] who ran the playground and coached Duke Snider [later a great Dodgers center fielder] in three sports but who always had the time to shoot free throws for Cokes with you. You hung around in the summer and you got up a touch football game or you played some tennis, and in between Schliebaum had us hopping in the school yard.

It was date nights at the Arden Theater with the malt shop next door. Girls were just something that were there. You would date them,

but then you switched the next time out. You knew you were supposed to take them somewhere, so you did it. But it was never a big deal.

What Duke Snider did for our high school teams in Compton was a big deal for us, and when Pete, who worked part-time for the Long Beach newspaper, wrote about Duke and we got to read it in the paper, that was a big deal. You know, in high school they played on the same basketball team. And the biggest days of the fall were about running home after school to hear about the World Series on the radio. Now that was the biggest deal of all.

And amazing as it sounds, I can't recall ever seeing one of us—any one of us—hit somebody. Fights? It was something that just never happened.

De Long also remembered that a mutual friend named Louie Joseph had an older brother who had a car. "He would drive us into Los Angeles to the magical attraction of Gittleson's Twin Links, which to us was the Augusta National of miniature golf courses." There, among the tiny windmills and the metal chutes, they would battle for a quarter a man, winner take all. "You won't believe the way Pete could concentrate. We would stand behind him and jump up and down and yell, but we could never psyche him out in those matches. The thing is I never met a competitor so intense as he was. Even in college he played hearts as though it were life and death."

When they were in high school, oratorical contests were a big thing in Southern California. What made them an even bigger attraction was the fact that you could get time off from school to prepare. There was that and the monetary prize that the American Legion gave to the top three finishers. "Just about the time a big one was coming up, a bunch of us tried to get him to go ice skating," De Long recalled.

That was a big thing to most of our bunch, but I doubt that Pete had ever even been on ice skates until that day. He didn't want to come because he was working on his speech, and I guess you could say we actually kidnapped him.

Anyway, he gets to the rink, and we helped him around a few times, and then we put him on the end of a whip. Then somebody said, "Okay, turn him loose. He's on his own."

So he staggers off, and the next thing you know, there's this tremendous crash, and he goes down face-first and there's blood all over the ice. So now we get him home, and his mother is really furious at us. Then she wipes the blood off his face and sees there's a tooth missing. For a minute I thought she was really going to kill us.

That was on Friday, and the contest was on Sunday. His folks took him to the dentist, and they got him a false tooth. Now he goes in the bathroom and looks in the mirror and starts to practice his speech, and he sounds like Donald Duck. His dad said he practiced all night and all day Saturday.

And darned if he didn't go to the auditorium on Sunday and compete. He didn't win, but it shows you how determined he was about anything and everything he ever wanted to do.

Determination and commitment. It didn't happen by accident. Decades later when he was interviewed at the National Academy of Achievement, he spoke extensively about his father's influence:

He did so much with what he had. He never went to college more or less because of the Depression. My dad had a great influence on me, particularly later, because I was so impressed with what he did with his life. He was already a young man during the Depression, and he had this local grocery store and before that, when I was very young, we had an earthquake—1932—while he was the manager of another store. He went down there during the after-shock and he couldn't believe how bad it was.

Everything was shattered. He swept the Rinso and Oxydol together; sold it as Earthquake Soap. It was as though it were almost against his religion to waste anything. My mother and father made do with what they had and I'm not quite sure how they did it but, tough as it was for them, they gave my brother and me a genuine middle class home. They never made a big deal over money in front of us but we knew they were struggling and I have to say that my father, just through

his example, gave me a terrific sense of work ethic as an obligation without ever lecturing.

The Rozelle home was at 3705 Agnes Avenue, and they moved into it after two previous rental homes. When they made the move into their version of the Lynwood American dream, Pete was five years old. It was the only boyhood home he remembered.

"I am," his father, Ray Rozelle, told me when I visited him there, "the longest continual resident of Lynwood, and since I don't feel like going anywhere, I guess I'll hold that title a little longer."

He shared a lot of photos with me. They were yellowed by the passage of time, and as he spoke his vivid memories made it clear how important it was to him and his wife to create a family environment even in the toughest of times.

If you had to characterize Ray and Hazel, who had passed away in 1972 before I met him, you'd have to say they were part of a tough, proud slice of America that looked the Great Depression in the eye, went crashing to the canvas, and struggled to their feet before somebody could run over and give them a mandatory eight count.

In 1919 Ray Rozelle came out of the U.S. Navy and hustled for a job as a machinist. Then he met Hazel Healey, whose parents had come west from Illinois four years earlier, virtually at the start of America's California-or-Bust migration. A year after that they were married. Eventually, they gambled their small savings on a neighborhood grocery store they called the Pacific Market.

Pete was born in 1926 and a younger brother, Dick, in 1929. That was the same year that America made a sharp economic U-turn. The Depression slammed across the face of America. Suddenly, Ray and Hazel were struggling to save their store. Ray told me:

I guess anybody who was around at that time recalls the way it was. The big crash hit. We tried to survive. What money I had, I put in three different banks. Nobody had much, and there wasn't much you could do if you were in the grocery business except to give credit to the people who needed it, and there were so many of them . . . too many of them.

Well, you know how it was. I just gave too much credit. Then two of the three banks we had the money in went bust, and then FDR closed the third one when he shut them all down in 1932. I was working every night until after eight or nine, so I didn't get to spend much time with my boys in those days.

On top of that we had a terrible earthquake that destroyed half the town that same year. We managed to hang on until '39, and then I just saw there wasn't any way, so I went over to Alcoa and I was twenty-six years with them until I retired.

It is a fact of life of the Depression generation that the economic problems of the parents shaped the sons. The Rozelles, like many other parents in what then was a basically farming community, clung to the belief that none of this might have happened if they had been able to get more formal education. The academic competition among that generation's children, therefore, was intense all across the country.

Because there was no money in their homes, all of them hustled and studied and then hustled some more. Pete and his friends all mowed lawns and delivered groceries, but when he entered Compton High School, something happened that changed his life forever. He discovered journalism. A blend of circumstances and motivation turned him into an incredible part-time bread winner. It also gave him a sense of the power of communication that was so much a part of the incredible success he would eventually become. "Once he started doing work for the *Long Beach Press-Telegram*," Ray Rozelle recalled, "he always had money. There were times he could have maybe four hundred dollars in his drawer. Of course, part of that was because he never seemed to spend much. Living in Lynwood didn't require that."

But on the eve of Pete's scheduled matriculation at Compton High (Lynwood was still too small to have its own high school), Ray and Hazel made a decision that had a profound impact on his life. The principal of his elementary school had proposed to move him up an entire grade because of his gifted academic record.

Pete was athletic but undersized. The Rozelles wondered if his academic achievements might surpass his social life and his maturing. They were concerned that there might be a social gap between him and his classmates.

"Well, we had some neighbors who had moved to Modesto the year before," Ray recalled. "They had this ranch, and we thought why couldn't we hold him out a year and let him go on up there and work on the ranch so he could fill out physically and do some social maturing? He went up there for ten months, and he worked with horses and pigs and cows. He set up a basketball hoop to improve his game when he had time off. When he came home we were amazed. I think he crammed two years of maturity and physical growth into those ten months."

The sabbatical from school had another far-reaching effect. It put him into a social group of classmates that created the bond with friends like De Long and Joseph and a number of others that lasted all through their adult lives.

Both his father and De Long remembered the adolescent Pete Rozelle as a kid with an enormous drive to get things done but with little interest in ego or ceremony. As a case in point, it is worth noting that neither of them attended their subsequent graduations from Compton Junior College after the war. They chose, instead, to go fishing.

Back when they were seniors in 1944 at Compton High, Lynwood, like the rest of their generation all around the country, began to change. Familiar faces disappeared, scattered to the battlefields of Europe and the Pacific. World War II was breaking up that old gang of Pete's.

"I remember," Rozelle told me, "that when we were juniors in high school, Myron had gone to one of those grade-B movies at the Arden—I don't recall which one, but it was probably a 'John Wayne in the Pacific' kind of flick—and the next day he told me, 'This is personal for me now. I got to get into the navy.' Well, I felt the same way. My dad was navy in World War I, and Myron and my other friends had their minds made up, so I guess mine was made up, too."

Rozelle tried to enlist three times and was turned down all three. But a challenge to Rozelle was like a debt unpaid. Because the military's left hand never seemed to know what its right hand was doing, Rozelle finally got his wish.

"It was the damnedest thing," his dad told me.

He got rejected each time because he was color-blind. They wouldn't let him enlist, but then they drafted him. So Pete goes over to the draft board in Los Angeles, and there is this huge line. It must have stretched out longer than a city block.

Well, it was getting near lunch, and one of the guys comes out a side door and sees Pete and he hands him some money and asks, "Will you get me a quart of milk?" and Pete says he will if the guys saves his place, because Pete is thinking that maybe when he gets back, the guy will let him in early.

When he comes back with the milk and knocks on the side door, the fellow takes him inside and asks what he wants—army or navy. The guys tells him, "Okay, it's navy if that's what you prefer, but all these other guys are going into the army." After three tries, he gets a guy a quart of milk and he's in the navy.

After his basic training he was assigned to a ship—and what a ship, a rusty old bucket of bolts called the *Gardoqui*, named after a Spanish gunboat captured during the Spanish-American War. The navy converted it into a class of tanker called the Double Eagle but did not rename it. It had been refitted, and its keel was laid down at the Kearny shipyard in New Jersey in 1921. The uss Missouri it was not.

"It was an old standard tanker," Rozelle recalled, not exactly the pride of the Pacific fleet.

What it was was kind of a seagoing filling station. You go out some-place and wait, and sooner or later people came to you. It was hardly the stuff of which war movies were made.

We had a small crew (seventy men including officers), and every-one had to stand wheel watch. It was so old; it wasn't electronic and

it was a big, old heavy thing, and you were forever trying to compensate because it was so tough to keep it on course.

Right after the war ended, they sent us into Tokyo Bay, and that became kind of a dramatic thing. We were getting close to the mainland, and a lookout spotted a floating mine that had broken loose from its mooring. It was headed straight toward us, and I remember we had to make a hard right to avoid it. But, really, that was the highlight of my career as far as danger was concerned.

Two months later we had discharged our cargo and headed back to sea, back to Pearl Harbor, through the Panama Canal to Mobile. We arrived in January. That's pretty much my entire navy career.

"Not exactly," I suggested. "Myron De Long told me that you ran the football pools on the *Gardoqui*. Did you?"

"Well, I don't quite remember that," he said, but his face lit up in the kind of aurora borealis of a smile that was a Rozelle trademark.

I will admit that on at least on one occasion, I did engage in a little freelance bookmaking.

I knew a little more about football than most of the crew did. Most of them were Catholic, and they were great Notre Dame fans. That's all they were talking about that November because Note Dame was getting ready to play Army. Now this was the Blanchard-Davis era, and Army was loaded, one of the best college football teams ever.

Well, all these guys did was talk about the Irish this and the Irish that, and so I said, "Well, suppose I take Army, and I'll give you and the Irish eight points."

Rozelle laughed again and said it was the easiest money he ever made. Army won by a mere 49–0.

"Isn't that gambling?"

"Well," he said, then he paused and threw back his head and laughed, "not if you knew football."

So here came Pete Rozelle, retired yeoman, retired "bookmaker," and hungry young man, marching home after the war, and if you studied him closely at that stage, you would have had to conclude

that there was very little difference between him and millions of other young men in the same circumstance. At loose ends and thinking about a career in journalism (his dream was to become sports editor of the *Los Angeles Times*) and entitled to financing from the GI Bill, Rozelle returned to Compton and enrolled in the local junior college.

Among the returning servicemen in that freshman class was his old buddy Myron De Long. "A lot of things began to happen that year," De Long recalled. "They obviously shaped his life, and in a way they shaped mine as well, because when they were over, I knew what I didn't want to be."

The event that had the biggest long-range impact on Rozelle's ultimate calling was taking place a continent away in New York City. Even as the old *Gardoqui* was docking in Mobile for decommissioning, the NFL owners were meeting to vote on a request by owner Dan Reeves to move his Cleveland franchise to Los Angeles.

The Rams had beaten the Washington Redskins a month earlier to win the 1945 league championship. But theirs was a typical NFL story for many owners. Champions or not, the team had lost fifty thousand dollars that year. And the future did not look any better.

The rival All-America Football Conference's Cleveland Browns were for real. Their league was headed for NFL merger, and the Browns were the hottest football team in either league. The prospect of two Cleveland football teams was unacceptable. It scared the hell out of Reeves.

With a guaranteed lease offer from the Los Angeles Coliseum in hand, Reeves sought permission to move. He was denied on the very first vote. Enraged, he threatened to walk out and sell the club. Then one of the lodge brothers wondered how they were going to explain that the NFL, still seeking a significant fan base in many of its cities, had lost its championship franchise.

Off that rare burst of logic, they took another vote, and the Rams were headed to Los Angeles. Compton Junior College had a nationally acclaimed football program with appropriate facilities. The Rams set up their preseason training camp there.

Meanwhile, Rozelle and De Long, on campus with tuition paid by the GI Bill, were hustling once again. They had set up the Compton News Bureau to add to their walking-around money, with Compton JC football as the vehicle.

"A guy named Maxwell Stiles was doing the Rams' publicity," De Long recalled, "and Pete knew him from the days when Pete was working part-time at the *Long Beach Press-Telegram*. So he walks into our office and asks us to put together the programs for their preseason games."

That's when Rozelle first met Tex Schramm, who would have a major impact on him within a few years, and Reeves, who would have an even bigger one.

"So the Rams came down to Compton that summer," De Long said, "and it was like we woke up suddenly in the middle of Fairyland. I mean, here we were, two kids just out of the navy, and now we were running around the practice field, rubbing shoulders with Tom Harmon and Kenny Washington and Bob Waterfield. And there was Jane Russell, Waterfield's fiancée and Hollywood pinup queen, at every practice."

For De Long, this was heady stuff. But for Pete, it was another step in valuable on-the-job training. He was learning his job, and as a bonus he got fifty bucks for putting out the exhibition-game programs. To quote De Long, "Pete was in football heaven."

Then the Rams left for LA to start the season, but they didn't miss a beat because Compton had a terrific football team that year. They did their publicity and covered Compton for the local papers. "We felt they were good enough to represent the West in the Junior Rose Bowl," De Long said. They were right. They were young and eager, and suddenly they were caught up in an aura of self-importance. "I'd be a liar if I said we didn't feel like that," De Long admitted. Here they were just a few months out of the service, giving out radio interviews and going into newspaper offices and planting stories. "Looking back now, I can see what was happening," De Long said with genuine insight. "Pete was getting ready for a career, and I was just having a hell of a lot of fun."

The following year we were so sure that Compton would be back in the game that we sat up all night writing press releases and stuffing envelopes. Cameron College [of Oklahoma] was the visiting team. Then Pete calls down to the newspaper to see if the selection committee has made a decision about the home team. The guy tells him they did, and they didn't pick us. They picked Chaffey Community College.

I think that over all the years I've known him, that's the only time I ever saw him really angry. Angry? Hell, he was furious. We were tearing up all the press releases and cursing and stomping. Looking back, I can see that both of us acted as though it were some kind of directly personal insult.

They took it so personally that the heart went out of the Compton jc News Bureau after that. With graduation on the horizon, they shut it down. But before they did, an unexpected opportunity would step out of the shadows to put the future czar of professional football's life on the road to his place in history.

Indirectly, it began with Louis Joseph, the young man whose brother, Emile, had been the wheelman on those pre—World War II expeditions in Compton to play miniature golf. Joseph, a determined but never gifted athlete who had played on the Compton High School basketball team with Rozelle and Snider, desperately wanted to go on to college. Through sheer self-discipline, he had made himself an acceptable player. With a plan that would have done honor to the legend of Frank Merriwell, it was his idea to enroll at Notre Dame, try out for basketball, and win a free ride.

But fairy tales usually remain just that. He didn't make it, but while he was there he met a young man from Milwaukee who was trying to do the same thing. His name was Paul Schramka, and along with Joseph he was also cut, but a friend told him that Pete Newell, the coach at the University of San Francisco, was looking for what he euphemistically called "physically motivated" players. Schramka, who never threw an elbow he didn't like, headed for the city they were beginning to call Baghdad by the Bay.

Newell found a use for his limited skills. Later when Rozelle

and De Long would wind up on the USF campus, they dubbed his forte "the Schramka Sacrifice." It was a highly complex maneuver worthy of a caveman. The opponent had the ball . . . the opponent had the shot . . . and then the opponent had two free throws, because Schramka had put him up in the eleventh row, and it is very difficult to shoot from there with a guy from Milwaukee attached to your sternum.

So Schramka became a substitute and a scholarship player with the USF Dons. That season Newell took the team south to play the University of Southern California (USC). Rozelle and De Long were at the game, and because Schramka had heard about him from Louis Joseph during their brief stay at Notre Dame, he introduced them to his coach.

Newell asked them about the Compton News Bureau and how it worked. Then he told them, "I may be calling you guys. We are going to need some help with publicity."

Joe Kuharich, a new football coach, had been hired. Newell's basketball team was on the brink of big-time results, and both would play a major role in Rozelle's future.

The future commissioner of the NFL always did think a jump or two ahead. "We both wanted to get our four-year degrees," Rozelle recalled when I asked him what motivated them to head for USF. "I didn't think the academics were going to interfere with the job. I knew that sports were really my life. I got good grades. I got mostly As and some Bs all through school, but I really crashed to get them. I didn't stay up with my studies as I should have to really learn. I'd cram for a test and get an A or a B. So now if I could get a degree and a salary [he would get both] and still stay in sports, I figured USF would be a good deal."

"I don't know what he got," De Long told me, "and I really never cared. I was working toward a degree, getting five bucks a month for laundry, and I was single and we had the GI Bill. I was having fun, and in my heart I just wanted to knock around until I figured out what I really wanted to do with my life. With Pete, it was different. I'm sure he already knew."

And as would happen so often in the future, he was headed for the right place at the right time. Swept along by the postwar boom, a group of local businessmen were interested in making USF a major sports attraction for the city. You can find similar groups at almost every major college in America. They are called boosters, and they believe that winning teams will make their schools something special. This group had money and influence. There were five of them headed by a local construction tycoon named Charlie Harney. Newell, who saw where the school's athletic program was headed, convinced Harney to interview Roselle and De Long. Realizing they wanted degrees and the money was secondary, Harney hired them.

"Right from the start," Rozelle told me, "San Francisco had a special attraction for me. It's a tight geographical city like New York, and I like that. I like a well-ordered place."

All his adult life, it remained a favorite for him. To use his word, what he liked the most was its "character." But his arrival at USF was not an "I Left My Heart in San Francisco" kind of social thing. It was 1948 and he felt he was on his way toward something, and through yet another set of strange circumstances he had come to the place that would be the next vehicle for it.

The University of San Francisco is a Jesuit school located near Golden Gate Park in the heart of the city. Like the whole American spectrum in general and urban colleges in particular, both its scope and its role underwent massive changes in the years immediately following World War II. For a time the returning GIS even changed the way they dealt with that mission.

These were young men in a hurry. They had been ripped summarily out of the mainstream of the educational process. Some of them had been to places their geography books forgot. Some of them had seen things that once viewed would change their lives forever. Now they were back in school. They were not the kind of freshmen whom sweet varsity Sue used to dream about.

On the plus side, the colleges saw a sudden glut of tuition money generated by the GI Bill. Schools like USF were particularly affected.

Building space had always been at a premium for urban campuses. Suddenly, patchwork fields of surplus army Quonset huts became America's new halls of ivy.

Populated with mature students, dreaming of the kind of physical and academic expansion that never before seemed possible, USF followed the route so many others of its type undertook. It was determined to generate new attention and prestige through athletic success.

Newell was already ensconced as the basketball coach. He was joined by Kuharich, a terrific recruiter of football talent. He would prove it eventually as the head coach at Notre Dame and with the Cards and Eagles in the NFL. Newell was so successful he would eventually jump to the University of California at Berkley. They were Rozelle's first master mentors.

So, this is the way it was, therefore, when Rozelle and De Long arrived on the USF campus, fresh from the minor league glories of Compton JC that, as De Long explained, "we were young enough to have secretly thought we were responsible for." The year was 1948. It was a time of infinite hope and excitement all across America.

Within the span of that first year, two things happened that convinced Rozelle that there was a very special and personal thrill when people suddenly sat up and took notice of you. And the unlikeliest early example came from the USF soccer team, who won and won in total secrecy.

Then Rozelle found the Prince. Well, there was some debate as to whether he was actually a prince. Rozelle thought he was. De Long told me he was not as sure. But he was, indeed, wearing tribal robes when Rozelle found him waiting tables in the campus dining hall. Things being what they were with USF soccer, if you were trying to promote it and one of your players said he was a prince and you thought people would like to see a prince play soccer, then you didn't stop to ask him to let you see the royal birthstone.

Rozelle and De Long hit the office mimeograph machine so hard it's a wonder it didn't explode. By the time they had a full

head of steam going, the prince had become a daily item in all the Bay Area papers.

"Well," Rozelle told me, "the truth is that we were pretty darn good. The school thought so, and it went out and rented Kezar Stadium. We had never drawn a crowd over, say, five hundred until then, but we worked like hell. We played Temple there, and we drew ten thousand people. It was then that I realized, if you sold it to the media properly, people would come."

At the same time, the city of San Francisco awakened one morning to discover it had a basketball team. It may have been the first time the town paid any attention to that game since Hank Luisetti—credited with invention of the running one-hand shot—led Stanford past Long Island University before a crowd of more than seventeen thousand at Madison Square Garden.

But now it discovered—through the dedicated efforts of Pete Rozelle and Myron De Long—that basketball was, indeed, alive and well and very much worth watching in the City by the Bay. It was not the kind of team the school would offer the city later when Bill Russell would arrive, but it would do very nicely.

Led by a big, strong kid named Don Lofgran, who later would have a brief whirl at pro basketball, and a pint-size guard named Rene Herrerias, the Dons would move on to New York City and win the National Invitational Tournament (NIT) at Madison Square Garden. Rozelle made sure that the nation's media capital knew who they were even before they were invited.

In fact, what he did helped them get invited. They would finish the year at 25-5 under Newell, but long before that he got the attention of Madison Square Garden's key officials. Rozelle launched what De Long referred to as his "Mutt and Jeff campaign," sending out pictures of six-foot-five Lofgran with his left arm extended horizontally well above the top of the five-foot-six Herrerias's head. He named the duo after a pair of popular comic strip heroes who had a similar height difference. Newspapers everywhere picked up the photo.

It was a beginning, and as the ball began to roll, Rozelle sensed

that something even bigger was surely going to happen. Actually, it was already in motion across town at San Francisco Junior College.

A local kid named Ollie Matson was a 9.6 sprinter and the best power runner Kuharich had ever seen. Earlier as a high school kid, he had competed in the national 400-meter trials for the Olympics. Four years later he would qualify for the Games in Helsinki and win two medals. The staff was shocked when Kuharich suddenly announced that Matson was coming to USF. De Long remembered:

> It happened so fast we couldn't believe it. We used to play poker with Newell and Pete Woolpert, his assistant, and some of the football coaches, and all they talked about was Matson.
>
> Football recruiting was almost impossible here because we were up against all those California glamour schools getting the real good kids. How do you compete for Saturday's heroes with Stanford and Cal Berkley and further down the coast with USC and UCLA [University of California at Los Angeles]? We were an urban school with no league affiliation on top of that, and we had trouble just putting together a schedule.
>
> Getting Matson really stoked Pete's imagination. He said, "If he comes here, this place is suddenly going to be crawling with guys who can actually play the game."

Rozelle demonstrated there was a touch of the prophet within him. As soon as Matson set foot on campus, it seemed like an army of huge young men in search of educational enlightenment and football fame flooded the campus. Their high school reputations were spectacular, and the names fall off the tongue like the roster of a college football Valhalla. They included future all-pros such as Dick Stanfel, Bob St. Clair, Gino Marchetti, Ed Brown, Red Stephens, Ralph Thomas, Roy Barni, and Joe Scudero. And, of course, Ollie Matson.

Kuharich had a football team and a half in the making. And Rozelle realized the future was his—but with a set of incredible problems to overcome. He was promoting a team that he was sure

would bid for national attention, but it was a squad with no home field of its own and no schedule that could make any money.

The West Coast teams, with the exception of Loyola of Los Angeles, which was in the same bind, wouldn't dream of risking their prestige against a football team like USF. It was De Long's recollection that Rozelle's efforts to overcome those handicaps nearly drove him bananas. "He would do almost anything to get USF into the newspaper—any newspaper. Studying was never a big deal with either of us, so we'd be sitting around the room at night, and suddenly he'd say, 'Why don't we go over to the office and do a special story on that third-string tackle from Hammond, Indiana, so we can send it to his hometown paper?' So we would go over to that drafty old army barracks that was our office, and I'd write it and he'd look at it and make me rewrite it. I mean, he just never stopped."

In 1951 the Dons came east to play Fordham University. Fordham was no longer the Fordham of Sleepy Jim Crowley and Eddie Danowski and Vince Lombardi. But it was a prestigious name, and, more important to Rozelle, this was New York City, the communications capital of the world. He had seen firsthand what it had meant to USF when it came to town for the NIT a few years earlier. Now he was pounding on the doors of every newspaper in town, knowing he had a quality product to sell.

So what if the game would be played in a battered old relic called Triborough Stadium, a facility as vital to Manhattan as, say, the Burma Road was to Boston? Reporters would be there—reporters from all over the Great Megalopolis. They would get to see Ollie Matson, and Rozelle was sure their response would be staggering.

A crowd mercifully announced at fifteen thousand found its way to the crumbling old ballpark. People who knew the level of Fordham football at that time insisted that half of them were actually confused motorists seeking directions to the George Washington Bridge.

But with a little help from Mr. Matson, the secret was out. USF could play virtually any other college team in the country if

they had the guts to schedule the Dons. Matson took the opening kickoff and ran it back 94 yards. In the fourth quarter with the game tied at 19–19, Matson took another kickoff and ran it back 90 yards to win it.

Afterward, an erudite sportswriter from the *New York Herald Tribune* named Harold Rosenthal wrote, "For once a college press agent told a reporter the truth about one of his school's football players. Pete Rozelle promised earlier in the week that Ollie Matson would prove he is special and yesterday he did." It was the first time Pete Rozelle's name had ever appeared in a New York newspaper.

The Dons went undefeated that year. Matson scored twenty-one touchdowns and gained 1,556 yards. Among the team's victims were the San Diego Naval Training Center, Santa Clara, and Loyola of Los Angeles, the "other team" the big boys would not play because of its quarterback, Don Klosterman, later a scout, general manager, and close friend of Rozelle.

Loyola was relegated to the same lower tier as USF. Klosterman was so versatile he could embarrass all of the neighboring big boys if they agreed to play Loyola. The same was true of USF, and its talented roster neighbors like Cal, Stanford, and Santa Clara refused to schedule them.

But down in Stockton, California, the College of the Pacific, once a Rose Bowl team, smelled money. A full house for Pacific's games was rare. It saw the value in a David versus Goliath game. When it agreed to play USF, more than forty thousand people sardined into the local ballpark to see the "mystery" Dons take on what was then the College (late to become University) of the Pacific, the most prestigious foe a USF football team had ever faced. Also in the crowd that day was the Orange Bowl selection committee.

Rozelle, his propaganda machine, and Kuharich's players were on the verge of a miracle. The Dons were awesome that day. They rolled to a shockingly easy 47–14 victory. Rozelle went out and bought suntan lotion, and, look out, Miami, the Dons are ready.

All they had to do was wait for the bid. They were all dressed up but, as it turned out, with no place to go. They turned down the bid when the Orange Bowl insisted that two players—Matson and Burl Tolar (later hired by Rozelle as an NFL on-field official)—stay home. They were African Americans, and the committee didn't want them anywhere near the segregated Orange Bowl.

They were denied their ultimate moment in the spotlight. But eight members of that team were later chosen in the upcoming NFL draft. The pros had noticed them despite their unbelievable triumphs without a home field or a major league schedule.

Rozelle had successfully mounted a brilliant publicity campaign with an incredible sense of purpose. "We had worked like hell," De Long said.

We had this ancient typewriter and this mimeograph machine that weighed a ton, and we would lug them to the top of Kezar for our home games. We were among the first to provide play-by-play for our writers. We never stopped planning.

His big scene was the eight-piece band he put together to play "Goodnight, Irene" after each touchdown while the student body waved white handkerchiefs at the other stands. But what I really know is that he wanted to feel that he had been able to help create *his* All-American—take a kid at a little school like this and make him more important than stars at Notre Dame or usc.

From the moment that Matson first showed up here, Pete worked day and night on him. He once told me, "Don't laugh. He is going to be *my All-America*." He played it that way whenever he got the chance.

Matson was a great runner in the Olympics later on. Pete must have read that story about Jim Thorpe going to a meet and the other coach blowing up and yelling, "You mean your school has a two-man team?" and Thorpe said, "No, the other guy is the manager." "Well, Pete, so he tried it with Matson. He entered him in the Fresno relays as the usf track team, and he wasn't lying because usf didn't have a track team. Ollie was it and Pete paid the entry money, and Ollie went out and won his events."

They were exciting times. Rozelle was a regular visitor to Bay Area newspapers, and he often recalled those times as golden. He acquired his first car, a battered old Plymouth, but dating was hardly a formalized thing. There was very little of a social life except for the nightly hearts games that De Long recalled as "pure aggression. We played for very little money and a lot of blood. The cursing and the table pounding were rather intense. One night we pushed our next-door neighbor, Father Houk, to the limit of Christian tolerance. He knocked softly on the door and said 'Gentlemen, I really hate to say this, but I think your language is getting a bit vivacious.'"

And then there was the day Rozelle picked up the office phone. Newell was on the other end. He had a handkerchief over the handset, and the conversation went like this:

"You have a praaayer name Wirree Wong?"

"Yes, sir. We have a player named Willie Wong. Who are you?"

"Yesss. I am Mr. Woo of China Press. People of Chinatown demand you say why Wirree Wong no praaay in games."

"Well, sir, he's only five-foot-five and . . ."

"Wirree Wong no praaay because he Chinese."

"Oh, no, sir. Nothing like that. Our coach, Mr. Kuharich, would never . . ."

"Then why he no praaay? You tell big rie."

It was Newell, with a handkerchief over the phone's speaker. He had Rozelle squirming for a half hour.

For De Long, it was a time of self-discovery. For Rozelle, it was something very different, another set of emotional landmarks on the road map that was taking him to what he was meant to do. But even as the two grew closer in understanding each other, they were drifting toward their separate destinies. According to De Long, "I never really wanted journalism, and he wanted to be the sports editor of the *LA Times*. I wanted a career in education. It was time for me to move in that direction. And Pete, well, he was perfect for what he finally became."

2

Moving On

Where the hell is Van Brocklin?
—Pete Rozelle, the day he showed the Rams who was the boss

When you work for [Pete Rozelle], you start to think like him.
—Bill Granholm, who worked for him with the Rams and the NFL

Suddenly, like a senior-prom orchid a week after the dance, the golden days at USF were simply a season whose time had passed. At the close of the 1951 football campaign, it became clear to the school's administration that a nomadic odyssey in search of windmills might be fine for Don Quixote, but it sure played hell with a small college's athletic budget.

Artistically, the Dons were hoisted on the petard of their own excellence. To schedule major opponents, they had to prove they belonged. But after proving it, the big-money schools were doubly sure they didn't want to play them. If they had to lose—and the Dons of 1951 proved they could beat anyone—it wasn't going to be to a team with no stadium and no national tradition.

Rozelle had battled Cal-Berkley, Stanford, and the NFL 49ers for space in the local papers. He got the space, but with rare exception the attraction could not draw enough customers. The rent at Kezar Stadium was becoming too heavy a burden.

To the South other independents such as rival Loyola were beginning to feel the same strain. And around the country a large number of Catholic colleges were of the mind that if big-time sports were key to more prestige and income, economics and common sense dictated the same thing could be done with basketball for

28

the price of ten sets of colored underwear, two hoops, and none of the staggeringly expensive equipment that football required.

Despite the fact it was coming off a perfect nine-game season, USF bowed to the inevitable. It announced it would no longer field a football team. Not that the old gang would have held together much longer anyway. Rozelle wanted to create his own All-America, and Ollie Matson completed the task for him as a bon voyage gift. Clearly, it was time for him to move on.

Shorn of his team, Kuharich accepted an offer to coach the NFL's Cardinals, then based in Chicago. Ollie Matson would be his first pick in the college draft. Newell, who had built the structure for a basketball program of national prominence, would leave the team intact for his assistant Phil Woolpert (he of the late-night card games with Rozelle and De Long) and surface as one of America's most successful coaches at the University of California, just across the bay. Myron De Long, the fellow traveler from Lynwood, would leave the "toy department" forever, forsaking the mimeograph machine and the typewriter for a teaching career of more than three decades.

And Pete Rozelle? Well, once again he would surface in the right place at the right time and, as De Long always said, would "know exactly what to do with the chance."

This time the trail led south, back to the edge of Lynwood, where it had all begun. Tex Maule, an erudite football guy who, later at *Sports Illustrated*, would chronicle much of Rozelle's public life, had resigned as public relations director of the Los Angeles Rams.

These were the same Rams for whom Rozelle and De Long as young student hustlers had produced preseason programs when the team trained in Compton. Tex Schramm, the general manger (GM) who was impressed with young Rozelle back then, was still the general manager. Once again it was as though fate had tiptoed in on tennis shoes and tapped Rozelle on the shoulder. Schramm hired him.

And, in typical Rozelle fashion, it was the right team in the right

town at the right time. No other football team and no other job could have presented him with such a spectacular opportunity to prepare himself for the future. The Rams were famous for that.

Over the years a steady stream of front-office personnel would learn under owner Dan Reeves, whose Rams organizations should have charged tuition for the way they schooled their executives. Bill Granholm had come to the franchise in 1949 as equipment manager. He was out of the University of Wisconsin locker room by way of a massive slice of overreaching known as the Chicago Rockets. They were a brief cog in an abortive palace revolution called the All-America Football Conference. Like most of their sister franchises and the league itself, all that remains of their existence is a line of agate type in an old record book.

With the financially undernourished Rockets, a man learned to make do with what he had, which was almost nothing. Granholm was amazed at the abundant options for success open to an equipment manager with the Rams. "I was the equipment manager, but, hell, football wasn't the kind of business it is today," he explained. "When the season ended all the equipment went into a warehouse, but you were still getting paid, so you worked. I worked in the box office, accounting, scouting. I moved around every year. It was that way with all of us." The pattern was set long before Pete came.

"The thing was you couldn't go to Dan and bargain for more money," Granholm told me, "because somebody had offered you a better job. If the job was really better, he'd advise you to take it and then help you get it if necessary. A lot of guys came out of that office and went to better jobs because of it, and the last thing each of them did as a Ram employee was to raid the 'closet.'"

"The closet" held every printed form the Rams ever used. It had expense vouchers, scouting forms, ticket forms—you name it. And everyone who left that office figured, "What the hell, I'm not going to find anything half as efficient where I'm going, so I might as well take some samples along." "I've seen those forms in a lot of strange cities," Granholm said. "You cannot possibly underestimate the impact the Rams had on Pete Rozelle."

What if it had been the Bears, where in order to requisition a dozen of anything he would have had to have had George Halas's signature a dozen times, or with the Giants, where the we-are-one-family syndrome of seniority was more prized than young ideas, or the Browns, where acquisition was whatever Paul Brown said it was and you damned well better not forget it?

Put handcuffs on a young, active mind with real drive, and you risk sending the mind in search of another career. But the Rams followed none of those procedures. They had moved from Cleveland in 1946, and with the exception of the business manager, Bill John, all the new recruits were California born and bred. John had made the move from Cleveland with Reeves, and even he was in his thirties.

The corporate structure of the team would also figure heavily in Rozelle's future. Reeves, whose money came from the sale of the Reeves Grocery Chain to A&P for eleven million dollars, had bought the team in 1941 for one hundred thousand dollars, along with a junior partner named Fred Levy. Five years later he moved it to Los Angeles and found himself in the middle of a battle of diminishing returns.

From the very beginning he believed that the Los Angeles area, properly worked, could be a gold mine, but the gap between the wish and the deed became a serious problem. After all, this was a college football town, and USC and UCLA had it all. He had to battle them for space in the newspapers and customers in the same stadium they used on Saturdays.

To complicate matters, the All-America Football Conference was still breathing and had put a team of its own, the Los Angeles Dons, into the city. As a sea of red ink threatened to drown the franchise, Reeves sought a lifeline by bringing in a money man named Ed Pauley, who had made his fortune in the oil business.

It was about to be as tacky an alliance as the marriage between Anne Boleyn and Henry the VIII. Daily closed-door battles between them were a way of life by the time Rozelle arrived as the new press agent.

This was 1952, and the Rams were coming off a World Championship season. When they assembled at Redlands University for preseason training, Rozelle looked forward to meeting the press on team picture day. The Rams had instituted this ritual long before Rozelle arrived. Players even received little booklets when they checked in each year, advising them of the importance of cooperating with the press. But ironically, on picture day, Rozelle suddenly faced his first challenge in the job—and it was as big a one as he would get.

The team was gifted with two marvelously talented quarterbacks. The first and local hero was Bob Waterfield, who had been an All-America in nearby Westwood at UCLA. He could run and punt and throw, and he could even place kick. Sharing the quarterback duties was Norm Van Brocklin, a fanatical competitor with a cannon of a throwing arm and a hair-trigger temper.

Photo day turned out to be especially hot, a Death Valley kind of heat. Rozelle, looking tan and cool and relaxed as usual, strolled over to a group of photographers. Naturally, each photographer who had braved the noonday sun wanted a separate shot of his own of the two quarterbacks. "Certainly," said the young press agent. "Here's Waterfield and here's . . . here's . . . here's . . . Where the hell is Van Brocklin?"

Van Brocklin had simply walked off the field. The place to which he had walked was the locker room showers. Well, where did you expect a smart prima donna of a quarterback to go on such a day? The sauna?

Among all the legends generated by newsmen about the personality quirks of America's Sunday heroes, the saga of Norm Van Brocklin's temper gets a high and legitimate call. When harassed by an unblocked lineman in those days before players wore those birdcage-type face masks, the Dutchman, as he was called, often put things back in perspective by firing the football directly into the lineman's unprotected face.

The heat of the practice field at Redlands University in July did not figure to ease the fires deep within the Dutchman.

"Where the hell is he?" Rozelle asked the players.

"In the shower," they eagerly responded.

"I never did find out exactly what was said," Granholm told me, "but in less than three minutes Van Brocklin was back in uniform, having his picture taken. I won't claim he said 'Cheese,' but he damned well was out there with the rest of them."

The Rams failed to get into the title game that season, but they got a hell of a lot of pictures in the Southern California newspapers.

If there was any significance to the two years Rozelle spent as the Rams' press agent, it was that he had come to pro football with a forward-thinking organization, that he had made no front-office enemies despite the white-hot feud between Reeves and Pauley, and that without knowing it he had laid the groundwork for a much larger step.

But despite the respect he earned, the truth is that he was growing bored. The challenge was no longer a challenge. At USF there had been the drive to earn the school recognition, but here everybody knew the Rams. They were California's glamour team. As in the past, he enjoyed his relationship with sportswriters, but the sense of urgency was missing. He knew he was becoming restless.

"We went to preseason camp in 1954," Granholm remembered, "and, for me, it was like any other camp. I mean, hell, it was fun, and I was just glad to be there. But one night we are out having a drink, and I remember that all of a sudden he tells me he wouldn't be surprised if before long he decided to give up this job. Now I don't know if I can really explain this, but this was a real shocker to me. I mean, it was like I suddenly found a traitor. I mean, we were a small group and a young group, and we were having fun and it was like it was going to be you, me, Dan, and the Rams."

The resignation of a publicity man attracts little attention. As quietly as he had come, he was gone. In 1955 Pete Rozelle returned to San Francisco. He never dreamed that within two years, he would return to the Rams.

In every relationship, all the way from his miniature golf outings with friends in junior high on up to the selling of the USF Dons,

Pete Rozelle had always been the leader. Triggered by a lot of trial and a few errors, he had managed to shape himself in the direction he wanted. Now for the first time, he was to meet someone who would do the shaping for him. And when the business side of their relationship was finished, it would add the last dimension necessary to catapult him into what would become a meteoric rise.

Back in 1949 when the USF basketball team had come east to the NIT in the Garden, Pete Newell had taken his publicity man out to dinner. They were joined by a man named Ken Macker. At the time Macker owned an advertising agency based in San Francisco. Its primary account was Trans World Airlines. They immediately hit it off.

If Macker hadn't been as good as he was at what he did, they probably would have spent a great deal of time together, but the high-priced accounts Macker serviced called for personal attention in many places, and he was constantly on the road.

Meanwhile, Rozelle forgot Macker. At the time Pete was immersed in the making of his All-America (Ollie Matson), the challenges of USF athletics, and his own personal life. He had just married Jane Coupe, an artist from Chicago whom he had met while he was in the navy.

But about a week after USF dropped football, Macker called to offer him a job. Rozelle chose the Rams instead. Two years later Macker called again. Impressed with the money he offered and Macker's charisma and bored with the redundancy that marked his job, Rozelle accepted.

The offer came about because a man named Andre Soriano had hired Macker to promote Philippine Airlines, which was still in its postwar infancy. The account never became a big thing for Macker, but it enabled him to hire Rozelle and expand his agency.

"Sometimes," Rozelle told me in his Park Avenue offices, "I do wonder what really might have happened to me if I had stayed with Ken. A couple of years later he bought the English-language paper in Manila and took over as publisher. That might have opened all kinds of intriguing possibilities."

With Macker Rozelle was thrust into an entirely different side of public relations, far removed from the time when a successful day's work was measured by a mention of USF in Prescott Sullivan's column in the *San Francisco Chronicle*.

When Pete joined him Macker was representing the City of Victoria, Australia. The country had landed the 1956 Olympics, and using his Victoria contacts Macker landed the right to represent Qantas Airlines, the official carrier for the Games.

It wasn't football, but it was a challenge requiring the same ingenuity he had developed during his USF days. He was in the forefront of developing the Qantas campaign, and he needed some part-time help that was familiar with sports. He instinctively returned to the "Lynwood connection." Myron De Long was back on his team.

"I wasn't all that serious about it," De Long recalled, "because I had already picked my real direction in life. But it was good money and I needed it, and I always had enjoyed working for Pete. Well, we felt that Qantas needed a symbol. You know, some kind of character that we could make stand for Australia the moment you saw it. And, of course, Pete did it. He chose the koala bear, and I think it's still featured in their commercials more than twenty years later."

Suddenly, De Long was in a position to see Pete as he had never before seen him. It was a far cry from the hearts games next to Father Houk's room. "When he worked for Macker," De Long said, "part of his job was to wine and dine celebrities who were connected with Macker's accounts. So he would be out all night and going pretty good, and he might get home at 3:00 a.m. He would be back at his desk 8:00 a.m. His energy was as much a factor in his success as his creativity. The incredible thing was that I can never remember him being sick or complaining he was tired. I think he learned a lot from Macker."

"It was," Rozelle confirmed, "a very close relationship. I think in my personal life one of the hardest things I ever had to do was to leave that job. I know it took a lot of thinking. I didn't want to leave the job, and I didn't want to leave the town. I have always had a fondness for San Francisco."

But the Rams called on him again, and his return to the team was hardly accomplished under ordinary circumstances. Halfway down the state, echoes of the old war drums were growing louder. Reeves and Pauley hardly ever spoke to each other in a civil tone. Schramm was sick of being caught in the middle. He left to go to CBS, which was developing its sports television division, and later, after Rozelle had become commissioner, he would leave CBS and be the guiding force behind the newly minted Dallas Cowboys.

In any event with Schramm gone, tensions increased in Los Angeles, and all hell broke loose when Levy, the third stockholder, jumped sides and formed an alliance with Pauley. There had been a tense meeting in New York's Scandia restaurant at which somewhere between the entrée and coffee, Reeves lost his directorship of the team. Now, the day-to-day operation was in jeopardy.

Bert Bell, the NFL's commissioner, understood that a smooth operation was necessary in Los Angeles—one of the league's three glamour franchises. The other two were New York and Chicago, both of which were solid anchors. Left with no choice, Bell stepped directly into the battle.

He did not know much about Rozelle, but he did recognize his skill as a diplomat. He knew Pete had already worked with Reeves and that Pauley had no objection to him. In fact, because of his earlier tenure in Los Angeles, virtually all the front-office staff knew and liked him. With the exception of Sid Gillman, the latest in a long line of Rams coaches, Rozelle had worked with all of them.

Ray Rozelle remembered getting a telephone call shortly after his son met with Bell: "I think it was on a Monday," he said. "He called down here to Lynwood and told me that Bell had offered him a job, but he wasn't even going to consider it. He knew about the Reeves-Pauley feud, and he knew that Bell had the muscle to force Pete on them as a compromise for two reasons. First, both of them liked him, and, second, each knew that to keep the status quo would destroy the value of the franchise. I told him," Ray Rozelle explained, "'Well, you make pretty good money up there

with Macker, but you are going to learn that it isn't how much you make but how much you have at the end of the year.'"

This was a strangely incisive insight into the lifestyle required of a high-powered press agent. It may have been so incisive that Rozelle stood back and took a different look at himself. "I don't think I would ever tell him what to do," Ray Rozelle said, "because he was then in a position to make a lot of money off Macker's clients. He had a big-money deal and Macker's clients had a lot of money, and you know there's an old saying that you can't be around money without some of it rubbing off. Friday night of that same week he called and told me he was going to go back to the Rams."

The result was not necessarily the economic thinking of his father. The son was thinking in other terms. He saw a sudden twist in direction that could take him to a spot he had wanted all along. He was, after all, the product of a Southern California home and a Southern California attitude.

But first he needed guarantees. He explained to Bell that he didn't see how this could work if he had to bounce back and forth between Pauley and Reeves like a ping-pong ball. It was obvious that whatever Reeves wanted, Pauley didn't, and whatever Pauley wanted, Reeves would fight. Against that backdrop and the need for a cool head running this important franchise, Bell assured Rozelle that he alone would have the final say, and as commissioner he would back him firmly in those situations.

So Pete Rozelle at age twenty-nine signed a four-year contract for twenty-five thousand dollars per year to run one of the most glamorous franchises in the history of professional football. He was given total control. Once again a unique and unexpected set of circumstances began to shape the kid from Lynwood. Had the franchise been Green Bay, Detroit, or the then Chicago Cardinals, he might have been just another general manager or—more probably—eventually would have returned to Macker. But the opportunity with the Rams was golden because the organization contained some viable employees who would make a contribution to Rozelle's education. He would go out and hire even more.

In Bill John, the Rams' business manager, Rozelle was to have firsthand contact with a man who knew the business side of pro football as well as anyone in the league. He inherited a woman named Kay Lang, who long before the advent of either women's lib or quota hiring was to prove herself so adept at her job that Schramm would hire her to run the ticket operation when he moved from television to the Dallas Cowboys.

Then there was a PR man named Bert Rose, who would later land in various jobs with various expansion teams at Rozelle's urging. The loyalty that Pete expected of him was born and nurtured in Los Angeles. Granholm taught Rozelle so much that later when he became commissioner, he brought him in as a special administrative assistant.

Among this group in Los Angeles he also found Ed Kotal, a man rarely written about even today, but who, in a very real sense, was a kind of godfather to the modern scouting system. It was Kotal, who long before Rozelle had become general manager, had discovered Grambling College, a small all-black school in Louisiana's red-clay country. He had visited Grambling—the only scout to visit any all-black school in those days—for four straight years, and he nurtured a relationship with the coach, Eddie Robinson, and college president, Dr. Ralph Waldo Emerson Jones.

The payoff would be the signing of an incredible football player named Paul "Tank" Younger, the first pro player to come out of an all-black school. No other franchise and no other scout even thought about that potential talent pool. But the Rams and Kotal (for the base pay of six thousand dollars) landed a remarkable athlete. He would make all-pro on offense as a running back and, a year later, all-pro defense as a linebacker.

Kotal remained a Ram under Rozelle's tenure, and it is not stretching things to say his breaking the no-black-school players taboo was not lost on the new general manager. The lesson about race stayed with him long after he became the league's commissioner. He believed—and proved it—that to eliminate a man because of race was absurd.

As commissioner he hired the first African American on-field official, Burl Tolar, who had been a key member of Pete's USF Dons, and Buddy Young, the first in the NFL's front office.

But in Sid Gillman Rozelle, for the first time, would be coming into daily contact with a strong, willful man whose professional background was superb and who was very much determined to make his own decisions about everything. In their first training camp together, the area of who decided what was delineated in forceful terms by the neophyte general manager. It happened on the most trivial of battlefields. For years the Rams had earned national attention from, of all things, their helmets.

When the club moved west from Cleveland, it had a running back from Utah named Fred Gehrke. He played only four mostly unremarkable seasons for them, but he left a legacy that impacted every team that played pro football from that time forward.

He was also a commercial artist in the off-season, and in 1948 he convinced Reeves that it would be great if he painted the helmets in the kind of dramatic fashion that had never before been seen in football. He created a look that stunned everyone. It was a blue helmet with gold trim, but the trim, about which he told nobody, was a pair of yellow Rams horns—one on each side of the helmet. "You can laugh if you want," said Mark Duncan, a Rozelle loyalist later hired by Pete as the NFL's supervisor of officials, "but when I was an assistant coach with the 49ers, we used to hate those helmets. We would go down to that big Coliseum where they were the glamour team. We would psych ourselves up, but then they would come pounding out of that tunnel and onto the field while we watched them. They were big and the sunlight used to pick up those Rams horns, and I swear the more we looked at them, the more they started to look like the real thing. It was a gimmick and it worked, because in our minds they seemed to give the Rams an extra fierceness."

Gehrke's creation made the Rams the first team to have insignias on their helmets and was the forerunner of today's NFL decals, but in their time the helmets were absolutely startling. No other team decorated its helmets until much later.

In Rozelle's first season as GM the "Gehrke helmets" were the same as they had always been. The sporting goods firm with which the Rams dealt expected to be turning them out forever. "But Gilman had a friend in the sporting goods business," Granholm recalled,

> and he had discussed the possibility of landing the Rams account with him. The guy went out and made several demonstration models. I remember one of them was blue with white stripes. Anyway, one day I saw Gilman coming out of his room at Redlands on his way to the practice field with the new helmets under his arm.
>
> I was sure he had discussed them with Rozelle, and I was equally sure Rozelle decided to keep the ones they still use today. Now, football players are very funny, and I know because I was an equipment manager. I don't doubt that if Gilman had casually let them have a look, some of them would have told Rozelle they wanted them.
>
> Well, I saw Sid step out of the room with the helmets, and I saw Pete coming out of his room, and he was gaining on Sid with every step. Then I saw the two of them talking, but I couldn't hear them. The next thing I know, Gillman is going back inside the building, and he comes out three minutes later without the helmets. I never saw them again.

Clearly, in matters both large and small, there was no doubt who was going to be the GM on this club. The three seasons in which he held that job were hardly artistic successes. The first, in 1957, the club went 6-6. The volatile Van Brocklin and equally opinionated Gilman were suing for divorce.

The 1958 team made a run at the title, but the team they were chasing was the Lions, with Bobby Layne. Their 8-4 record wasn't good enough. The following season they fell far, finishing 2-10. But it is worth noting that before the season began, Rozelle swung a trade that was one of the most daring in NFL history. He got his old USF All-America Ollie Matson from the Cardinals for eight— count 'em, eight—players. Matson became a Hall of Famer.

At the end of that terrible season, Gillman and his staff quit.

Interestingly, Rozelle and Gillman respected each other professionally, but otherwise for years there was little warmth between them. Gillman wound up in the American Football League and in 1963 won the league title by routing the Pats, 51–7. He immediately wired Rozelle, suggesting his Chargers play the NFL champions. When Rozelle ignored the request, Gillman, who is Jewish, wired him, "Even Pope John forgave the Jews." Rozelle responded, "Yes, but it took 2,000 years."

Certainly, Rozelle's won-lost results as the Rams' GM were hardly spectacular. So how do you evaluate Rozelle's tenure as the Rams' GM? Well, you evaluate them not from the wins and losses but rather the way he solved the team's financial problems and its vendetta at the top. Bitter and tense as the Reeves-Pauley war was, he never let it get out of hand at a time when it could have ruined the franchise. "I think in a way it was the making of Pete as an administrator and a forceful man," Granholm insisted.

He couldn't, after all, ask either owner for an opinion unless he wanted opposite viewpoints. So he just went on, did what he felt was right, and made it stick afterward. Another thing he learned was how to delegate authority. He couldn't (and didn't try to) coach the football team. He knew that wasn't his job. But he had good ticket people, good press relations people, good administrative people. He let them do what they were hired to do, and if they couldn't, well, then and only then he would step in and handle it. He was the same way as commissioner.

He had the knack of learning without letting you know it. I think in a way that was always one of his strongest points. He does his homework, and you don't realize he's done it until you have to debate him.

I never saw him with a briefcase. I never saw him with notes. But I have rarely seen him without an answer. When you work for him, you do not go to him often because you start to think like him. Like him, you learn not to paint yourself into a corner.

Now, without knowing it, Rozelle was about to stand at the biggest crossroads of his life. Without the Rams job he would not have

been ready. Looking back after he became commissioner—a job he did not seek—Myron De Long put the qualities that brought him to the top in clear perspective: "Everything he did really prepared him for what he finally became. The journalism background gave him a sense of order. The USF thing taught him to improvise. I don't know much about the GM year, but I think the time he spent with Macker gave him a totally different look at life. I think it enabled him to bring a dimension to the job of commissioner that accounted for the way he could be equally at home dealing with owners, television people, and the United States Senate."

He would soon need each of those skills. The biggest challenge of his life was rushing toward him.

3

The Accidental Coronation

All government is founded on compromise.
— Edmund Burke, "The Thirteen Resolutions" (1775)

I voted for him back then only because I thought he was just another harmless ass-kisser.
— Carroll Rosenbloom, fifteen years after Rozelle became commissioner

Bert Bell was gone, dead of a heart attack the year before. They had lost the last point man of the old guard. It had been Bell, who had gone from player to team founder (Eagles) to NFL commissioner, who had taken the league through the challenges of a major gambling scandal, survived the economic threat of the upstart All-America Conference, and protected their stadium ticket sales by pulling the television plug on home games that weren't sold out.

Eight years before his death, with that one explosive scandal in mind, Bell had hired a former Federal Bureau of Investigation (FBI) agent named Austin Gunsel as a watchdog for the league's integrity. Gunsel was promoted to treasurer, and when the commissioner died, the twelve owners had made him their interim choice for commissioner.

It was assumed that when the owners met in January 1960 at the historic Kenilworth Hotel in Miami Beach, the job would become permanent. Hard by the Atlantic Ocean, the Kenilworth was a beautiful site. It had more than its share of history.

It was the resort that Arthur Godfrey made famous and later owned. It was also the only resort within the city limits that for

years had a sign that read: "This Is a Restricted Hotel. No Jews or Dogs allowed." The sign was long gone when the NFL assembled there for nine days of fumbling and bumbling that accidentally created the history that changed the course of all sports in America forever.

Almost by sheer luck they elected a leader who taught every sports group how to use television, how to lobby the most powerful lawmakers in the world, how to make friends and allies of what had been an only casually interested media, and how to set the pace for every innovation that followed anywhere in America's professional sports.

But amazingly, when the owners of the twelve NFL franchises assembled in Florida on January 26, 1960, nobody in the general public even suspected that there was an unsettling undercurrent of discontent boiling beneath the surface in what appeared to be this 100-yard Eden. Some of it was personal. Some of it was regional. Together they produced a nine-day emotional tug-of-war that was part filibuster, part stubborn anger, part tunnel vision, and total confusion.

The most obvious clash of personalities was between the two most powerful personalities in the league—pioneering owner George Halas of the Bears, whose entire agenda was geared toward expanding the number of franchises from twelve to fourteen, and George Preston Marshall, whose Redskins owned the entire country south of the Mason-Dixon line and who would fight like hell to keep his radio and television monopolies intact inside his private Cornpone Curtain.

George Halas had always been a visionary. As player, coach, and owner of the Bears, he had stood in the rain and the snow outside Northwestern Stadium in the 1930s, passing out flyers that read: "If you liked today's college game then come see the Bears play professional football tomorrow at Wrigley Field." Now it was 1960, and a new threat called the American Football League was about to start play. Halas sought to cut it down to what he considered appropriate size by competing with it for the Dallas market with a new team.

He was a ferocious advocate of expansion. He had already secretly selected an oil millionaire named Clint Murchison to run the Dallas franchise when it was activated. He didn't care who got to be commissioner. His powerful personality had handled every commissioner the league ever had. He believed he would handle this one as well. At the moment he was more interested in not angering any of the lodge brothers while he lined up expansion votes.

On the other side was George Preston Marshall, the man who owned the Washington Redskins. He and Halas were bitter rivals on and off the field. A consummate showman, Marshall created the nationally famous Redskins marching band, complete with feathered war bonnets.

His team originally first played in Boston and was known as the Braves. He had once hired a Native American named Lone Star Dietz as his coach and had a theatrical makeup artist decorate the players' faces with "war paint." But it rained so hard that day that the makeup ran down their faces and into their eyes, and the players revolted.

When he moved the team to Washington, he launched his radio network into every corner of the South, as far as Florida and Texas. He did the same when television came along. Today, their battle hymn ends with the words "fight on for old DC." But back then the phrase Marshall used was "fight on for old Dixie." He viewed the possibility of inserting a new southern team in Dallas as a threat to his revenue stream. Consequently, he wanted an "old guard" commissioner who would respect his team's "divine right" to own the South. Austin Gunsel was his candidate.

Both men came to the Kenilworth Hotel meetings with separate but equally strong agendas. Halas would vote neither for nor against any candidate for commissioner for fear of impeding his expansion plan. Marshall would vote for Gunsel simply to keep the status quo alive, feeling Gunsel could be an ally.

Meanwhile, a small but vocal coterie out of the West—the 49ers, the Rams, and the Chicago Cardinals—nominated Marshall Leahy, the 49ers' in-house counsel, who pledged to move the league head-

quarters from Philadelphia to San Francisco. This was a critical campaign promise to the western owners. They felt everything was weighted toward their eastern counterparts, including the schedule making by Bell's office. Leahy's most powerful supporters included the Packers, the Rams, the 49ers, the Browns, the Cardinals, and the Lions. As a gesture toward finding league unity, the Giants joined them.

On the first ballot the rest of the owners—Washington, Baltimore, Philadelphia, and Pittsburgh—stuck with Gunsel. But George Halas stunned them all and proved that this was going to be far more complex that any of the other owners realized. The Bears voted second, following Baltimore. When the roll was called, Halas calmly wiped his glasses, leaned forward, stuck out his rock of a chin, and, with fiery determination punctuating each word, intoned, "The Chicago Bears pass."

Before this nine-day marathon would run its course, Halas would pass on all twenty-three ballots for commissioner. It was as though a voice in the back roads of his mind was chanting, "You guys can pick the commissioner. I can handle whoever it is, just as I always did. Just get me a team in Dallas." With Halas, still a very powerful voice in league meetings, in a self-imposed exile, the battle lines were drawn. The first ballot tally read: Leahy seven . . . Gunsel four . . . one abstention.

On the second ballot Leahy picked up a vote from Pittsburgh's Art Rooney, giving him eight. Again, Halas did not vote. On the third go-round, Gunsel got just two votes. On the fifth three Gunsel votes shifted to a new nominee, Edwin Anderson, general manager of the Detroit Lions. Why Anderson got them, much less why he was nominated, nobody seems to even remember. In any event the stalemate held until the sixth ballot.

It was then that Carroll Rosenbloom acted like, well, Carroll Rosenbloom. Of all the egos gathered in that meeting room, Rosenbloom could have given six points to any of them and still won by two touchdowns. His was an ego based on the business accomplishments that built his personal textile fortune.

When Bert Bell approached him about buying the Baltimore franchise in 1953, his immediate response was that he viewed the NFL (compared to Major League Baseball) as a nickel-and-dime league. "I don't have the time to spend on it," he said. Bell responded, "Look, I've got a guy who can do it for you. I'll send him down there, and you won't have to be bothered."

Bell had been an assistant coach at the University of Pennsylvania when Rosenbloom played halfback there in 1927 and 1928. They had become friends. It didn't hurt that the man he sent to "help out" was one of the greatest athletes Penn had ever produced. Don Kellett was a nine-letter man in football, basketball, and baseball and even went on to play a year with the Boston Red Sox. Rosenbloom knew who he was and made him the general manager.

The Colts became winners under Kellett as GM. They won the first sudden-death championship game ever played in the NFL in 1958 and won the title again in 1959. Around the league Kellett was extremely popular. And around Baltimore he was elevated to the role of municipal icon. He had become the spirit of the Colts.

He and not the owner got the credit for the two titles. Those who knew Rosenbloom best understood that what Kellett had achieved flew in the very face of what had always been Carroll Rosenbloom's immutable law. More than a few of Carroll's friends knew that however unintentional it was, Kellett had broken Carroll's rock-solid dictum: "Nobody upstages the boss."

This may well explain the sudden impulse the unpredictable Rosenbloom followed just before the sixth ballot at the Kenilworth. He placed Kellett's name in nomination. There are two schools of thought on why he did it. The first was the notion that should Kellett win, he would have a friend in the commissioner's office. The second, and most plausible to those who knew Rosenbloom, was that he didn't want to share Baltimore's adoration with anyone. He wanted it all and would get it with Kellett out of the local picture.

On the twentieth ballot it was down to Leahy (seven votes), Kellett (four), and Halas still abstained. Then Rosenbloom switched again, pulling all the Kellett votes with him as they moved back

to Gunsel. Why did Rosenbloom switch? "Probably," said Ernie Accorsi, who knew Carroll well, was a respected general manager with the Browns and the Giants, and was once the Colts' PR director, "because he wanted to prove he could. You had to know Carroll to understand that theory."

Meanwhile, Rams owner Dan Reeves remained loyal to Leahy. As he had explained to his young general manager, Pete Rozelle, five ballots earlier, "I know him. I respect him, and I gave my word. I will continue to cast our vote for him."

Rozelle was not surprised. He knew Reeves well. If Reeves was a Leahy man, it was good enough for him. He watched the power plays with interest but no actual voice.

But one man could watch it no longer. Paul Brown had voted for Leahy all along, but he had begun to find the bickering against his nature. To him, it seemed to tell the public that the men who controlled the only game of its kind in America looked very much as though they didn't know what the hell they were doing.

This should have surprised nobody if they remembered the way his Browns, a power in the now defunct All-America Conference, prized professionalism. When merged into the NFL just ten years earlier, his Browns battered the defending champion Eagles in their very first game. Afterward, he had interrupted his team's postgame celebration to tell his players before he allowed the dressing-room doors to be opened, "Remember who you are and what you represent. Act like you've been here before."

The longer this debate wore on, the less professional Brown felt he and his colleagues had begun to look. He was caught center stage in a road-show version of the theater of the absurd, and it angered and frustrated him. So he was more than a little receptive when Reeves accosted him after the deadlocked voters broke for dinner. He knew Reeves was a Leahy man, but he listened: "This will never end if we don't do something. I think you need to nominate Pete as a compromise. I will not vote against Leahy, but if you put Pete up, I promise I will leave the room and not vote at all."

Brown immediately sought out Wellington Mara and asked him

to help electioneer. Shrewdly, he took what appeared to be Rozelle's biggest weakness—his youth—and turned it into his strength. First, he pointed out to Mara that while the voting blocs had frozen into polar opposites, nobody in the entire room considered Rozelle an enemy. He might have added that was probably because hardly any of them knew who the hell he was. Fortunately, he did not, or they might have been stuck in Miami counting votes until the swallows returned to Capistrano. Then as a faith builder he pointed out that it was the popular Bell who had engineered Pete's hiring as the Rams' GM.

Mara, eager to end this marathon, agreed and immediately recruited Art Rooney, who relied on his son Dan for critical advice in this case because the son knew Rozelle and the father did not. Tired and wanting the ordeal to end, Rooney took his son's endorsement and immediately signed on.

With these powerful allies in his pocket, Brown then played a brilliant hole card. Without telling Mara, he enlisted Rosenbloom. "I want you to nominate this fellow so we can get the hell out of here," he said. By declining to mention Mara and Rooney's intention, he let Carroll jump to his own conclusions. It was the perfect maneuver. Rosenbloom could play the hero. It wasn't until more than twenty years later that he confided to me on the patio of his Beverly Hills home that he had since experienced a total change of heart: "It was a mistake I shouldn't have made. He [Rozelle] thinks he is an emperor in that Park Avenue palace of his, and I plan to stop him. I voted for him back then only because I thought he was just another harmless ass-kisser."

But back then Rosenbloom was eager to step back into the spotlight with his nomination. He had voted against Leahy because "nobody had even asked me on his behalf, and I am, after all, an owner in this league." He had decided to vote for Gunsel until he could figure out what he wanted. Next came his failed ploy with Kellett. But now he could leave for dinner, believing that Brown had crafted a solution for him as a hero sent straight from 100-yard heaven.

Reassured by Reeves's promise of neutrality, Brown met Mara and headed for Rozelle's hotel room. "I just looked at them," Rozelle later recalled. "Here I am, thirty-three years old, and I'm making twenty-five grand a year, and I figure this will be it for the rest of my life. Suddenly, they lay this on me."

Brown told him not to answer but to think it over. "Have dinner with your boss [Reeves] and see what he thinks." The dinner that followed was even more ludicrous in Rozelle's eyes. Reeves spent two hours telling him why he had to take the job. "Of course," Reeves said, as he picked up the check, "I can't vote for you."

In the final session Rosenbloom made his nomination speech, and Rozelle was elected by a needed two-thirds vote of eight to one, with three abstentions. Reeves walked out before the vote, as planned, and the Bears and the Lions abstained. San Francisco cast the lone vote for Leahy.

They called in the media, and Rozelle, who had been hibernating in the bathroom, washing his hands each time a reporter came in, held them up and said to the assembled pencils, tape recorders, and cameras, "As you know, already, I come to this job with clean hands."

At the same time, a continent away, the telephone rang in Myron De Long's house. It was a classmate from USF, telling him about Rozelle's election. "I heard it on the radio and then half an hour later, a mutual classmate from USF called to tell me. The first thing he said was 'It figures, doesn't it? I mean, we always knew he was headed to the top of something.' Personally, I don't think it surprised any of the Lynwood or USF group," De Long said, looking back. "We lived together at USF. I was in on the romance that led to his first marriage. As close as we were, I can never recall him talking to me about a personal goal. What I always felt was that if he had one, he'd reach it."

The men who owned the National Football League didn't even think of Rozelle as the combination of Halas (the football maven), Marshall (entertainment genius), and Moses (the parter of a sea

of red ink) necessary to keep them artistically and economically afloat—all of which he would become. At the time they weren't even sure what they wanted. But Rozelle, the reluctant candidate, knew what they needed once he became the commissioner. Time and again he would surprise them, to the point that they eventually rarely questioned his wisdom.

Years later, Rozelle told me something else about the long night following his election. Long after the voting and long after the exhausted palace guard had staggered off to bed, he and Reeves sat alone in a hotel room, drinking and recalling memories of their shared past with the Rams and the uncertain future of the young man now in charge. "I'm going to move the league office out of Philadelphia and to New York the first chance I get," Rozelle said. "It's the media capital of the world, and we need the media."

Reeves agreed. They talked for a long time. And then, just as the first shaft of light from the Florida dawn began to slant through the window, Reeves cleared his throat, looked over at the new commissioner, and said as mentor to student:

> Look, Pete, I hope you don't take this the wrong way, but you're a total California kid . . . a product of a different kind of culture. New York, well, New York is different. There are things you really need to know if you are going to move the league office to New York.
>
> Don't take this the wrong way. I don't want to embarrass you, but you have to know the lifestyle there is different. It's not at all like California. How you dress is important there. You need to buy a hat immediately. Only the most important people would dare go without one up there.

On the day he moved the operation to New York, he bought a hat, handed it to his secretary Thelma, and said, "Hold on to this for me." She did for about thirty years. He never wore it.

Clearly, the lord high everything of professional football both started and finished as very much his own man.

4

The Boy Wonder Takes Center Stage

I never thought of a career like this. What I really wanted to be was the
sports editor of the *Los Angeles Times*.
 —Pete Rozelle on his boyhood dream

No son of a bitch who steals my song is going to get into my league.
 —George Preston Marshall on his opposition to a new team in Dallas

They were still in Miami. They had agreed on the wunderkind of
Los Angeles as a compromise choice for commissioner. He had yet
to set foot in the league office, but the morning after his selection,
he chaired the final agenda item of the Miami meeting—the fate
of a proposed expansion team in Dallas and one to follow a year
later in Minneapolis—St. Paul. They needed a unanimous vote,
and the battle still matched the two old street fighters, George
Halas in Chicago and George Preston Marshall in Washington.

 Halas was an unlikely choice to spearhead the attack to bring
the league into the future; a player-coach-owner of the team that
moved from Decatur, Illinois, to Chicago in 1921, Halas was as old
school as the single wing. Yet, ironically, at the end of the 1959 sea-
son, the "old" Halas had actually forced pro football into a major
geographical shift. The Chicago Cardinals, his cross-town rivals,
were nearly bankrupt, and their South Side location at Comiskey
Park, where attendance was sparse, didn't help the situation. Wal-
ter Wolfner, their owner, had come up with a brilliant solution.
He would move the team to the far more comfortable venue of
Northwestern's Dyche Stadium, just north of Chicago.

 "Like hell you will," Halas told him and then forwarded to Bert

Bell a document signed by Halas and by the previous Cardinals owner that agreed the Cardinals would never play north of Madison Street and the Bears would not play south of it. Bell sided with Halas, and later in 1960 Wolfner moved the Cards to St. Louis and gave the league a brand-new territory.

With the AFL soon to play with a Dallas team as a charter member, you would think that Marshall, the entertainment maven of the league, would be on board with Halas's plan. But while Marshall, selling an excursion train for away games in New York and Philadelphia as a kind of hotel on rails and with his 110-piece marching band, was all for innovation, his economic philosophy was "not on my block."

In sports as in business, economics always trumps the aesthetic. His was the only professional team in all the South. He owned Dixie radio rights, TV rights, and fan loyalties all throughout the Cornpone Curtain.

Rozelle who knew that harmony was the reason Halas never cast a single vote in the bitter election for commissioner that week and understood that he could not afford to make an enemy of either of the two most powerful owners in the league. The only NFL franchise for which Rozelle had ever worked, the Los Angeles Rams, was, itself, the product of territorial expansion. Unlike a number of his owners, he was not blind to the coming challenge of the embryonic America Football League.

But he made no attempt to flex his brand-new muscles during his first day in office. If these two had a fight, he knew he could play the role of King Solomon and take the ultimate bow after they took the blows.

He believed that a new day was coming to this league, and its beginning ought to be the fruits of the Halas plan to put a team in Dallas, where the AFL already had one ready to play, and in Minneapolis—St. Paul, which was set for the AFL but not signed, sealed, and delivered. In truth he was already thinking about a way to steal that city for the NFL before it jumped off the AFL drawing board.

Halas was an able advocate, much to Rozelle's delight, because

the future general manager of his planned Texas franchise was there in the Kenilworth Hotel that week and highly visible. His name was Tex Schramm, and he was the guy for whom Rozelle had once worked.

The newly minted commissioner wanted a team in Dallas, and he wanted his old friend to control it. But Schramm had nothing to do with Marshall's anger. It was Clint Murchison, the oilman and potential owner, who enraged Marshall, and it was his loss of his Redskins monopoly throughout the South that fueled him.

And then there was "the song." "Hail to the Redskins" was Marshall's battle hymn. He unveiled it in 1938, the year after Marshall moved the club from Boston to Washington. According to the credits the music was written by a society bandleader and bandmaster of the Skins' marching band named Barney Breeskin, with words by a former showgirl and movie ingenue named Corrine Griffith, who was married to Marshall. The tune sounds strangely like the opening bars of an old hymn, "Yes, Jesus Loves Me," but nobody challenged Barney. The original lyrics, in the best tradition of 1930s racism, included, "Scalp 'em, swamp 'em—We will take 'em big score / Read 'em, weep 'em, touchdown!—We want heap more!"

When Corrine divorced George she wanted the rights to the song. According to the late *Washington Star* columnist Mo Siegel, "Corrine got the rights in the settlement. Breeskin had never gotten paid the original price of one hundred dollars. Murchison secretly bought the song from Breeskin for twenty-five hundred dollars and threatened an injunction against its playing by the Redskins marching band and any other musical group performing at Redskin games."

Everyone around the league relished Marshall's discomfort, and everyone except Marshall agreed that Murchison had a world-class sense of humor. You do not make fun of the big chief in Washington, threaten to ban his war hymn from being played in his own stadium, and expect him to forget or forgive.

Just before the Dallas expansion vote, Halas had demanded to

know why Marshall was opposed to opening up that franchise, and, according to Siegel, Marshall shot back, "No son of a bitch who steals my song is going to get into my league."

Halas, impressed by Murchison's ability to find the soft spot on Marshall's chin, laughed and then negotiated the release of the Redskin "anthem" with Murchison. Marshall, who loved his song and delighted in leading his Redskin marching band and an army of DC fans up Eighth Avenue to the Polo Grounds when they played the Giants, swallowed hard and voted for expansion.

Rozelle, now in control, took a very Rozelle-like approach. He watched and listened, as he always did, and later in the day when Joe Foss, the AFL commissioner, threatened a lawsuit because the AFL had already announced its plan to put a team in Dallas, Rozelle made his first public announcement as commissioner: "They moved into our territory in New York and Los Angeles and San Francisco. Why shouldn't we be allowed to move into Dallas? We will do just that." His fire was intended as a wake-up call to his constituents. The owners had elected a fellow they thought could keep the seat warm until they figured out what to do with it. With that pronouncement—like it or not, and some did not—it was clear that the lodge brothers had gotten a leader, not a follower.

When they finally left Miami and headed home, it was not without a serious amount of uneasiness. They had turned over the future of their business to a man whom most of them knew less about than their team equipment managers. He was their employee, and, for the most part, they were strong, willful men who did not believe that the future was very complicated. Their reluctant choice of commissioner reflected the thoughts of Carroll Rosenbloom, who explained later that "I just wanted to get the goddamn thing over with."

With the major exception of Halas, they looked at the AFL as though it were the last mosquito of summer, an irritant at worst that they would dispatch as they had always historically prevailed over other gate crashers in the past. But Rozelle clearly understood the threat. He would deal with it in more detail at the right time,

but with approval for Dallas and the Twin Cities out of the way, he was ready to deal with more immediate issues on his agenda.

Just as he and Reeves had discussed on the night of his election, it was imperative to anchor the league's operations in New York. Bell had pioneered the league's television policy—away games on local air and home games blacked out when all the seats weren't filled. It was a start. Rozelle would take television, and with refinements that nobody had even imagined, he would turn it into the cash cow that would fund the NFL's march toward national ownership of Sunday afternoon.

In the past the commissioners of all leagues had set up shop in their hometowns as a matter of pure convenience. For that reason Bell's headquarters were anchored in Bala Cynwyd, a suburb of Philadelphia. He was the overseer of twelve teams (as compared to thirty-two today), and, using a large checkerboard as a visual aid, he drew up their schedules on his dining room table. He had also been firm in various controversial stands. Compared with commissioners of other leagues, he was by far the most progressive. But pro football's idea of progress until Rozelle came along was measured in yards. Rozelle's plans called for movement in light-years.

Just two years earlier the greatest bonus in the league's history had been dumped in its lap, and nobody even remotely understood it, much less knew what to do with it, until Rozelle came along. The championship game of 1958 between the Baltimore Colts and the New York Giants tiptoed up to the collective psyche of America's sports fans as simply the end of another season. But once on center stage, it brought a new kind of drama to what was its largest national audience ever. More than forty-five million people watched it. There would have been hundreds of thousands more, but the stadium did not sell out and under the "blackout rule" nobody in the Great Megalopolis without a ticket got to see it. But the rest of America, through what had previously been the underutilized red eye of television, did.

Second—and of far more importance—it was the first sudden-death title game in league history. Consequently, it generated the

greatest media attention the NFL had ever had—for a couple of weeks. Then it went back to business as usual, at a time when cities without franchises barely covered professional football.

This was unacceptable to Rozelle and symptomatic of what he saw as the league's biggest immediate obstacle. Each week Bert Bell's office had sent out a single release (most of which ended in garbage pails in various newspaper offices) about who would play where that week, starting times, and the league standings. Reading one of them was about as exciting as spending an evening watching a fly crawl up a drape.

That was publicity pre-Rozelle style in the collective mind of Bert Bell and the team owners. Actually, Rozelle had put together a far better local PR team back with the Rams. With that in mind, he couldn't move the NFL out of its isolated mom-and-pop headquarters fast enough. For starters he took the entire operation up to Manhattan and a small suite of offices located in Rockefeller Center with a staff of just seven people. Today the NFL has roughly eleven hundred employees in offices in Manhattan, Los Angeles, and Mount Laurel, New Jersey.

The times they were, indeed, a-changing. In January John Fitzgerald Kennedy, the youngest president in history, would breathe new optimism into America with his inauguration speech when he challenged a nation looking for direction.

It was contagious. Within that decade Americans would walk on the moon, and the gross national product would double. For Pete Rozelle, both an organizational and a marketing genius, 100-yard nation building would begin within the walls of the tiny new suite of offices that the league would outgrow two years before the decade would end.

The meteoric growth of his past would provide the prologue to his future. He knew the message of the impact of that marvelous overtime game in Yankee Stadium two years before he rose to power. In its simplest form it was: "To love us they have to know us."

It was a lesson that first took root in his arsenal back at USF when he discovered the soccer-playing Prince's story and lured ten thou-

sand people to a game that should have drawn only a couple of hundred. Now he would make the NFL story so compelling that the interest generated by that overtime title game would flower into America's autumn passion.

Before he left the battlefield in 1989, he spread the gospel of who and what the NFL was across the face of the continent, including exhibition games in Mexico and Canada, preseason games to be played in Tokyo and London. Under his guidance the league would expand to twenty-six franchises. And by the end of his first decade in office, he would take the NFL and the AFL in his hands and shape them into one league with liberty, justice, and guaranteed serious profits for all. He would win the most expensive and dramatic interleague war in the history of American sports.

But before that day he would need an army that could act and think as he did. If he couldn't inherit it, he would create it. Why not? Without realizing it, he had been recruiting one much of his adult life. From the Rams he brought Bert Rose out of his old PR department and Bill Granholm, the equipment manager, who, when with the Rams, started to think as Rozelle did and developed skills that would leave the locker room behind. Granholm would become the most important nuts-and-bolts guy in his headquarters.

And, of course, there was one of his most key hires, a woman named Thelma Elkjer, who worked for both Tex Schramm and Rozelle in the Rams office. She declined Schramm's offer to come east when he left for CBS. But she saw something in Rozelle that others in the organization seemed to see. She agreed to work for him in New York. Schramm always said he couldn't understand why she spurned him for Pete.

Thelma was his executive secretary on the NFL's table of organization. That didn't even begin to tell it. She was the gatekeeper to both Rozelle's inner sanctum and his telephone. If you didn't get by her, you might as well have been standing downstairs on the street with nowhere to go.

She was also confidante, mentor, role model, and friend to Anne Marie, Rozelle's daughter from a failed marriage of whom he had

full custody. It can be said without fear of contradiction that Elkjer's role in that matter made him a better commissioner because I have never known a man who took being a single father more seriously.

From the Denver Broncos he plucked an assistant coach named Mark Duncan, who became his supervisor of officials. Later, when the AFL was merged, he added Mickey Herskowitz and Val Pinchbeck from its publicity staff. To plan for the future after the merger, he created the jobs of assistant to each league president, which was simply a Rozelle-regimented training ground for the future. Among those recruits were Ernie Accorsi, a Baltimore Colts PR guy who became general manager both in Cleveland and with the Giants; Al Ward, a Dallas Cowboys PR guy; and Jan Van Duser, from the Vikings. Like winners of fellowships, they came to Rozelle Tech, studied under him, and ultimately went off to other franchises, preaching the Rozelle Way. From the Associated Press came Don Weiss, a key lieutenant. Jim Heffernan, later head of PR, was a Philadelphia beat writer.

At one point every league official in a policy-making position was a former public relations expert, and the others in key jobs had to been trained to think like Rozelle. "He brought them in, trained them, and then shipped them out to play key roles around the league," Accorsi says.

> He had an ability to attract good people and make them feel wanted and important. I think each of us would have sacrificed our own careers for him if he'd wanted that, but he didn't.
>
> I remember we had this meeting . . . Weiss, Pinchbeck, Harold Rosenthal, myself, and a few others. We are sitting around this big table. He wanted our opinion about something. He asked each one of us, and he sat there and listened. Then he said, "I want you to know I really appreciate your input. Now, here is what we're gonna do."
>
> Well, none of us had even thought of the plan he came up with. So we're leaving the room, and I said to Rosenthal, who used to write for the *Herald Tribune* and who knew Pete as far back as his USF days, "How the hell did he come up with that when none of us had a clue?"

And he laughed and said, "Because, Ernesto, he is smarter than the rest of us."

Hell, he was smarter than anyone else we knew. But he never made you feel that way. What he did was to listen . . . always listen. . . . Sometimes at owner meetings he would stop and say he wanted to take a straw vote on some issue, and I knew that was because he wanted to make sure when they took the real vote he would win and also because that would tell him which owners he had to work on.

He hired and shaped the greatest PR staff and the greatest administrative staff any sports general ever had. But in the beginning there was the man Rozelle always referred to as "my offensive and defensive coordinator." His name was Jim Kensil, and for sixteen years he was the commissioner's alter ego. In 1961 Kensil, who was a jack of all trades in the Associated Press sports department, also wrote a Sunday column on sports and television called "The Sports Dial." On this particular day he had scheduled an interview with Rozelle to discuss what plans he had for the league and expanded television. It was, indeed, an interview. What Kensil did not know was that after the first five minutes, it was Rozelle who was doing the interviewing. By the time they finished he stunned Kensil by offering him a job.

From Pete's top public relations guy, he rose to the title of the NFL's executive director. His hiring freed Rozelle to spend more time getting to know his way around the halls of Congress. It was there that he would score his first major victory. He needed congressional approval for a plan so simple it would revolutionize the revenue stream that television's sleeping giant could provide his product.

As a visionary Rozelle surpassed P. T. Barnum, but unlike Barnum he always sold reality, not illusion. He looked at the haphazard business model with which the league's individual owners had sold their television rights. Each team controlled its own destiny in that area. None of them knew what their rights were worth, and a few of them couldn't even sell them. Who, for example, would

put up big money to televise the Green Bay Packers with their tiny stadium and their limited television territory?

He conceived of a package where everyone would make money; everyone would sell their games, because everyone would sell out of the same store to the same retailer. As always marked his style, he knew how to identify and recruit just the key allies to serve as the point men to make it possible. The men he needed to sell the other owners on the plan were Jack Mara and Wellington Mara, who owned and ran the New York Football Giants. "When Pete approached me," Wellington Mara told me,

> individually we were making more money off television, little as it was, than anybody else. After all, we were the only game in New York. And New York was the key city in any sport.
>
> Still, it was a gamble. But what he was saying was that it was good for the league, and Jack and I always felt we had to consider that because the league was more important than any one team. Without the league what did we have? If other franchises were in trouble, then so were we. This was our philosophy, no matter what the issue was.

The brothers Mara immediately spread the gospel of TV as Rozelle preached it. There were no holdouts. Now all he had to do was get Congress to grant a limited exemption from the antitrust laws. He lobbied hard, establishing relationships with senior congressmen and senators that would benefit the NFL for years to come.

Once again that groundwork was helped by Rozelle's time at USF. The city-side reporter for whom he always left football tickets had his own meteoric rise after both of them left the City by the Bay. He was now John F. Kennedy's press secretary. For years, when asked if Pierre Salinger helped the new commissioner get the votes and urged the president to sign the bill, Rozelle would consistently reply, "Not really." Perhaps. But as your mother used to say when asked about the benefits of chicken soup for head colds, "It might not help, but it couldn't hurt."

Kennedy signed the exemption into law and changed the way all professional and even college leagues would eventually operate.

5

How Do You Tell Vince?

You are made to feel special when you are very young. . . . And it's often hard not to start believing it.

—Frank Tripucka, former Notre Dame and Denver Broncos quarterback

Then we found this bar, and [Vince and I] sat there and we talked . . . and we drank scotch . . . We drank scotch for four hours.

—Pete Rozelle after he told Lombardi he planned to suspend Paul Hornung from the NFL

It was 1963, and in his heart the commissioner knew he ought to be concentrating on the challenge of the American Football League. It was three years now since the ragtag "Don Quixotes" of that other league had staggered off the drawing board and onto America's sports pages. They lacked both adequate playing fields and liquid capital. Newspapermen favorable to the old-guard NFL referred to the embryonic league's contests as aerial volleyball matches, a reference to both the lack of finesse and an incredibly limited view of defense.

But they were still alive, with their own ABC television contract. Now the head-to-head war was about to move into a new and ugly phase, one closer to home. When a group of shrewd sports-oriented businessmen had picked up the bankrupt New York Titans AFL franchise for the price of its debts—a mere one million dollars—Rozelle knew the AFL was moving into a new phase. The new group was led by David Sonny Werblin, a show-business and sports entrepreneur, whose Music Corporation of America's (MCA)

clients had included Guy Lombardo, Frank Sinatra, and Ronald Reagan. In addition, his television contacts (he had *Wagon Train* and *Bonanza* at numbers one and two in national popularity at the same time) made his new team, the Jets, a formidable problem for the hometown Giants.

It was April 1963, and Rozelle knew he should have been thinking about Werblin and the mounting legal costs of the interleague battle. He should have been thinking about the college draft and what share of the precocious heroes of America's fumble factories would sign with his league. He should have been thinking about expansion and the moves he needed to make.

But "should have" and "could have" are very different animals. "Could have" had become impossible with the impact of a well-kept secret with which Pete Rozelle secretly grappled. He had known for some time that the sort of problem that terrifies every commissioner, every owner, every college president with a big-time athletic team and every coach, was dangerously hanging over his world.

And he knew that it had to be dealt with swiftly and decisively to preserve the NFL's integrity. Without integrity, the NFL could have no product.

This is a country where gambling has always been a fever in the national blood. I remember as far back as when I was a kid in New Jersey, you could dial WE 6-1212, and a recorded voice would tell you that this was a report from the National Weather Service and that there was a 20 percent chance of rain. In what other country on the planet did the national government make book on April showers?

We are a country of gamblers. We always have been and always will be. This is no secret. Just think back to Yeoman Pete Rozelle's Army—Notre Dame caper as an amateur bookmaker aboard the USS *Gardoqui*.

We are also a country that will make an icon out of a young man who can throw a football sixty yards, hit a baseball four hun-

dred feet, or dunk a basketball from a half-mile above the hoop. That adoration can have a profound impact on how such gifted athletes view themselves.

I grew up with a great quarterback named Frank Tripucka who was an All-America under Frank Leahy at Notre Dame, an all-league quarterback in the Canadian Football League, and the first quarterback of the AFL's Denver Broncos. One day after he retired we were discussing how hard it can be for young athletes to keep themselves in perspective when the boys become men. "You are made to feel special when you are very young," he explained, and he knew because he had been there.

> Newspaper guys write terrific things about you. Boosters want to give you things in college. Later when you are a pro, hometown fans reach for your restaurant tabs. They all tell you how special you are. And it's often hard not to start believing it. For those who do, the rules become something for someone else to respect.
>
> When I was a pro, I knew one thing. Let someone buy you drinks long enough, and he will probably want a favor. That favor could be anything from going to a friend's wedding or . . . well . . . The way you avoid that is to eat and drink only with your teammates on the road, and then nobody can put you in a compromising position of any kind.

With the growth of football betting in America, an intriguing new form of merchandizing by bookmakers posed an escape route to players who wanted to have things both ways. It was called the point spread and established what the winning margin had to be to win a bet if you took the favorite. By keeping a team under that margin and still winning, a player could say and believe, as a New York University basketball point-shaver said to me after a major 1961 scandal, "Well, nobody got hurt except the bookies."

Now the briber did not have to get a player to lose a game. All he had to do was make sure his team did not cover the spread. With that possibility it didn't have to be a fact for rumors to cast doubt on the game's integrity. Proof positive that the betters believed

this to be true came with the myriad of telephone calls they placed to the NFL switchboard on Monday mornings after some place-kicker had missed a thirty-yard field goal and impacted the spread.

Rozelle knew all of this. And he knew that to permit a player to gamble at all was to flirt with disaster. He understood how easily gambling debts or free drugs for players in the fast lane could threaten the honesty of his games. He knew how it had happened before and how the fix had materialized in big, bold headlines about scores of college basketball games, hundreds of prizefights, and, yes, even once in the National Football League.

He never met bookmaker Alvin Paris, a man short in stature but huge in negative impact on the NFL. But he knew all about the impact he had on the sport in 1946. Paris had been the kingpin that made Bert Bell's worst nightmare a reality. He also became the very real ghost of things that could happen again if the lesson were ignored. Ever since pro football's mill-town days, people had bet on football. It was more an exercise in chauvinism than greed. Because gambling had always been there and because there never was a confirmed shred of evidence that the NFL's games were anything but honest, the league paid little attention to what the man on the street did to back his loyalties.

World War II had been over for a year. The boys came marching home. New cars rolled off the assembly line. A bright, new day was here, and with it a return to a form of normalcy long forgotten. The Giants and the Bears, two of the most bitter rivals in pro football, had earned their way into the title game. In the euphoria of a postwar rush back to the future, 58,346 football fans would pack the Polo Grounds.

It was then before the 1946 championship game that Alvin Paris, a man who left no other major mark on society, brought pro football face-to-face with its first horrifying moment of truth. That would be on Sunday. But only after all hell broke loose on Saturday.

Bert Bell, the commissioner, had always been uneasy about what

could happen with a gambler determined enough and a couple of players venal enough. Paris planned to broker that marriage.

Shortly after three on that Saturday, Mayor William O'Dwyer called Tim Mara, who owned the Giants. "Something has happened, Tim, and you and Steve [Owen, the Giants' coach] should know about it."

Thus, with no warning, began the longest day in the life of Tim Mara, a former legal bookmaker in the pre-tote-board days and a pioneer in the NFL's stepchild era. He had seen his team rise from the bottom to the top. He loved all things New York, and his Football Giants certainly were. As his cab took him to Gracie Mansion, the mayor's residence, he had no way of knowing he was on the threshold of the twenty-four cruelest hours of his life.

Arthur Wallender, the city police commissioner, was already there. As Mara and Owen listened, he explained that Merle Hapes, the Giants' starting fullback, admitted he had been bribed by Paris to fix the game. Hapes also claimed that teammate and tailback Frank Filchock had also been approached. Each, Hapes insisted, would get twenty-five hundred dollars, and, additionally, Paris would bet one thousand dollars for each of them on the proposition that the Bears would win by more than (remember the point-spread school of betting) ten points. Filchock denied his involvement. Bell agreed to let Filchock play, pending his own investigation, but Hapes was immediately suspended for not reporting a bribe attempt.

The Sunday papers were filled with the story. As the Giants clattered down the ancient stairs that led from clubhouse to field the next day, Filchock was greeted with thunderous boos. He had lied to Mara and Owen. Only he and Paris and Hapes knew that. But the crowd was publicly commenting on the possible lack of integrity of the game they were just coming to understand and love. It was a barometer as to how quickly the public would believe the slightest taint of scandal.

In an effort to redeem himself, Filchock played the best game of his life—even after he broke his nose. The Bears won. Then

Filchock confessed that he, too, had been offered money. Bell moved swiftly. He suspended both men. Neither ever played another game of football in the United States.

History remembers only the bribe attempt and not the final score. The gravity of that was not lost on Rozelle, who was a keen student of history. And there was something else. Two years before Rozelle became commissioner, the Colts had beaten the Giants in a sudden-death overtime title game. It was the game that vaulted pro football on its path to establishing itself as the new number-one sport in America. But it was also a game that fed into that myth of suspicion with which the commissioner now had to grapple.

The books had made the Colts a three-and-a-half-point favorite. On the game-winning drive in overtime when Johnny Unitas threw on second down, although an easy winning field goal was within reach, it triggered a nasty rumor. Carroll Rosenbloom, who owned the Colts, was a man who loved to gamble—cards . . . fights . . . perhaps even football. Rumors spread that he had bet on his Colts and needed a four-point spread to win that bet. A field goal would not have provided that. The Colts, instead, played for the touchdown.

When Unitas was challenged by the media afterward about the play he responded with: "It's not dangerous. If you know what you're doing, you don't get intercepted." And his long string of successes is evidence enough to prove that he knew what he was doing.

Despite that Rosenbloom's reputation as a gambling man was still alive when Rozelle had to consider the first major crisis of his tenure. On January 3, 1961, George Halas requested a formal investigation by Rozelle into what he termed betting by a member of a "midwestern franchise." The player to whom Halas had secretly alluded was Paul Hornung, the so-called golden boy of the Green Bay Packers. The investigation would open a Pandora's box of serious problems. Before it was finished, it would indict the entire management conduct of the Detroit Lions, uncover more

players who bet, and result in the suspension's of Hornung and the Lions' Alex Karras. Only by a stroke of luck, lack of aggression by the hoodlum fringe, and Rozelle's PR brilliance was Rozelle able to wipe out the long-range impact of a scandal that could have threatened the league's very existence.

The Rozelle probe generated fifty-two interviews with persons connected with eight of what were then fourteen teams. The scope could be this effective because of a growing relationship between the league, first with Bell, and then on into the Rozelle years with law enforcement officials.

What had begun with Bell in 1949 and the 1950s, checking with local Philly bookmakers about "erratic action," had become an effective intelligence-gathering operation. Pete began to have relationships with law officers and ultimately even staffed hirings in his security department from among former FBI agents and police officials.

In 1956 Hornung, a Notre Dame senior, was invited to play in the East-West Shrine Game in San Francisco. That week he met a young California businessman, and the two hit it off so well that when Hornung returned home, he promised to keep in touch. Over the next three years of occasional meetings and phone calls between the two, the recurring theme was the friend's desire for information about this player or that and this game or that.

By the summer of 1959 Hornung was an established member of the Green Bay Packers, and the friend's questions about "this game" had evolved into "these games." The telephone calls had become weekly, and Hornung was now placing his own bets on college and pro games through his friend. The bets were usually one or two hundred dollars but occasionally were as high as five hundred dollars.

The betting continued on into 1962, when for some unexplained reason it suddenly stopped. But by Hornung's own reckoning in his later talks with Rozelle, he generally broke even, although he did recall that one year he had made about fifteen hundred dollars. None of his pro bets involved the Packers.

Among other pieces of Hornung information that reached Rozelle through law enforcement sources was the anecdotal recounting of a harmless chance meeting with a Kansas City mafioso whose ties were unknown to Hornung. But it illustrates what Rozelle perceived to be the potential danger to the league's reputation.

In 1959, even before Rozelle became commissioner, Hornung's name appeared in an FBI report through no fault of his own. Hornung had been in a bar when a friend of a friend approached him and told him there was a guy who would like to meet him. The next thing he knew, Hornung was having a drink with a guy the feds call Needle Nose, whom he had never heard of and to whom he was obviously introduced by his square name.

He bought Hornung a drink and told him how much he enjoyed seeing him play and how much he admired the Packers. That was the end of the sports talk. After that they probably talked about broads and drinks and the weather, and it was over so fast that Hornung probably doesn't even remember it today.

The feds had no interest in Hornung, but the reason the story eventually reached Rozelle was that they knew enough about Needle Nose to put a permanent tail on him. That agent reported to his boss the next day that Needle Nose "had met with a professional football player at a bar, bought him a drink, and discussed subjects unknown."

It was Rozelle's belief that NFL players had to be so far above reproach in their social dealings as to make Caesar's wife look like a Las Vegas hooker. The possible impact, he told me, of law enforcement reports like what he called "the Needle Nose Papers" was serious if they became public knowledge.

His public relations instincts told him that there's always a Needle Nose trying to get close to a superstar. He may just want to buy a ball player a drink because he is nuts about football, and most of them are. He may just want a little information to help him make his own bet. That happens with people in all professions. Or he just might want something more. "Unfortunately," Rozelle told me, "you can't stop the public from jumping to that last conclusion."

To compound the situation in Rozelle's mind, Hornung, who had been Player of the Year in 1961, was, to say the least, artistically erratic the following fall. He was obviously limping from a knee injury at the same time that strange things were happening to the Green Bay point spreads—not for any nefarious reason but because lack of information about his injury was a major factor in establishing a proper line each week. "I knew the Packers were not appearing on the betting lines some weeks in certain cities," Rozelle said.

> So I had people contact certain persons [euphemism for bookmakers] to find out why. The answer made perfect sense. It was twofold. They couldn't tell how much Hornung could play at top speed with a bum knee, and what we found to be more important was the peculiar psyche of the Green Bay team. It could beat almost anyone in the league 49–0 if it chose to do so, but it rarely wanted to humiliate anyone. As a result there was too much guesswork involved in making a line on the Packers, which was the reason they occasionally did not.

He knew that in addition to Hornung and Karras, there could be more to this story. But at no time did he say that he did what he had to do to prevent a larger scandal. Instead, he took a necessary PR approach. "I believe in the men in this league," he later explained. "The decision to suspend Hornung and Karras was mine alone, and it had to be done. The main thing is that back in January, I reported the situation to the owners in a very general way without being specific, and one club owner told me, 'There is no evidence of wrongdoing beyond breaking a rule against gambling. Of that I am certain. . . . No evidence of point-shaving. But we might have both those problems in a couple of years if we don't follow this investigation all the way down the line.'"

Rozelle already knew where it would lead. He knew of Hornung's bets; he knew that he had documentation to prove that Karras had bet six times through a business associate beginning

in 1958. At least one of those bets had involved the Lions against the Packers when Karras had backed his own team.

But more important, the Karras issue had led Rozelle into a larger and more dangerous situation. It uncovered the fact that five other Lions (allegedly at Karras's instigation) had bet on a Packers-Giants game along with Karras. Rozelle also came into possession of Detroit police reports that had been first directed to Lions management, warning it of players' association with known local hoodlums who often obtained sideline passes or sat on the Lions' bench. The Lions' management took no action.

And finally it led to a Detroit gin mill nicknamed the Lindell AC that was owned—or so it appeared—by the Butsicaris brothers. Its clientele was eclectic. In addition to local athletes and newspaper guys, it offered a group of other folks you would never find on the NFL's red-carpet list. Karras, it developed, owned a piece of the bar, which he would later sell.

The Lindell AC bothered Rozelle. Its co-owners, Jimmy and John Butsicaris, ran what may have been America's first sports bar. It began in the fleabag Lindell Hotel at Cass and Bagley, when the area was Detroit's skid row. It moved up the block the same year that Karras was suspended. Rozelle claimed his evidence indicated that the Lindell was a hotbed of illegal gambling activity and forced Karras to sell his share of the bar. It was across the courtyard from an apartment house called the Town House, where a bunch of Lions and assistant coaches lived in season.

Pete Waldmeir, a terrific columnist who moved from sports to city side at the *Detroit News*, recalls the joint in its first incarnation, which was when the Lions and others among Detroit's famous were first attracted to it.

They would walk across an alley and through the back door of the Lindell. They partied a lot. Bookmakers used the telephone. I remember they had hookers in the joint, and one of them used to do crosswords during her "downtime"—and cheat.

But not many Mob guys hung out there. They were down in Greek-

town at the Grecian Gardens, which was a Mob place owned by the mother of a mafioso named Dominic Corrado, whose father, Machine Gun Pete, had been deported to Sicily, where he died.

The joint was just a couple of blocks away from police headquarters, and it was notorious for paying off cops to look the other way on assorted gambling and liquor violations. The owners couldn't get a state license anyway to serve alcohol because of their criminal records, so they served whiskey to the regulars in coffee cups. They also made book on horses, football, whatever else moved, and they ran a Greek card game called *barbut* upstairs. Karras was not exactly a stranger to the joint.

But the thing that kind of locked the Lindell and Grecian Gardens together on Rozelle's undesirable list was a bus trip from Grecian Gardens to Cleveland on August 18, 1962, where the Lions played a preseason game. "They ran the bus to away games," Waldmeir told me, "and called it the Blue and Silver Bus, which were the Lions' colors. Well, on this trip the passenger list included Billy Jack Giacalone, Dominc Corrado, Anthony Zerilli, Carl Thomas (a convicted murderer), Sam Giordano, Peter Vitale, the night manager of the Grecian Gardens and bag man for police payoffs, who later was a suspect in the disappearance of Jimmy Hoffa. Also along were assorted members and Detroit underworld players from the Licavoli family."

An hour and forty minutes later, the bus arrived at the Bunkhouse Café in Toledo, known to law enforcement as the hub of gambling in Toledo and owned by local hood Ray Gentile. When police sought to identify the passengers, they declined to comply. Authorities later learned they were joined on the return trip by Karras, John Gordy, and Darius McCord, all of whom played for the Lions that day.

"As if that wasn't enough to jolt Rozelle," Waldmeir said, "the behavior of the Lions' coach and management raised a lot of questions with him. On Wednesdays, Mike and Pete Larco, Mob-associated brothers who ran an Italian restaurant on the west side

of Detroit, would just walk into the locker room after practice to deliver a huge vat of minestrone and socialize with the players. The Larcos and other known mobsters were issued sideline passes on game day. One of them once sat on the bench."

Rozelle had more than enough evidence on the gambling charges and in Karras's case association with known felons. But in both cases it was clear there was no nefarious point-shaving scandal here, much to his relief. Now it was time to act. Rozelle knew there were risks here. For one, he would be fining the Lions' ownership for its lack of attention to policing its sidelines and locker room. But he knew he could handle that. The players were not going to be able to dispute the evidence. So he knew he could handle them. But there was one other character in this morality play.

He was the strongman of the National Football League. He could be the commissioner's most powerful ally or his most dangerous adversary, depending on how he reacted. His name was Vince Lombardi. He was the creator of everything Paul Hornung had become on the playing field. Rozelle had no idea what Lombardi would say or do when he learned he had lost the golden boy.

When Lombardi took over at Green Bay in 1958, he took one look at films of Hornung, a superstar at Notre Dame and a failure at Green Bay, and he shook his head. Management did not know what it had. Hornung was obviously a runner who could throw the ball, not a quarterback who could run it. So he took Hornung and made him into a shining star who was as versatile on the field as he was gifted. He put in a halfback option, as he had done for Frank Gifford as the Giants' backfield coach. Hornung turned it into a thing of beauty. He ran him in the Green Bay power sweep and turned him into a weapon calculated to strike terror into a linebacker's heart.

Off the field Lombardi tolerated more from Hornung than all of the others who dared to test his spartan rules for curfew. In a sense you could almost detect a touch of envy in the coach for Hornung's lifestyle. He became the father vicariously watching the son prove that youth is not always wasted on youth after dark.

Lombardi spoke often but in a joking way of his feelings toward Hornung, whom he tolerated at times like a wayward son who still managed to make him proud when it counted. Above all, the coach who some said threw praise around as though it were a manhole cover, did not hesitate to extol both Hornung's natural talent and his critical role in the Packers' offense.

Knowing all of this, it was with great trepidation that Rozelle picked up his private line and called Lombardi with a request he knew the coach would challenge. "Will you please come to New York immediately? It is extremely urgent that I speak with you."

"I am coaching a football team," came the response. "I don't have time. What do you want?"

"What I want," Rozelle said, "is to see you in my office."

Lombardi said he would be there the next day.

"I sat there waiting for him the next afternoon," Rozelle told me, "and I kept asking myself, 'How do I approach him? . . . What do I say? . . . How am I going to set him up? . . . How am I going to win him over?' He was one of the most honorable men I have ever known, and he had a grasp of loyalty and organization. I decided I would sit back and let him make up his own mind."

When Lombardi walked through the door, Rozelle said nothing. He simply took a massive manila folder off his desk and handed it to him without comment. "I remember," Rozelle said, "that I watched him read it."

Neither of us said a word, but I could tell he was really shaken. Then he closed it very slowly, and he looked at me and he said just four words: "You have no choice."

Here was this strong-willed man, and I knew what Paul meant to him . . . not only as the star of his team but as a person he had tried to guide. I didn't know what to say, so all I did was nod my head in agreement. And then there was another long silence, and I could see the pain in his eyes, and I said, "Let's go have a drink."

They went down the elevator in silence and walked east on Forty-Ninth Street. "Neither one of us could say much at first,"

Rozelle recalled. "Then we found this bar, and we sat there and we talked . . . and we drank scotch . . . We drank scotch for four hours."

Lombardi left town that night, still unclear on what action Rozelle would take. Now events were moving swiftly toward a conclusion. The penalties were already clear in Rozelle's mind. Arriving at them was difficult, but implementing them would be even more precarious. It had to be done swiftly so that the story did not leak to the press. It would have to be done decisively so that the American public, which held the future to the product he had been chosen to protect, would not turn against the league.

He wanted to do it diplomatically as well, so that he did not get into a public brawl with the defendants. "I felt the first thing I wanted to do," he told me, "was to speak with Hornung."

> I had already planned to do this thing the next day, and I didn't want him or anyone else to learn it through the newspapers. I found him through his mother, Loretta, in Louisville.
>
> Apparently, he had told her a little bit about what was happening because when she found out who was calling, she indicated that she knew it had to do with my final decision.
>
> I told Paul what I was doing and why. I know he was deeply disappointed. I don't know whether he and Vince had discussed it, but he showed so much class that night, and he would do it again the next day on television.
>
> The other guy [Karras], well, we had a very tense conversation. All I can recall these days was his anger—and it was considerable.

Conversely, Hornung had actually written the commissioner a letter after his suspension ended and told Rozelle he believed the commissioner had done the right thing except for the case of Lions management, which he thought got away far too easily with what he told Rozelle was a slap on the wrist.

"Vince called me before I knew anything about their meeting," Hornung told me, "and said Rozelle would be calling and maybe I should also go see him."

Neither of us knew what the penalty would be. I knew they had tapped my phone. I didn't know whether that was legal or not, but I never called an attorney because I knew what I did was wrong. I knew of others, but I didn't give a damn if it was just going to be me because I was wrong. So I didn't mention anyone else, and I never will.

He was the best commissioner any sport ever had. He told me that I was to stay away from casinos and race tracks and that meant the Derby, too, and you know I live in Louisville and hadn't missed one since I was twelve. But I listened. I dotted my *i*'s and crossed my *t*'s, and I still think he did the right thing.

But I did have a little fun with him. After both of us were out of football, I went to Del Mar Race Track with my buddy D. Wayne Lukas, the trainer, and I looked down from our box, and I saw him below. So I ran down there. He was glad to see me, and he asked how I was doing, and then I said, "I just want to know one thing. Can I make a bet on a few horses today?" He actually roared he laughed so hard.

After he called Hornung and Karris, Pete Rozelle did not sleep well that night. That figures. Nobody ever pleads the executioner's case. He has to work it out on his own. He knew that within twenty-four hours, he would be looking squarely into the jaws of the moment of truth. It would be the day the NFL and its young commissioner would learn how much clout it really had with the American sports fan and his hot little disposable sports dollar. He tossed and turned until finally he said the hell with it and rolled out of bed at 5:15 a.m.

The morning fog was just beginning to lift when he finally hit the street. It was April 17, a warm spring day. As he walked he could see the UN complex in the first flush of light, reaching toward the sky. A soft breeze came rolling in off the East River, and he paused for a moment to watch a snub-nosed Moran tug groan its way against the current, a generation of soot plastered against its weary side. It was not yet 7:00 a.m., and the rush hour was still an hour away. For a time he paused and watched the river, and then he turned away to walk the fifteen blocks to his office near Rockefeller Plaza.

For some time he had contemplated moving the offices from the cramped quarters in the General Dynamics Building to much roomier digs. Now he regretted he hadn't done so. He was still a journalist at heart. He knew the television crews with their heavy equipment would be a problem, the still photographers with their aggressive psyches perhaps even more so, and an army of reporters jockeying for space and one-on-one interviews would be the greatest challenge of all.

By the time he arrived his mind was already clicking off marching orders for the staff. First, there would be the sharp metallic clicking of the keys on the office TWX machine, and when the short, terse message of no more than three sentences (he still hadn't figured how to frame it) was finished, all hell would break loose.

How do you tell the world that Vince Lombardi's golden-boy prodigy is at the heart of the biggest gambling scandal in league history? How do you tell the owner of the Detroit Lions that not only are you suspending one of the greatest defensive linemen in the history of football but that you are also fining other Lions and the Detroit management?

He stepped into the empty elevator and rode toward his office. It was time to do the laundry.

The press conference was the most masterful piece of media manipulation I have ever seen as a working newspaperman. Shortly after Rozelle relayed his state of the penalty-box message, Kensil was already telephoning newspapers and the electronic media. As Rozelle had expected, the cramped quarters could not even begin to accommodate the seekers-after-NFL-truth. Within an hour even standing room was at a premium.

Rozelle began with a simple statement of fact. Hornung and Karras were suspended indefinitely. Five other Lions—guard John Gordy, defensive back (DB) Gary Lowe, All-League middle linebacker Joe Schmidt, linebacker Wayne Walker, and defensive end (DE) Sam Walker—were fined two thousand dollars each for the bets they had placed. And, finally, the Lions' management was fined four thousand dollars because Coach George Wilson had

failed to forward a Detroit police report to the proper authorities on his club and failed to properly police his own sideline.

The shock of Hornung's and Karras's involvement had overridden the much larger problem of what had happened on the Lions' sideline and inside the locker room. Those management violations in their way were potentially the seeds of a far greater problem. Had it not been Hornung and Karras but two lesser players, the media would have focused far more on the Lions' management.

Was the penalty for this serious problem so light because Rozelle would have been disciplining one of his own bosses? Perhaps.

But I have another theory. Jerry Greene of the *Detroit News*, one of three daily newspaper reporters to have covered every Super Bowl, told me years later that after the merger between the AFL and NFL he had asked Rozelle if the Lions would be one of three NFL teams forced over into the AFL. Rozelle had responded by answering Greene with another question. Did he know that the Ford Motor Company was one of the league's primary television sponsors at the time?

And then there was what he did not say. Where does Ford live? Michigan. Who else lives in Michigan? The Lions. Who owned the Lions in 1963? William Ford Sr. Who got away with murder in this whole gambling mess? It wasn't Hornung and Karras.

Karras got the official word in the Lions' office that day. "I haven't done anything I'm ashamed of," he said, "and I'm not guilty. I have retained a lawyer."

Meanwhile, back in New York as the press conference droned on, somebody asked Rozelle how he would characterize Karras's reaction to the commissioner's phone call informing him of the penalty. "Angry," Rozelle said. "Very, very angry." And if he had to find a word for Hornung? "Stupid," somebody in the back of the room shouted. "Disappointed," Rozelle responded.

Rozelle was the ringmaster, alternating between the press and television, shuttling from the makeshift press section to a small ante room where TV crews came and went with the precision of

an automatic punch press. The big topic of discussion relative to Hornung and Karris was "How long is indefinite?"

"Can you excuse me?" Rozelle asked the multitude, picking up on a signal from Kensil. "Paul is on television and I'd like to listen."

On the screen in the corner of Rozelle's office Hornung was saying all the right things. He was sorry. He was sorry that he had let his teammates down. He was sorry that he had been so foolish. He was sorry that he had let his fans down.

"One more sorry," a guy in the back whispered, "and 'indefinitely' will end by noon tomorrow."

"I'm sorry," Rozelle said, and everyone looked to the ceiling to see if a duck with a ten-dollar bill in its beak would drop down, proving that "sorry" was the old *Groucho Marx Show*'s magic word for the day. "I'm sorry," Rozelle repeated, "for the interruption. Where were we?" Not that it mattered. The show was over.

"It was," Rozelle told me that day, "the hardest decision I ever had to make. Now that it's over, all I can tell you is that I have a tremendous feeling of relief. There has to be when you live alone with something like this."

Hornung, as America's favorite, could have been a problem, but he handled the party line perfectly. Rozelle had handled the legal problems perfectly by announcing the suspended players were free to play elsewhere, knowing full well that no AFL team would dare to sign an admitted gambler at a time when it was fighting for respectability. And there was little trouble Karras could make once the team management fell in line—which it couldn't do quickly enough once it saw how light the penalty for management was.

Karras remained as volatile as ever during the suspension. A friend of his who actually may have been one of the fellows mentioned in the Detroit police reports told me that during the ban, Alex flew to New York City with him on business and bumped into Rozelle on Sixth Avenue.

"How are you?" Pete said.

"Fine. I really want to get this suspension over with. I've changed my lifestyle. I'd like you to meet my new business manager."

Which is how, without ever knowing the truth, Pete Rozelle happened to shake hands with a bookmaker in broad daylight in the middle of Manhattan.

And you also have to say this for Karras: he had a sense of humor. After the ban ended and he was back in football, he walked to the center of the field for the coin toss to start a game against the Vikings.

"Mr. Karras," the referee said, "you are the visiting captain. Will you please call the coin toss now?"

"No," Karras said.

"I beg your pardon?" the referee said. "What did you say?"

"I said no. I won't call the coin toss. I'm sorry, but the commissioner says I'm not allowed to bet."

Shortly after the suspensions ended, Rozelle hired his first chief of security, Jim Hamilton, the cop who had founded America's first police intelligence-gathering unit in Los Angeles. "I want them to know you are watching," Rozelle told him.

The week that his hiring was announced, Hamilton was seen in the Giants' dressing room before the game. But members of the Colts insisted that he was in Baltimore that day. "We saw him after our game. He can't be in two places at once."

"Oh, no?" Hamilton told me when I repeated what the guy had said. "Don't tell him, but that's why trains run between New York and Baltimore."

Rozelle always loved that story.

6

Heads They Win, Tails He Loses

From Dallas, Texas, a flash apparently official, President Kennedy died at
1:00 p.m., Central Standard Time.
 —Walter Cronkite, cbs newsroom, November 22, 1963

I felt badly over all the criticism Pete took because I think he did the abso-
lutely right thing. He didn't cancel the games. I played that Sunday in New
York, and I believe, at least in this city, it got us all moving again.
 —Frank Gifford, in defense of why Rozelle did not cancel the nfl
 schedule

It was the kind of media honeymoon that would melt a politician's
heart. From the time that Pete Rozelle became commissioner of
the National Football League on January 26, 1960, until the day
all of America froze in horror on November 22, 1963, he had been
viewed as a kind of 100-yard Mother Teresa, cleaner than dirt and
purer than a Green Bay snowfall.

From his radical television policy to his shrewdly ignoring
the rebel afl until he believed that his ownership was finally
ready to fight, from the suspension of Golden Boy Paul Hor-
nung and Black Hat Alex Karras for gambling to his personal role
in the forced integration of the Washington Redskins, Ameri-
ca's media virtually applauded his every act. He was, they uni-
versally acknowledged, the best-looking, most articulate, and
brightest of all the commissioners that had preceded him in all
of America's sports.

And then came that horrendous day when President Kennedy
was assassinated in Dallas that struck at the very heart of all Amer-

ica. That was on a Friday afternoon around noon, local time. He died within the hour at Parkland Medical Center.

The country was paralyzed by that act. By nightfall those same circumstances would force Rozelle to make a decision that would bring down an avalanche of acerbic criticism upon him no matter what he did. There was, for him, simply no way to win. For the first time in his career, the commissioner who seemed to always plan for every contingency was thrust into the teeth of a lose-lose decision. With a beloved president assassinated and a nation in mourning, the question that caught Rozelle flush on the jaw was "to play or not to play."

The mood of the country more than reflected the tragedy—it lived it. The AFL in conjunction with NBC, which carried its games, immediately canceled its full schedule. In some minds that put the National Football League at a public relations disadvantage.

Like all Americans, I remember clearly where I was when the events that set that weekend in motion began to take shape. On the morning of November 22, 1963, I drove across the George Washington Bridge from New Jersey, exited onto the Major Deegan Expressway in the Bronx, and went on to Yankee Stadium, where the NFL Giants were preparing for their Sunday game with the St. Louis Cardinals.

It had been a year of ups and downs for Sam Huff, the middle linebacker, who had become a New York City hero since he had joined the club seven years earlier. I planned to build my Sunday column around him, so I watched practice, met with Sam in the locker room, and headed back down to Manhattan. By then I was already the lead columnist with the *Star-Ledger* in New Jersey, but I spent so much time in New York City that I was in the habit of stopping by my former newspaper, the *New York Herald Tribune*, to write and file my column.

I was halfway through the piece when this tremendous commotion broke out on the other side of the city room. People were

running toward the glass-enclosed alcove where the wire-service machines were housed. Copy boys were sprinting toward the elevators and then disappearing into various saloons and restaurants to haul angry editors and rewrite men away from steins of beer and half-eaten sandwiches and back to the office to work on one of the biggest stories in the history of American newspapers. The president of the United States had been shot.

Who among us cannot recall the sounds and sights of the immediate days that followed, the constant drone of the radios and television sets, the sadness . . . the tears . . . the anger? For those of my generation (since Kennedy was one of us), it was the single most traumatic event of our lives at that time.

And in this chaotic time, Rozelle had to make a decision. CBS, which carried his games, was waiting for it, and it couldn't wait too long. The media, conscious of the AFL cancellations, were watching. What made the urgency for action from Rozelle even more demanding was the fact that due to travel arrangements, television plans, and ticket holders, his clock was clicking at a furious pace.

In Cleveland, Browns owner Art Modell picked up the phone, called Rozelle, and expressed an immediate opinion of his own. "I had spoken to some people I knew in the White House, and, of course, I had my own feelings.

"I deeply felt the games should not be played out of respect. Pete had his own opinion. What made it worse for both me and the city of Cleveland personally was that the team we were going to play at home that day was the Dallas Cowboys.

"And what hurt me was the fact that the AFL, which at the time had no stature, had made what I considered to be the right decision."

Modell was not alone. Nobody ever took a straw poll, but clearly the issue left a house divided. As for Rozelle, what would influence his decision most was not surprising. As he always did, he reached back to old friends for their opinion. Pierre Salinger, the city-side reporter from the *San Francisco Chronicle* for whom Rozelle always left tickets for USF football games, had remained close to him through the years. He had also become Kennedy's press secretary.

Salinger seemed to speak for the whole Kennedy family when he told Pete that he was sure Kennedy would not have wanted the games canceled. He said that Bobby Kennedy had personally said as much to him. Within hours Rozelle announced that the NFL would play as scheduled. When he made that announcement, the commissioner immediately became the target for a tsunami of public condemnation that even his gifted public relations instincts could not divert.

For me, the game-day drive that Sunday across the Macomb's Dam Bridge that fronts Yankee Stadium was like a journey through the twilight zone. It played hell with normal visual perspective. Looking at the big, concrete saucer of a ballpark, it seemed as though some alien Gulliver had swept a giant hand across the horizon and totally rearranged the skyline.

And then I realized what it was. The flags.

They had always been a constant, ringing the top of the stadium as a kind of landmark. But now they were at half-mast, they hung limply in the November wind, dramatically changing the entire configuration of a view that I had seen hundreds of times before without really seeing it.

The emotions and the events of the day were staggering, not only in the Bronx but all across America. Out in Cleveland Modell had invited a few reporters into his box to watch the news telecasts from Dallas as the teams warmed up. There—as in the Yankee Stadium press room, where I was watching—we saw Oswald shot and killed on live TV being transferred from police headquarter to the county jail. Modell recalled the horror he and the reporters in his press box felt when "we were watching a second damned murder."

The irony for a number of sportswriters was staggering because Oswald's killer, Jack Ruby, as a strip club owner, often picked up the tab for local cops at his Carousel Club. In addition, he was a virtual sportswriter groupie, visiting our hotels and handing out free-drink cards. Most of us had met him. Each time he left his parting words were "Don't forget to tell the other guys they're welcome at the Carousel."

Back in New York, before the Giants-Cardinals game, Jack Mara, then the team president, offered refunds for any season ticketholder who did not attend. There were no takers, and there were no protesters.

I did not agree with Rozelle's decision at the time, but apparently most football fans did, because 62,992 of them showed up at Yankee Stadium. There were seven games played that afternoon, and the only drop in expected attendance was in Minnesota, where the weather and not grief was the key factor.

So the crowds did show up, leading to the conclusion that at least for America's NFL fans, Rozelle had made the right decision. Even today, however, I am convinced that much of the country did not agree at all with what he elected to do.

But I could not help but wonder if the cancellation of a week's worth of NFL football would have affected CBS or NFL profits and what the impact on both corporations would have been of the need to extend the entire schedule deeper into the calendar by rescheduling the week's games. In other words, was money a factor?

And what if Dallas or Washington had been scheduled to play at home? What would the NFL have done, faced with the incredible nonfootball things happening in those two cities on that day?

In New York the crowd was so quiet and reflective, I wondered again, "Why are they playing this game?" Modell said that in Cleveland there were close to 60,000 fans on hand, but "it was the strangest day I ever experienced at any stadium. They were so quiet. The best way to describe the whole day is 'eerie.' What made it even worse was the fact that of all the teams in the league we had to draw the one from the town where it happened."

And there was something else. It was the time of America's love affair with the transistor radio, and at Giants stadium, like in every other venue, they seemed to grow in number through sheer osmosis. Usually, you saw them because football fans like to hear the radio announcers explain things they cannot quite see. But on this day their bulletins from Dallas turned the crowd positively schizophrenic: the Giants complete a screen pass and the crowd wants

to cheer, but then the radios tells them that Lee Harvey Oswald has been shot. The Cardinals score and the crowd wants to groan, but the radios report that the late president's body is on its way to Washington. The Cardinals begin a drive and the crowd wants to chant "Defense . . . Defense . . . Defense . . . ," but the radios tell them that Lee Harvey Oswald has died.

And an hour earlier Martha Wright, the Broadway star, sang the national anthem, and for the first time in my life I heard 62,992 people sing along with her in unison. New York sports fans are not by nature singers of the national anthem at any event. But on this day they sang. I didn't have a clue as to what that meant in terms of Rozelle's decision, but I suppose there was some kind of message in it.

It was on that day and still is Frank Gifford's contention that Rozelle's decision was "the best thing that could have happened for the city of New York and its people. The whole thing was so horrible that we all seemed to be standing still. I played in that game, and I honestly believe it was a release. I think the city started moving forward again with it behind us. We had to get back to living."

After the game I went to look for Rozelle. He had elected to come to the Giants game because, well, because he was Rozelle and he had made a decision, and I knew he would not take the easy way out. Earlier, in a formal statement he had said, "It has been traditional in sports for athletes to perform in times of great personal tragedy. Football was Mr. Kennedy's game. He thrived on competition." That was the NFL publicity machine's explanation, but I still wanted to hear something from him.

I found him in the long, cold tunnel underneath the grandstand on his way out about a half hour after the game. It was chilly, and I have a vague memory that he was wearing a light-colored trench coat. I remember telling him I thought he had been wrong and then asking him how he made his decision. This is what he said:

It's your right to think what you like, but I do not believe you have the right to tell me how to mourn any more than I have the right to tell

you or anyone else. Each man has to mourn in his own way. I went to church this morning. Nobody made these people come here today. They wanted to come. I think it [playing the games] was a good thing for them and for the country because it kept some form of order for them and gave them some kind of relief.

I don't think playing the games was disrespectful. I don't think I made a mistake. I know that some feeling has developed since I made the decision on Friday. We got a lot of phone calls that were critical at the office. But I believe it was good for the country.

And money quite honestly had absolutely nothing to do with that decision.

But what if Dallas had been scheduled to play at home? Or Washington had? "What would you have done then?"

"That would have changed everything—completely. But it wasn't that way. It's not unfair for you to question me about it, but with that a nonfactor, I honestly believe I did the right thing."

Except for Modell most owners did not express opposition to Rozelle's decision. Back in 1963 they pretty much supported just about everything he did. John Mara's recollection was that Wellington never even discussed it with him until the subject came up after the attack on the World Trade Center thirty-eight years later.

It was odd that we never had discussed it before then, but I certainly had no memory of his position when it happened. But after the attack on the World Trade Center it was unanimous among owners not to play, and I do recall that my dad said then that it had been a mistake to play the JFK game.

He was adamantly opposed to it, but he understood that Pete did it with the best of intentions to try to get us all back to normalcy. But in retrospect my dad thought it probably was the wrong thing because people were still grieving and there was no way to judge that.

Rozelle surely defended it during that brief one-on-one we had after the game. But later he continually and publicly stated that in retrospect, he had come to regret that decision. Still, over the

years I have not been clear over what Rozelle really thought. Did he really come to regret it? Did he think he was wrong, or did he believe deep down that he had actually done the best thing possible for the league and for the country at large?

Joe Browne, who later became the league's top PR man and its vice president for government affairs, probably still has the best read on it:

> In 1989 when he was leaving, someone was interviewing him and asked him to go over some of the things that pleased him most during his career. He talked about the growth of the Super Bowl into a huge national event and the day Art Rooney won his first Super Bowl. And then the guy asked him about the Kennedy game and he went along with the idea that he regretted playing it, but I don't think he meant that.
>
> The guy had asked him about his biggest regret or disappointment, and the truth is that he had so few as commissioner that I think he went along with the idea that maybe the Kennedy game had been a mistake.
>
> But later he told me he still believed it was the right thing to do and remember Pierre Salinger had advised him that it was, and his old tie to him and their days in San Francisco I am sure convinced him.

It was, arguably, the first time popular opinion over a Rozelle decision was split so passionately. It would probably be the last.

The war between the NFL and the AFL was about to ignite in full fury. But as the two leagues battled, Rozelle's got no heat because there were really no tangential issues that forced America to take sides beyond plain, old-fashioned municipal chauvinism.

It wasn't the need to bring professional football to growing cities that had been left out of the mix that would trigger serious trauma for the commissioner. He knew expansion was coming, as his subsequent acts showed. That it would come through heated competition didn't worry him, either. After all, competition was

ingrained deeply within him, with a serious passion going all the way back to those quarter-a-hole matches at Gittleson's miniature golf course.

Pressure had always seemed to bring out the best in him. But now he was about to be pressured to compete as never before. There was a new gunslinger in town. His name was Al Davis, and nobody before or after would get his competitive juices flowing as intensely and for as long a period of time as this new player in America's 100-yard game would.

The old guard of the National Football League would face the biggest challenge in its history. Never were the stakes as high as the ones for which Rozelle and Davis would go head- to-head—on the playing fields (both collegiate and professional) and ultimately in the courts.

Some would say, well, it wasn't personal. What it was was business. But even after it had run its course and a new combined league morphed out of it, and for as long as Rozelle was the commissioner and Davis was the gadfly, it was, indeed, very personal.

7

The 100-Yard Armageddon

Let them raise enough money to buy a football.
> —NFL commissioner Elmer Layden, when asked how the All-America
> Football Conference would fare in the entertainment field

What's bigger than a giant? A titan, that's what.
> —Harry Wismer on the naming of his AFL franchise

He knew his history, which is more than you can say for some of his owners, who seemed to believe with an almost religious fervor that the roots of their 100-yard monopoly had something to do with Mount Sinai and stone tablets.

Pete Rozelle fully understood that those who ignored the failures of past history were destined to repeat them. And when it came to rival leagues failing, there was no shortage of messengers. He knew that for all the failed attempts, there were two that had a tremendous impact on what the National Football League had become.

In 1925 George Halas had struck the single biggest positive blow for solvency in the history of the fledgling NFL when he signed Red Grange, a magnificent running back out of the University of Illinois who had captured the nation's imagination. The architect of his inspiration had been a man named C. C. (Cash and Carry) Pyle, a press-agent entrepreneur, whose later brushes with immortality would include a coast-to-coast walkathon he creatively named the Bunion Derby. The signing of Grange, a home-grown hero, brought the Chicago Bears as close as they had ever been to solvency.

As an aside Tim Mara, whose Giants were playing in their inaugural season, gave away five thousand tickets each Sunday and still

couldn't draw customers. Over the first ten games, he couldn't clear the ten thousand dollars a game he needed to break even.

But Mara had scheduled the Bears and Grange for game 11. On that day they broke the fire laws. Roughly seventy-three thousand people paid their way in. A visiting superstar had made the Polo Grounds the place to be in New York City.

It was that way everywhere Halas took the Bears. But the love affair between Halas and Pyle soon generated into one of pure hate. The year after the Polo Grounds milestone, Pyle suggested a new arrangement. The thing he wanted to rearrange was the Halas bank account. He demanded a 50 percent ownership stake for Grange, who was his client.

After Halas threw them both out, Pyle ran around the country seeking cities for a rival league, with Grange as its centerpiece. Grange would be co-owner along with Pyle of a team in Yankee Stadium. Pyle's circuit was called the American Football League, and it was an economic disaster.

The semirise and meteoric fall of that league was best summarized by Wellington Mara, whose dad owned the Giants. The Polo Grounds was directly across the Harlem River from Yankee Stadium. On game days the teenage Wellington would sit in the Giants' center-field clubhouse and train his field glass on Yankee Stadium.

Decades later he would recall for me the time his father stormed into the room and ranted in four-letter words about how Grange was keeping the Giants' crowds down by playing on the same day. The teenage Wellington replied, "Don't worry, Pop. There's nobody over there, either."

The NFL survived its first serious challenge to exclusivity by understanding it was in a war. Over the next two decades, the NFL found a niche driven by the heady octane of monopoly. The Pyle-Grange American Football League was just a long-gone memory.

Then a new rival called the All-American Football Conference (AAFC) emerged in the 1960s to challenge the status quo. The NFL's attitude toward it would be fueled and encouraged by the contempt

and narrow-mindedness of an old guard that had learned nothing about business competition since the war of Red Grange and C. C. Pyle. "There probably wouldn't have been this new league," a man named Sam Cordovano once said, "if the NFL had treated us decently, that is to say if Don Ameche, the actor who wanted a franchise in Los Angeles, Tony Morabito, who wanted one in San Francisco and myself, who wanted one for Buffalo had been treated with respect.

"They could have accepted our bids for entry into their league after World War II ended," Cordovano said. "But what they did instead was an insult. Now it's going to cost them."

And it did—particularly because after all the fighting and money spent, Los Angeles and San Francisco ultimately became NFL cites anyway.

The new league was called the All-America Football Conference. It received massive media exposure through the enthusiasm of Arch Ward, the *Chicago Tribune* sports editor, who was so influential that earlier he had actually created the Major League Baseball All-Star Game.

The league began operations in 1946 with franchises in New York, Buffalo, Chicago, Cleveland, Los Angeles, San Francisco, Miami, and Brooklyn. Its determination to sign college prospects and its impact on the cost of doing football business should have been apparent right at the start when Dan Topping, owner of the NFL Yankees, withdrew from the league and accepted a franchise in the AAFC, giving the AAFC the added edge of having a team in Yankee Stadium.

The shortsighted handling of the situation by the NFL and its commissioner, the old Notre Damer Frank Layden, almost enabled it to snatch defeat from the jaws of victory. It laughed at the thought of the two West Coast franchises. It compounded its disrespect when Layden commented about the new league's future, "First let them raise enough money to buy a football."

The war lasted until December 1949. It cost the old guard two million dollars, and in those days that was considerable money. Before it was over one NFL owner, Alexis Thompson of the Eagles, would even sell his team, declaring the fight just wasn't worth the money he was losing.

Looking back it is legitimate to understand that the acceptance of Morabito's San Francisco bid would have averted the whole thing. The NFL had actually gone to LA because Paul Brown's AAFC Cleveland team had chased the NFL Rams out of town. Out of sheer self-defense the NFL took in the 49ers, the Browns, and the Baltimore Colts, to create the peace it thought would last forever. When it was achieved key owners around the league publicly vowed this would never happen to them again. Right.

Within a decade they would again ignore two newcomers that logic, geography, and common sense said they should have accepted, a kind of twin reincarnations of Tony Morabito. And this time the battle would last twice as long and cost the kind of money that defies counting. Their names were Lamar Hunt and Bud Adams.

Who is to say they would have been ignored if Pete Rozelle had been the commissioner? But Rozelle was out in Los Angeles as general manager of the Rams with nothing to say in such matters. The gathering storm that Bert Bell, then commissioner, had failed to see on his 100-yard horizon would morph into Rozelle's inheritance.

As for Hunt and Adams, very few people outside of the state of Texas had ever heard of either of them. Lamar was the son of H. L. Hunt of Dallas, an oil baron, whose fortune in 1957 was speculated to be at least between four hundred and seven hundred million dollars. Nobody actually knew what he was worth or, for that matter, the financial worth of his son, Lamar. But when somebody told the old man that Lamar could lose another forty million dollars a year with his football venture, the old man replied, "Well, that only gives him fifty years to make it."

Bud Adams, the son of another oilman, had a similar story. Both wanted a little sunshine for their egos. As their point man they

sought out another Texan, Davey O'Brien, who had been an All-America tailback at Texas Christian University, following in the footsteps of another TCU All-America, Sammy Baugh. O'Brien, the smallest quarterback in the NFL with the team least likely to be able to protect him, played three years with the Eagles and then joined the FBI. He was so battered by his team's lack of an offensive line that today instead of the FBI, he probably would have sought out the witness protection program.

Hunt believed that demographics, geography, and a growth heavily fueled by oil money would dictate that the NFL look to Dallas for what he thought would surely be its expansion. Since the economics of travel and so forth could only be helped by the inclusion of a second Texas team, why not the inclusion of the "other oilman's kid," Bud Adams over in Houston? And who better to introduce him to Bell than a Texas All-America turned FBI agent, who had actually played for Bell in Philadelphia?

O'Brien did his part, and Bell listened because at first Hunt sought simply to buy the financially troubled Chicago Cardinals. That deal fell through, so in 1959 he and Adams formally met with Bell in Philadelphia to make their case for expansion. They were told that the NFL had absolutely no interest in either expansion or Texas or even them. Confused and frustrated, Hunt told Bell that he and the other oilman's kid just might start a league of their own.

Coincidentally, since Bell had already been scheduled to testify before Congress about the NFL monopoly, he smiled and said for public relations purposes, "It's up to you. After all, competition is the American way."

Hunt went home and began calling local sportswriters to see if they knew of any other cities that had tried to get into the NFL and failed. He uncovered failed bidders such as Bob Howsam in Denver and H. P. Skoglund and an old-line sports promoter named Max Winter in Minneapolis. Both cities wanted in.

And then, with absolutely no warning at all, Harry Wismer, a man who could make Charles O. Finley sound like Saint Francis of Assisi, telephoned Hunt from New York (knowing Harry,

the wonder is that the call didn't come collect) and proclaimed in decibels loud enough to shatter all the glass window in the original Notre Dame: "There is no longer cause to worry. Your new league will have a team in New York that cannot possibly fail because I will be the owner."

When Bert Bell, in an effort to show that the NFL was not the big, bad monopolistic monster that some said it was, leaked the news of the new league during a congressional hearing, it took less than a day for Hunt to hear from yet another petitioner.

Ralph Wilson, a wealthy insurance man, had always dreamed of owning an NFL team in Miami, but the University of Miami had a lease for its football team to play at the Orange Bowl and told him in no uncertain terms that it would never let him in. Convinced that there would never be room at the NFL's inn, Wilson saw Hunt's experiment as a real possibility. He told him he wanted to come in to the new league with a team in Buffalo, a city many insisted had been shafted during the AAFC-NFL merger. Ultimately, Buffalo's response would prove that the earlier critics of this northern outpost were incorrect. It would, indeed, be a hell of a pro football town.

Next came Barron Hilton, the hotel king, who opted for Los Angeles, and finally Billy Sullivan, who capitalized his venture with the public sale of ownership stock in his Boston Patriots. In the early days Sullivan would spare no expense to bring players into Boston from as far away as, well, Boston.

All of these unfolding events in 1959 meant little to Rozelle. He was still the general manager of the Rams and fighting his own war, trying not to get caught in the vitriolic cross-fire between Reeves and Pauley that grew more intense day by day. At league meetings Reeves and not Rozelle was the Rams' spokesman. "Those meetings were nothing like the ones we had much later on," Rozelle recalled. "The big thing was that Marshall and Halas would argue over things like whether the team rosters should be frozen at thirty-two or thirty-five men. Some of us thought they did that to keep most of us confused because on the big issues, except for expansion, they seemed to agree."

Surprisingly, the embryonic AFL was the subject of little conversation among the NFL owners. Even Paul Brown, the hero of the old All-America Football Conference, who, himself had forced that merger with the NFL, didn't really see how this ragtag band of upstarts represented any kind of major threat to the establishment.

In their euphoria nobody thought to look toward the heavens. If they had, they would have seen between the sky above and earth beneath a coast-to-coast, seemingly endless electronic orchard of television antennas. By not doing so, they failed to understand the biggest single hole card in the fledgling AFL's arsenal—a subsequent and totally unexpected AFL deal with ABC that would keep the rebels alive through its early financially challenged times.

In August 1959 Lamar Hunt, as president of the new entity, had indicated it would jump off the drawing board the following year with eight teams, one of which would be the Minneapolis—St. Paul franchise.

But Lamar had no idea that one player on the NFL side did not think the new league was a joke, and he was a player who held a powerful hole card. It was John Brodie of the 49ers, who was in the last year of his contract and ultimately played one league against the other for a payoff when the war settled of close to a million dollars to avoid his threatened lawsuit.

During the marathon election that ultimately anointed Pete Rozelle as commissioner, George Halas had consistently abstained from voting so as not to anger anyone who might object to his real agenda, which was NFL expansion. At that meeting he ultimately touted Dallas as his target and never mentioned another city that was also very much dead center in his crosshairs. When Rozelle appointed a subcommittee as his first act to study expansion with Halas as the chairman, the cagey charter member of the league was free to move behind the seasons and deal the AFL what he hoped would be a mortal blow.

One of the partners in the Minneapolis—St. Paul franchise announced by the AFL was a man named Max Winter, who had immigrated as a child from Austria with his family to Minneap-

olis and became Americanized enough to win a basketball scholarship to Hamline University. A businessman and restaurateur by trade, he became part owner of the Minneapolis Lakers of the NBA in 1947.

By the mid-1950s he attempted to induce the NFL to expand to Minneapolis but failed. When Hunt called to offer a franchise in the new league, Winter immediately accepted. But George Halas, the ultimate competitor, never forgot anything about football in general and the NFL in particular. He recalled Winter's earlier failed NFL bid and immediately contacted Winter with an offer he couldn't refuse.

Ironically, the AFL was that very week holding its organizational meeting in Minneapolis. "Stall them," Halas advised him, "and I'll take care of the rest." Halas delivered as promised, and the week after Pete's election Winter and his partner defected to the NFL to become the league's fourteenth franchise.

With that unexpected defection the AFL was off-kilter with seven instead of eight franchises. To bring it back into balance, it reluctantly awarded a franchise to Chet Soda and the Raiders, who seemed to have more partners than Methuselah had children. Actually, Soda had seven partners, and they are still fondly remembered for having threatened to punch each other out during a home game in their inaugural season. It actually happened in the press box, but all of them wondered the next day how the story got out.

And then there were the New York Titans. Their success, it was felt, would be critical. If you can make it there, as the song goes, you can make it anywhere. Remember, it had been their owner, Harry Wismer, who had called Hunt and promised him that the league's future was ensured because Harry would deliver all of New York from river to river. The truth was that Harry's printer couldn't even deliver tickets to the Titans on time because the printer had to wander around the east side of New York trying to find their office.

If you had set out to write a novel in which the antihero threw

obstacles in his own path, discovered empty six-lane highways, and then tried to drive on the shoulder of the road, Harry Wismer could have sued you for invasion of privacy. He was a man who would call a press conference to help sell tickets for Sunday's game and then, bloody Mary in hand, publicly abuse the opponent's visiting advance man because "your team stinks and we will bury you." His office (which was also his apartment) had a Park Avenue address, but its entrance was on Madison.

It was the summer of 1961 when I went to interview him, and I was convinced that somebody had stolen 277 Park Avenue. That was the address all the media ads listed for the offices of the newly whelped New York Titans. Even in Manhattan, where people are so obsessed with their own needs they step over heart-attack victims to get the next subway train, you'd think somebody would have noticed the kidnapping of an entire apartment house.

I was desperately looking for 277 Park. It was a steamy ninety degrees, and I had walked up and down the block eight times. Finally, an obliging doorman saved me.

"It's Madison Avenue around the corner," he said.

"Then why does it have a Park Avenue address?"

He responded with, "So why does New York need another football team?"

When I finally located the joint and rang the bell, I was greeted by a Swedish maid who demanded: "Vat you vant? You vant buy tickets? You vant job? You vant see Harry?"

When I stepped inside the office/apartment of the Titans, I was crossing into the Twilight Zone. The dining room was the ticket office. The coaching and scouting staffs met in his bedroom. Next to the kitchen, the publicity director, Ted Emery, turned out releases on an ancient mimeograph machine in an alcove alongside the bathroom. When I arrived he had just used that facility, causing the Swedish maid to turn her back to me and shout at Emory: "Dammit, Ted, I tell you ten times. Ven you use bathroom, open vindow. You stink up whole kitchen." And welcome to Chez Wismer.

When I asked Harry how he chose his team's name, he almost shouted at me: "What's bigger than a giant? A titan, that's what."

In his second year of operation, Harry called a news conference at which he accused *Daily Mirror* columnist Harold Weissman of discrimination against his league because he said the guy's son was a ball boy with the Giants. The man had no children, and I leaned over and told him, "Better call home. He may know something you don't." Then Harry went on a rant about the cowardice of the Giants and challenged them to an end-of-season bowl game for the city championship.

When the conference broke up, I asked Sid Youngelman, an NFL exile and a starter for the Titans, what he thought of Harry's challenge. He said, "I think he has insurance policies on all of us and is trying to get us killed."

Financially, the league's most important franchise began life as a disaster. Even though Harry announced crowds of thirty thousand a game, the truth was they were averaging a little more than four thousand. Cynics even doubted those numbers, referring to his crowds as people who were disguised as empty seats.

Small wonder the old guard of the NFL hardly felt threatened by Lamar Hunt's operation and had no plan of attack. It had every reason to believe the Oakland and New York franchises would do the job for them.

Rozelle, who was used to being an initiator, understood that until he could convince his owners that they were, indeed, in danger, his time was better spent in serious housekeeping. He cleaned up the potential Hornung-Karras gambling scandal. He spent much of his time in court, the biggie being the AFL's multimillion-dollar lawsuit against the NFL that Rozelle eventually won.

Then there were those cases that gave the lie to the popular adage that college football players learn nothing in college. If nothing else during this war between rival leagues, they learned how to write their names. They were so good at it that some of them learned to write them twice—once on an AFL contract and once on an NFL contract.

Rozelle knew firsthand how that went. In 1960, as the Rams' GM, he signed Heisman Trophy winner Billy Cannon of Louisiana State University and agreed to keep the contract a secret so Cannon could play for LSU in the Sugar Bowl. But in the end zone after the Sugar Bowl, he signed with the Oilers and shook hands with Bud Adams, the Oilers' owner, for the television cameras. The case went to court, and Adams won it after the judge castigated Rozelle, who had been a witness, saying he had taken advantage of "a poor naive, country boy." For years, each time the commissioner ran into Peter Finney, the gifted columnist for the *Times-Picayune*, who knew Cannon well, he greeted him with, "Hey, how's that poor, naive country boy doing?"

Another court battle between the Giants and the Chargers over Charlie Flowers, a Mississippi All-America and a statewide hero, did not end with such a forgiving attitude. Jim Lee Howell, the Giants' player personnel director, who had been called as a witness, told me: "I wasn't sure how the case was going until the judge said to me, 'Sir, are you comin' down here all the way from New York City to tell me that this fine Mississippi boy is a liar?' and then he turns to Flowers and he says in a very loud whisper, 'Now, Charlie, where did ya say y'all want to play?' I just got up and headed for the airport."

With that some of the NFL lodge brothers began to view the new league a little differently—but only some. Without a consensus that would dictate full warfare from his congregation, Rozelle—in typical Rozelle style—did not rush to force the issue.

He had, indeed, begun to formulate a battle plan. The Charlie Flowers affair had privately convinced him that one was going to be necessary. But as AFL attendance figures were still hardly intimidating, he knew he could afford to wait. Instead, what he did next was to clean up the last piece of business that the late Bert Bell had left behind. It would take a delicate balancing act because it would involve the close-to-home interests of George Halas, who could become either his tremendous ally or a serious enemy.

Chicago was the only two-team football town in the NFL. The

only other one had been New York, where both the Giants and the Brooklyn Dodgers (AAFC team, not the baseball Dodgers) over in Ebbets Field had shared the city. But the Dodgers were long gone. In Chicago the Bears were pretty much the soul of the city's football history, but the Chicago Cardinals were at times a thorn in George Halas's backside.

It was a rivalry with more history than equality. The Cardinals, like the Bears, were charter members of the league when it was formed in 1920. But only once in all those years (1947) had it won a clear league title.

In 1932 the late Charles Bidwill bought the team for fifty thousand dollars. He was the president of the Chicago Stadium Corporation, the owner of race horses, and the head of a local printing company. Ironically, he had once been a partner of Halas in a local basketball team and even loaned him fifty thousand dollars to keep the Bears out of the red.

Bidwill never did see the Cardinals win. He died earlier in their championship season, and his widow would later marry Walter Wolfner, who became the team's general manager. Wolfner did not defer to the man they called Papa Bear.

Halas and Wolfner did think a lot about each other. You could not call theirs a relationship. Try, instead, vendetta. Stuck on the South Side of Chicago in a deteriorating neighborhood around Comiskey Park, Wolfner's club lost more money with each passing year. To end the Bears' domination of the city, he even offered to pay Halas to leave Chicago. Halas laughed at him.

The bond between Bell and Halas was suspiciously strong. Year after year Wolfner always seemed to get the lousy home schedule. One year Bell, who made up the slate, scheduled him to open at home in the same park he shared with the White Sox on the day the White Sox opened at home in the World Series. In response to Wolfner's feverish telephone calls, Bell told him, "Work it out with the baseball team."

People did not flock to see the Cardinals. It is doubtful you could have "flocked to them" with a gun, a whip, and a chair. They were

a lousy team, playing in a crumbling stadium, and in three previous seasons they had managed to win three whole, entire games while losing twenty-eight.

It was Wolfner's idea that although he couldn't pass, catch, or run with the ball, he sure could do something about a venue. Or so he thought.

In desperation, while formulating a master plan to a better financial future, he signed a one-year lease with Soldier Field; at the time that big white elephant was a place in which the college all-star game, Army-Navy, and the city high school championships were the only football played there. The field was unsuitable. It should be noted, parenthetically as a measure of which team owned Chicago, that it was made reasonably usable for the Bears after the Cards left town.

But Wolfner did have a plan. He made a deal with Northwestern University in the nearby suburb of Evanston to move his home games there the following year. There was parking as well as a well-maintained stadium and comfortable seats. To Wolfner it would be a chattel mortgage on the 100-yard promised land for which he yearned—and take that, George Halas.

At least that's what he thought—until Halas delivered the fatal blow. George went back into the old safe and pulled out a document that Wolfner's predecessor, Bidwill, had signed decades earlier. In all of sports there has never been a signed document like this one. In it Bidwill agreed (for considerations never made public) never to play a game north of Madison Street, the traditional dividing line between North and South Chicago.

When Halas dropped his bombshell, everyone in the Cardinals' office six blocks away ran for the map of Chicago. They could have saved themselves the trouble. Nobody had to tell George Halas where Northwestern University was in relation to Madison Street.

Bell had only delayed the solution by ignoring Wolfner. The owner of the Cards would show up at league meetings to complain about the schedule Bell had forced upon him. They would vote, and the vote was always eleven to one against him.

It fell to Rozelle to find some way out of the mess. If Wolfner had to leave town, St. Louis, Rozelle reasoned, made the most sense. In a sense there were two reasons that swayed him. First, the population indicated that it could support a pro football team. Second, and in some ways more important to the commissioner, an NFL team in St. Louis would impact the growth of the rival AFL. It would shut the door to that territory forever. Measured against his feeling that it was time to get his constituents out of their lethargy and strike some blow against the AFL, it was little enough for Rozelle to do to start the war drums beating.

But to move a football operation under those circumstances drastically costs money. Among the major expenses, the remaining lease with Soldier Field had to be paid off. The tab to make it all work was figured at approximately five hundred thousand dollars. Wolfner, fueled by rage, immediately balked.

It was then, with little publicity and great skill, that Rozelle pulled off a major triumph. He prevailed upon an anonymous owner to pick up the major share of that tab for the good of the league. And who was that masked angel? George Halas. The commissioner had brilliantly put a ribbon around the entire package with that master stroke.

That was in March. By the summer the fledgling American Football League was staggering toward its first season. All that year Rozelle had been quietly waiting to see what line of attack the new league would take. Secretly, he hoped it would try to induce NFL players to jump to the new league, thus violating their existing contracts. That would have given the old guard a course of legal action against the newcomers. But the AFL had wisely chosen a different route . . . one that was twofold.

First, it would take the NFL to court over everything it could think of, from antitrust violations to jay walking. Second, it would make its stand with barrels of money in the annual collegiate draft, and that, too, as Rozelle knew from Flowers and Cannon, could also wind up in the courts.

But slowly, as it became clear that television money was a pow-

erful tool for the rebel league, Rozelle was inching toward the battle that would change the face of professional football forever. It would cost millions of dollars for both sides, and when it was finally finished it would actually give birth to a brand-new monopoly.

I remember the day the commissioner sat in his office and recalled the moment he knew that the gloves had to come off and the battle had to be taken to a whole new level. "I think the Flowers signing was the tip for me about what we had to do," he said.

> At that point, I didn't feel we'd lose our experienced players to them . . . at least not yet. But if they stayed in business, we would have a serious problem with the rookies.
>
> The thing that became clear was that we were going to have to protect the college kids we wanted to sign. And I knew they would try to do the same. The answer was that little by little, both sides got into this babysitting thing. With the Hornung case behind us and the American League starting to spend real money in their drafts, I'd have to say that 1964 and 1965 were the years we finally decided to go to war.

8

Sex, Lies, and Bringing Up Baby

This is Junius Buchanan. He's 6-8. He's beautiful and he's going to be all ours.

— Don Klosterman, general manager of the AFL Dallas Texans

The first thing you did was to find out what car they wanted, and off the top of my head I got to know the price of all of them.

— Gil Brandt, part of the NFL's babysitting high command

In all of sports there was never anything like it. Huge football players who, if provoked, could have pounded holes in the side of the USS *Forrestal* suddenly claimed to be kidnap victims, held against their will by men five-foot-eight, 145 pounds, forced to sleep with wild women, drink whiskey, accept automobiles registered in their name, fly to exotic places, and endure this kind of torture until they signed a contract.

This was the War of the Babysitters, and the truth is that Rozelle's old-guard army was late getting to the front lines. Right from the start the AFL came out with guns and checkbooks blazing. Don Klosterman, who had once been a star quarterback at Loyola of Los Angeles against Rozelle's old USF teams, and Al LoCasale, then with the Chargers, were among the best of the rebel league's body snatchers. Klosterman said, "When they evacuated the Congo, the last three to leave were two Belgian nurses and a Charger scout." He was stretching it a little, but in the beginning the AFL's deputized body snatchers seemed to be everywhere.

What compounded the NFL efforts to get its own babysitting brigade organized was the fact that there were still brothers in the

lodge hall who didn't trust each other. Rozelle admitted as much to me years later when he said, "We didn't sign guys to league contracts, and we didn't share costs. We did try to isolate guys so that whoever drafted them in our league would get the chance to see them.

"But we used NFL employees for that because we didn't want anyone else on our side to know where they were until we told them. We didn't want one of our teams hurting another one."

With that in mind, he did what he always did in such tight situations. He relied heavily on his associations of the past.

"It wasn't much different than what he had learned at USF from Pete Newell. Recruiting is recruiting," said Gil Brandt, who worked for Rozelle as a scout with the Rams and later become player personnel director for Schramm in Dallas and Kansas City and who as a high-placed babysitter for Rozelle would log enough frequent flyer miles to fly to Saturn and back.

> The principle was the same. In college you scouted the high school kids. What you did back then was to get an alumnus in his hometown to find everything out . . . what schools he leaned toward . . . what position he wanted to pay in college . . . did he need a car. Just like you couldn't sit back in the spring when other schools were making moves on the kid, well, it was the same thing with us on the pro level."
>
> Pete knew that game well, and he knew the people to make it work.

Bert Rose had been the sports information director at the University of Washington when Rozelle hired him to head the Rams' publicity team. He also knew a lot about recruiting. He later left the Rams to become the Vikings' first general manager, and when that didn't work out, Dan Reeves brought him back to run a modest scouting operation. He would be the guy Rozelle tapped to run his body snatchers.

Rose immediately set up a network of high school coaches, fringe professional football people, friendly college boosters, and just plain football nuts to serve as his field men. Two critical soldiers brought on board by Rozelle himself were Buddy Young, who would later

become an administrative aide to the commissioner and the first African American in the NFL's front office, and Brandt, who may have been the very best at it.

Young, a University of Illinois All-America running back and the National Collegiate Athletic Association (NCAA) sprint champion, was a football pioneer. Small at five-foot-five and 150 pounds, the flanker position was invented for him when he played for the Colts; he was the league's top salesman in the eyes of many black players. He delivered Gayle Sayers to George Halas.

He was also a point man for the NFL into the virtually untapped all-black colleges. Once, in the confusion of the NFL war room, Buddy answered one of what seemed like 254 telephones that were always ringing. "What you mean the boy's father just died?" he said to the man he had entrusted with the care, feeding, and isolation of a prospect in Mississippi. Has the boy been told? What are the arrangements?

"Don't worry about it," he was told. "It's all taken care of. I'm the only funeral director in town."

You can best understand Young's role as a babysitter as told to me by his wife, Geraldine: "Buddy never spoke much about what he was doing, but I can tell you that one day I looked around my home and realized I was cooking for thirteen college players—black and white."

"I didn't know much about what Rose and Young were doing because I was just a kid in the mail room at the time," said Joe Browne, now the league's in-house chief of governmental affairs. "All I knew about what they did was that it seemed to me that there was always a lot of cash around that office."

Once Rozelle determined to move the battle from team responsibility into league responsibility, he found himself at the apex of a system so complex that it wound up training people for a job that could only put themselves out of business if they were successful. "We barely paid these guys," Rozelle explained.

They were professional people or fans who really wanted to be around this strange game—and it was a hell of a fascinating one. We set up regional schools for them to learn what we wanted them to know.

We gave them sales kits outlining our sales pitch and the sales pitches of every club in our league. We taught them how to sign people, and we gave them blank NFL checks. Then they would call the club that had drafted the prospect, and the club would tell them what bank to fill in. We gave them air travel cards.

Now during the last period, you know the last week before the draft, they would be with the kid wherever he went. In some cases the kid might be out of school, so they would take him to some great places. Sometimes that would be great for the babysitter, too—plush hotel, palm trees, drinks poolside, the whole deal.

And sometimes, well, I remember one kid went home and our guy went with him and there was a blizzard, so the kid's old man sent him out to get the cattle in and there was that poor bastard babysitter running around and freezing his ass off with him.

There were, indeed, unbelievable stories. There was the time that Green Bay of the NFL and Kansas City of the AFL had each drafted a huge Grambling tackle named Al Dotson. Grambling had gone down to Miami to play Florida A&M in the Orange Blossom Bowl, and Dotson's AFL shadow had lost touch. So there was a telephone call to a friend who had another friend who had a third friend who was a Florida state senator and damned if the Florida State Police didn't cut off the Grambling team bus after the game so that the AFL guy could get on it and sit next to Dotson.

On a flight to West Virginia, Brandt sat down next to a lady who turned out to be the daughter of Vic Fusia, the UMass football coach. When he told her he worked for the Dallas Cowboys, she said her dad had been to the Chargers' camp and they had signed one of his players, Milt Morin—that's how the NFL learned that the AFL had held a secret draft.

The battle became more heated. There were fistfights. There were lies and massive examples of blatant deceit. Sex and booze

became major factors when luring players. The objects of all this pursuit caught on quickly. They learned to play the game in one hell of a hurry. For some it was played in sets of two:

The NFL motel weekend and the AFL motel weekend . . . the NFL offers of a car and the AFL offers of a car . . . and, both sides would privately admit to me, a girl or two if that worked. Everyone was riding the craziest merry-go-round in the history of sports.

Back at NFL headquarters there were ten supervisors, each with his own blackboard with five to ten names on it, depending on how important the players were and how much effort the league was willing to go to sign them. They would keep a running tally of vital information about the guy next to his name: college major, parents' occupations, girlfriend's name, address, and telephone number.

It was ludicrous. Both sides were operating with code words and aliases on hotel registers and logistical planning that would have done honor to D-day. A kid sitting in a Dallas motel would suddenly hear the babysitter suggest a trip to Las Vegas, and they headed out to the airport just about the time the rival babysitter was within sight of the motel.

Brandt delights in telling a special story about the NFL catch that got away. It was the night before Thanksgiving 1965, and Buddy Young and a babysitter-stockbroker named Wallace Reed drove to the Prairie View A&M campus northwest of Houston and picked up Otis Taylor, a great tight end that everybody wanted, and his buddy Seth Cartwright, a mediocre lineman that nobody wanted. Taylor insisted his friend come along.

The inducement was a weekend in Dallas. As Brandt recalls they were stashed at the Holiday Inn off the North Central Expressway in suburban Richardson. Buddy left, leaving Reeves to sit outside the front door while the two recruits inside were occupied by whatever the NFL had provided.

Meanwhile, when calls to Taylor's dorm room went unanswered, Klosterman called Taylor's mother and said he feared that people unknown had kidnapped her child. Then he called Lloyd Wells,

a Chiefs operative who was close to the Taylor family and had known the player since junior high school.

Reed, who had a little too much to drink that night, had fallen asleep outside the door in his chair. From the parking lot below Lloyd threw stones at Taylor's window. When Taylor opened it, Lloyd shouted up to him, reminding him of their kinship in pursuing women and the chance that Lloyd would lose his job if he couldn't sign him. He also spoke seductively of a red Thunderbird for which Taylor had expressed a desire.

The pair climbed out of the window, Wells took them to Kansas City, and Taylor signed and drove home to Texas in a red Thunderbird.

That same weekend Al Davis signed Fred Biletnikoff, a brilliant receiver at Florida State, immediately after the Gator Bowl. It was a scenario straight out of Groucho Marx. "I signed him," Davis said, "while his mother and people from the Lions who had drafted him were on the sidelines screaming 'Don't sign, Fred, don't sign.'"

Best of all was the story related by Blackie Sherrod, sports editor of the *Dallas Morning News* and the unofficial poet laureate of sportswriters in the Southwest. Blackie and his wife, Marilyn, were just sitting down to dinner in their apartment in Dallas's Oak Cliff neighborhood when the doorbell rang. It was Klosterman. "I want you to see something," he told them.

So they went upstairs to a vacant apartment in the same building that just happened to be owned by Lamar Hunt. Junius Buchanan was sitting on the couch. He is six-foot-eight and weighs several tons more than a small freighter. After Junius drops all of himself onto a couch, Lloyd's of London would be reluctant to insure the upholstery.

"He's beautiful," Klosterman said, "and he's going to be all ours."

For three days Claire Klosterman cooked for him. She cooked everything in Buchanan's apartment. Then she cooked all the food in the Sherrods' apartment for him. Three days later he signed his contract, possibly because the Klostermans and the Sherrods were the only humans he had seen all week.

But perhaps the most interesting dialogue of all was between Lou Curl, one of Ralph Wilson's insurance agents turned baby-sitter, and an Ohio State lineman named Birtho Arnold.

"Mr. Arnold," said Curl, who was five-foot-five and weighed 135 pounds, "I'm with the Buffalo Bills."

"Christ," gasped Arnold, who was six-foot-six and 310 pounds. "What position do you play?"

Because of the undercurrent of mistrust among some of the NFL owners, Rozelle made it clear that each of his supervisors maintain the secrecy of his "client's" location as if he'd taken a blood oath. The routine they evolved was for an interested team to call the NFL switchboard, which, in turn, connected him to the proper supervisor. Once the call was cleared, the supervisor would have the switchboard patch the caller into the location where the prospect was stashed.

"Thinking back on all this," Rozelle told me, "it's hard to keep from laughing. One day the supervisor got a call from the 49ers, and he patched him in to the Jack Tar Hotel where the kid was stashed. The 49ers' office was in the same hotel. They could have simply taken the elevator to see him. But, of course, we never told them."

If there was a winner during this period, it was the players. Basically, the two leagues battled pretty much to a standoff in the matter of collegiate superstars, although the NFL did a little better in the matter of middle-echelon players. In truth it was not the battle of the babysitters that would change the thinking of either side. Other factors were coming into play.

First came a deadly duo with the kind of hunger that would convince Rozelle that it was time to turn to diplomacy. Beating the AFL over the head with the collective NFL wallet was beginning to leave his side's wallet a little light. He never doubted the NFL could win that kind of battle, but everything he had experienced since he got into this league convinced Rozelle he could wind up with a devastatingly expensive pyrrhic victory.

All through his career he had made it his business to know all

the significant players in the game he was working, whether it was the battle for media space at USF and Los Angeles, the supporting cast in the Reeves-Paley feud, and key people in the AFL. But suddenly, two new major players would emerge as point men for the rebels. In Sonny Werblin and Al Davis he faced two men no less determined and no less equipped for the battle than he was.

Harry Wismer's reach continually exceeded his grasp. If adjectives, boasts, and hot air were decisive weapons in the battle, Wismer would have won by technical knockout (TKO) on the way into the ring. But they were nothing more than added burdens the AFL could not endure. Typical of Harry's operation was the day the towel man showed up after practice and told assistant coach George Sauer Jr. that if the Titans wanted to shower, they could roll in the grass to get dry.

"Harry will take care of your problems. Just give us the towels."

"Sure," Sauer was told. "Just give me the money."

Sauer paid out of his own pocket and was never reimbursed.

The day after Thanksgiving 1963, with Wismer a million dollars in debt, the league kicked him out and put the franchise up for sale for the cost of its debts.

A five-man syndicate headed by David "Sonny" Werblin bought the club in a bargain-basement deal not seen in the city since Peter Minuit paid what was to be twenty-four dollars for all of Manhattan, including the land on which the Titans' home field, the Polo Grounds, ultimately stood.

Werblin was coming from a milieu where financial hand-to-hand combat was a way of life and talk softly but carry a big stick was a hard-and-fast credo. He had been the president of the Music Corporation of America, a giant octopus of a monopoly that he had joined as an office boy. It was the most misnamed corporation in all of show business. It handled music, all right. It also covered actors, writers, directors, producers, film distributers, band leaders, booking agents, television sales, and so on, and on.

This is the way Werblin explained his early show-business experience to me the week he bought the club: "Julie Stein was the pres-

ident and I was out to impress him. He always started work at 8 in the morning and I would get there at 7:55 to impress him. When I did that he started arriving at 7:45 so I came in at 7:30. Then he came in at 7:15. Then he had called me over to demand why the pencils hadn't been sharpened. They had been but he deliberately broke every point. Welcome to the world of show business."

Werblin was sent on the road as a band boy for Guy Lombardo and his Royal Canadians to get him the hell out of the office. He would make all the stops from band runner to agent to supersalesman to president. Among his better-known clients were Frank Sinatra and Ronald Reagan. He became the single most powerful man in a business that thrived on power and devoured all but the strongest.

Werblin was a devoted sports freak. He was president of Monmouth Park Race Track. He was the number-one booster of Rutgers University football. And he was well aware that the Titans, whom he would rename the Jets, were scheduled to move into a brand-new stadium about to be built in Queens. With this background he was more than equipped to become a serious factor in the AFL's run to daylight.

He proved it that very year. At MCA he had become a close friend of Robert Sarnoff, the president of NBC, placing a number of shows on that network. Sarnoff's relationship with Werblin undoubtedly had something to do with what I learned almost by accident. In the summer of 1963 I was in Paris and bumped into Ralph Wilson and Lamar Hunt, who were having dinner together. They were ecstatic.

"You heard the news?" Wilson asked.

"No, I haven't."

"Well, we're celebrating. CBS just signed a $28.2 million contract for a two-year deal with the NFL."

"And this helps your league how?"

"You bet it does. NBC-TV has to stay in our game at just the right time."

"You're a reporter," Lamar said. "Figure it out and go ahead and report."

He was right. NBC came up with $36 million. Admittedly, it was spread over five years, but it was enough to become a critical factor, and it is a little-known fact that NBC then loaned various sums of money to different franchises to help them sign players.

And then along came Al Davis.

If Sonny was the point man to a new access to television boardrooms, Al Davis would add a set of much-needed brass knuckles on a very different level. You may recall the way he held off Fred Biletnikoff's mother and several Detroit Lions executives at the Gator Bowl and successfully signed Lance Alworth when he was assistant at San Diego.

That day he proved he totally understood how to deal with these college kids when he explained it was the bonus that made Alworth ignore his mother. He had been quoted as saying, "I asked him if he understood what he was signing and he said yes . . . yes but, of course, he didn't. You put $5–7,000 in front of them and that's what they really wanted."

Davis knew recruiting; as an assistant at the military college the Citadel, in South Carolina, he had made that team better. However, and the story may be apocryphal, he failed to explain to a couple of recruits that, the Citadel being the Citadel, they would be required to play toy soldiers in the afternoon. The message from the commandant, General Mark Clark, about what it meant to be a cadet there and the heat Davis is alleged to have taken made it clear to Al that an assistant's job at a military college was not a vehicle for him. He moved on to USC, and when that football program wound up on probation Davis was out of a job.

His first pro football stop was San Diego under a man Rozelle once fired, Sid Gillman. Meanwhile, the once fratricide-bound multiplicity of Oakland owners had faded away. Of those remaining, level-headed businessman F. Wayne Valley was in charge. He jumped at the chance to hire Davis.

Davis was a brilliant football mind, and he proved it. He could

coach and he could plan, and the Raiders became a power. Davis's Brooklyn accent, his dark glasses, his slicked-back hair, and his design for the team's new black and silver uniforms all spoke to a two-word résumé: street fighter—which was exactly what the whole damned league needed.

Sonny Werblin had dominated show business through MCA by the use of the star syndrome. Every top money earner in the MCA stable was a star, one who had often been created by Sonny. The Jets moved to Shea Stadium in 1964 and on opening night drew an actual crowd of more than sixty thousand. Werblin sat in the owner's box, pondering how to put an exciting face on his team, when the public address announcer did it for him.

The Jets had a rookie linebacker named Wahoo McDaniel out of the University of Oklahoma. He was a Choctaw-Chickasaw Native American. Several times in the first quarter Werblin heard words booming over the PA system: "Tackle by Wahoo McDaniel . . . Tackle by McDaniel . . . Tackle by Wahoo McDaniel."

Werblin raced down the aisle to the PA booth, hammered on the door, and hollered at the announcer, "From now on its just Wahoo and if he comes within 10 feet of the ball carrier, he gets credit for the tackle."

By the third quarter he would shout "Tackle by Who," and the crowd would shout back, "Tackle by Wahoo." Stardust had finally come to the American Football League.

And on the other coast, Davis created a PR juggernaut. He was a great coach, whose posture as the league's resident rogue came off as a kind of 100-yard Robin Hood who would steal from the NFL rich and give it to the AFL poor.

He was the league's coach with charisma. Valley would call him "my genius." Later, when Davis ousted him to win control of the team in a postmerger power struggle, Valley would call him something else.

But now with Werblin an immediate threat to the Maras in the East and Davis an equal threat to the 49ers across the bay in San Francisco, the pressure mounted for either all-out victory or com-

promise. That pressure began to show on Joe Foss, the war hero who had been chosen as AFL commissioner from its very inception.

I remember that when Foss was tapped for the new job, Harold Rosenthal, my colleague on the *New York Herald Tribune* at the time, had said to me: "Perfect choice. Absolutely no skeletons in his closet. The guy was the governor of South Dakota for crying out loud. Do you even know anybody else who lived there? And he won the Congressional Medal of Honor as a Marine pilot. He's a general in the Air National Guard. Who the hell is gonna write anything negative about a guy like that?"

Harold was right. But as time dragged on and the AFL desperately needed to do better than just stay alive, some of the owners were beginning to think he was too mild mannered and not aggressive at all. In the spring of 1965, he set out to disprove that notion. He planned to deliver the league's first expansion franchise.

Ivan Allen, the mayor of Atlanta, had already brought the Braves to the city from Milwaukee, and he was pushing hard for a football franchise to share the newly built Fulton County Stadium

A man named Leonard Reinsch, president of Cox Broadcasting Corporation, was coming to the AFL league meeting in New Jersey with $7.3 million and tremendous newspaper backing, seeking an Atlanta AFL franchise. Unfortunately, he forgot to lock up a stadium.

A week before that meeting, Arthur Modell stopped by the NFL office in Manhattan to tell Rozelle about Reinsch's mission. But not surprisingly, Rozelle already knew. Because he always studied the media, he knew that while Reinsch would seek a franchise in the name of the Cox Communications people, Cox had scrupulously stayed out of his two newspapers' policies.

Reinsch was coming on behalf of the *Atlanta Constitution*, but Rozelle knew that the sports editor of the *Atlanta Journal* would fight to convince his boss that the NFL was a better deal. Rozelle knew that Jess Outlar, the *Journal*'s sports editor, could be an ally. He told Modell what he wanted to do.

"What if I went down there and stole the city on the same day that the AFL was meeting at Werblin's racetrack?"

"That would be dynamite," Modell said. "But, Pete, what if you go down there and don't get the city and the story appears in the media? Think of how bad we'll look."

"He was right, of course," Rozelle later told me,

and I had to consider that. But I knew what a propaganda coup it would be for us if somehow we did lock up Atlanta.

So I went down there and toured the stadium on the same morning that the AFL was meeting in New Jersey. I told the stadium authority people that I couldn't give them a definite yes but I felt they had a real shot. I pointed out that the AFL would still be there as an insurance policy. I suggested to Mayor Allen that he not sign a stadium lease with anybody until we held our own league meeting.

He agreed so quickly I knew we had them.

That agreement to delay was the death knell for the Reinsch group. It may be said with a certainty that a funny thing happened to AFL commissioner Joe Foss that day. Somewhere between the conference room and the men's room, he lost the city of Atlanta.

He also lost his job. That wasn't official until April of the following year, when his written resignation was spiked with a defense of his tenure: "The league has come to the stage where problems are fewer and the owners have more time to get into mischief. . . . I have never been a dancing bear for the owners, and never could be. This is the time for me to leave."

I also remember something he said to me when I called him that day. He had always felt the big-city NFL writers were against him. He was a Congressional Medal of Honor winner and a war hero and the former governor of South Dakota, but I always believed he carried within him the doubts and sensitivity of a country boy dropped into the big city.

He confirmed that for me when he said, "Well, the New York media got what it wanted." He felt we didn't understand him when

in fact it was probably the other way around. We were not after him. We were after the kind of insight that an elusive commissioner could not provide.

His departure came in the spring of 1966, just two months before the two leagues merged. Davis was unanimously chosen as the new AFL commissioner the very next day. And he, every bit as much as Rozelle, became the reason the two leagues merged.

What had been a chess matchup until then immediately morphed into a dog fight, with the new AFL field general unleashing a pit-bull strategy of attack, attack, attack. Looking back, without him, there would never have been a merger.

With that in mind, it is worth backing away for a moment and taking a fresh look at the new heavyweight contender. Al Davis knew when he took the job that there was no shortage of trouble among his own people. One of his first official acts as commissioner, much to the delight of the media, was to break up a rolling, squirming attempt at a fistfight between Oilers president Bud Adams and a sportswriter named Jack Gallagher on the floor of the Shamrock Hilton. The *Houston Post* carried shots of the tangled combatants across seven columns on the front page.

Davis had always held PR folk in disdain, but the demeaning spectacle of one of his owners rolling on the ground with a writer was the last straw. Davis did not come to this job without a little serious study about the other army's general. It was his theory that Pete Rozelle's greatest single strength lay more in his PR ability than his football expertise. He respected that talent, but it did not enter his mind for a single minute that given the war chest and the support, his own particular natural talent was more suited to the battle.

To cut into Rozelle's enormous media advantage, he had already begun to hire a staff of experts. As Rozelle had done when he organized his first office, Davis immediately hired three men with public relations or newspaper experience. From the sports information office at Syracuse, his alma mater, he got Val Pinch-

beck, who had helped make Floyd Little an All-America. From the Angels' PR department (Davis was a fanatical baseball fan) came Irv Kaze, a well-liked and experienced PR guy in sports and television. And from the ludicrous fistfight he had halted he decided to seek out the *Houston Post*'s popular columnist Mickey Herskowitz, who said:

> The way it happened with me goes back to that mess with Gallagher and Adams. He called me at home that night and asked me how he should handle it. I told him to forget it. That it was already going to be in the papers the next morning and that anything he would do would keep it alive unless he let it die a natural death. Then he thanked me and told me I would be hearing again from him soon, which I interpreted to mean absolutely nothing.
>
> Then he called me back in a few days and laid it out for me. He said there would be management opportunities for me if things worked out because he indicated he planned to go back to Los Angeles with a new team to fill the void the Chargers had left when they moved to San Diego. He mentioned New Orleans, which was still without pro football, as a possible expansion franchise and even Chicago, where he thought the AFL could go head-to-head with George Halas.
>
> I had only met Al once at an Astros game when a pitcher named Don McMahon, who had gone to high school with Davis, introduced me to him. Davis was with the Chargers then and he had always been paranoiac about writers, but I assumed he thought I was a writer that his old friend trusted.
>
> Actually, that probably was all he knew about me. But he calls that second time and offers me a job. I was then the sports editor of the *Post*, and I was twenty-six years old and knew I couldn't go any higher because it was a family paper, so I asked for a week to think it over and he said, "Absolutely not. Have your answer when I call tomorrow."
>
> So he did and I said I was coming, and then there was a long pause and I thought he was having buyers' remorse, sort of like a guy who chases a broad, gets her consent, and then isn't sure he did the right thing. The pause seemed to last forever, and then he suddenly asked,

"Can you name the offensive line of the Denver Broncos?" and I said, "Can anybody? I'll look it up if you want," and then he said, "All right. Be in New York in two weeks."

Davis was like a heavyweight contender who finally got his title fight. In his first season as a head coach (1963) he had turned the Oakland Raiders, once the joke of the league, into the talk of the AFL and, in fact, all of football. His roster was a blend of over-looked veterans, a few future superstars, and players who were developed by him. He was the AFL Coach of the Year that season. Nobody ever dared to doubt that Al Davis had a brilliant football mind.

He was the perfect candidate to run the AFL's battle for survival. In truth the media, in general, did not feel this would be an even battle.

He was going to wage war against the most talented mind in the history of all sports administration. And make no mistake about it, he wanted this fight the way Frazier yearned for Ali. The analogy is not misplaced. Looking back, it can be said that inside the ring, those two made each other better than they had ever been and ever would be again.

It would be much the same with Davis and Rozelle. For his part Davis was absolutely convinced he would win. And he was, indeed, an imposing adversary who relished the role of the guy with the black ten-gallon hat.

His Brooklyn accent—he called his team the "Raiduhs"—his slicked-back hair, sunglasses. Years before we had a Darth Vader, we had Al Davis. As a case in point, there is the oft-repeated but possibly apocryphal story about the time John Robinson, the head coach at USC and a friend of Davis, invited him to watch the Trojans practice.

Afterward, he is supposed to have told Robinson, "John, see that apartment house over there? Anybody with binoculars could get up on one of the high floors and film your whole practice."

"Isn't that a little paranoid?"

"Sometimes in this business a little paranoia is a good thing."
Clearly, he was ready.

And it was a damned good thing, because on the day he was introduced at the plush Plaza Hotel as the new AFL commissioner, the NFL was meeting in Washington. Even the NFL owners did not realize that their own commissioner was about to up the ante. When they finally settled in, Rozelle stepped to the rostrum and in a well-modulated voice announced that the Giants had signed a new placekicker and he had approved the signing. The player's name was Pete Gogolak.

And then all hell broke loose because Gogolak was on the roster of the AFL Buffalo Bills. He had been the first placekicker in a decade or two to draw the attention he drew years earlier as an undergraduate at Cornell. He was the first of the soccer-style sidewheeling placekickers. He lined up as though he were facing the stadium comfort station but kicked the ball straight through the uprights from incredible distances with incredible accuracy. He also kicked it so far that opening-game kickoffs became a social event for Cornell students.

When he joined the Bills, he was the most exciting new weapon in all of professional football. He demanded more money, couldn't get it, and played out his option year. Now he was a free agent and willing to jump leagues for the right price.

Bitter as this war was, nothing like this had ever happened. Gogolak got himself an agent named Fred Corcoran, who had handled Ted Williams's affairs and was better known for his work with professional golfers.

Then Gogolak and Corcoran hired a lawyer named Michael Mooney. They contacted the New York Giants and told them that Gogolak was a free agent and willing to become the first AFL player in history to jump to the NFL.

The instant Rozelle announced to assembled owners that he had approve the signing, the joint sounded like the Tower of Babel construction crew on a very bad day.

Just before Rozelle made his announcement, Vince Lombardi

leaned over and whispered to Art Modell, "Arthur, I'm afraid one of my oldest friends has done something that's going to cause all of us a hell of a lot of trouble."

Modell thought the whisper had come from Lou Spadia of the 49ers on his other side and said, "Who, Lou?" But Rozelle immediately turned the floor over to Mara, who was speaking about the terms. There was no bonus, and nobody will ever know the rest because Lombardi was on his feet, shrieking at his old Fordham classmate. He was so loud it's a wonder he didn't peel the paint off the walls. Maybe he did, but nobody could have seen it because they were all yelling at once.

"I tried to tell them," Rozelle explained. "I had discussed this with Manny Celler [the Brooklyn congressman who had been helpful with congressional approval for the NFL's single-network television policy], and he agreed that when a player finishes his contractual obligation with one league, he is within his rights to move to the other one. I could not void Gogolak's contract."

Dan Reeves was upset. The Bidwill brothers were angry. Art Rooney and his son Dan joined in. Over the roar Lombardi released a fusillade at both Wellington and Pete. "That contract never should have been offered by you, Wellington, and never approved by you, commissioner. What are we paying you for . . . to put us all on the road to bankruptcy?"

"Yes," Rozelle later told me, "he was livid. But I think he was angrier at Wellington than he was at me for approving it. But I can tell you one thing with certainty. No matter what you may have heard, he never said my job was in jeopardy—absolutely never."

Modell jumped up and called for an immediate recess. "I wanted one, too, so the owners could break into smaller groups and digest what had happened," Rozelle explained. "I didn't like it that much myself, but we had no legal grounds to deny Wellington since Gogolak was a genuine free agent, and to deny it would have risked a huge lawsuit."

As Rozelle approved the adjournment, Lombardi came around the edge of the table next to where Mara was speaking, put his

quivering jaw maybe three inches from Mara's nose, and shouted, as Mara later told me, "'Wellington, I like you . . . You are an old friend . . . I respect you . . . But goddammit, you have no idea what,' etc., etc., etc."

During the recess Reeves, Lombardi, and Bidwill joined Modell in his suite, still not sure what to do. In the middle of a highly confused and emotional discussion, Tex Schramm knocked on the door, and someone shouted, "What now?"

"Look, guys," he said. "Before you pass judgment I think there is something you should know and you don't. You don't and Wellington doesn't. Nobody in this entire league does except the commissioner does. I've been seeing Lamar Hunt."

Or as they say in the soap operas, the husband is always the last to know. Nobody involved in the negotiations between the leagues bothered to tell Davis about them. He truly believed he was in a fight that his owners wanted him to win.

"I was absolutely furious," Modell later told me. "Here I am an owner in this league, and nobody tells me what's going on. I was outraged at Rozelle. Now I figure, the hell with Gogolak. I demand to know what's going on.

"Looking back now," he later told me, "Pete was right. All we needed was one slip and the whole thing would have crashed, and what I had forgotten in the heat of that moment was that Tex really couldn't have committed to anything. But that day with all that went on, I was steaming."

"Y'all can do whatever you want about Gogolak," Tex said, breaking the sudden dead silence that engulfed the room, "but I have to let you know something else about these talks. I think we just might almost be there."

Now, everyone in that room decided that they really needed a lot more time to think. And what they didn't know—not even Schramm knew—was that Rosenbloom had on his own initiative called Ralph Wilson in Buffalo and given him his best "We are all reasonable men" speech and had said he thought that the two leagues could merge under certain conditions and no franchises

would be moved. The AFL would pay twelve million dollars. Wilson said he's ask around and get back to him.

Rosenbloom, as usual, had gone off on his own. Wilson called back and said, "Yes to franchises and merger, but no to the money." Ever the diplomat, Rosenbloom suggested Wilson bend over and perform an anatomically impossible act.

Meanwhile, up in New York, at the Al Davis bar mitzvah ("Today I am a commissioner") press conference, they had no way of knowing that the NFL was not exactly totally united. Now Davis had begun to speak about what had to be done to put some teeth into its identity and some fear into the NFL when Jack Horrigan, the Buffalo publicist, had left the room to answer an urgent phone call. When he returned he whispered the news about Gogolak's signing to Davis.

Davis was visibly angry but not necessarily because he believed his league had been wronged. He was a pragmatist, and he could live with the loss of one placekicker—particularly with what he was already planning to do. He was angry because he felt that the NFL (read Rozelle here) with its keen sense of public relations and newspaper reaction had set out to eclipse his personal press conference, which is exactly what happened in the next day's papers.

Without so much as a pause, Davis personally delivered the news about Gogolak and then told the assembled press he felt the favor could be returned—indeed, must be returned. He had come to New York to wage war, and not one isolated defeat in which he wasn't even involved would change that plan.

With offices on the same street, there were metaphorically eyeball to eyeball . . . very different yet very much alike.

Rozelle: Smooth, tan, socially aware. White Anglo-Saxon Protestant, California. Determined to do what had to be done.

Davis: Husky-voiced, intense, all football all the time. Jewish, Brooklyn raised. Determined to do what had to be done.

What a fight. Only Don King was missing.

The one critical variable that no reporters considered was the unspoken truth that there were key AFL owners who wanted estab-

lishment acceptance and love even more than they wanted victory. But that would surface later

Now, from start to finish, neither Rozelle nor Davis would blink . . . not then . . . not after . . . not even for the next three decades. From the moment of the dueling press conferences, in the words of Sherlock Holmes, "Watson, the game is afoot."

9

Ain't Gonna Study No War No More

Oh, it can end all right, mister. It can end all right, if somebody does what he is supposed to do.
 —Vince Lombardi on his growing frustration

Here's two guys meeting behind statues and in the park and they're deciding our fate and we don't even know that it's happening. I'm steaming.
 —Art Modell on being left out of the AFL–NFL merger loop

This was the early spring of 1966. The NFL had just approved the Giants' signing of Buffalo's Pete Gogolak—the first case of an AFL player using his free agency to jump to the NFL. Now the National Football League had convened a great public relations gathering of coaches and general managers. During one long afternoon they spread them around at various locations in a large hotel banquet room, plastered posters of their teams on the walls behind them, and invited the press to stop by and visit. It was an ideal coach-to-writer chance for a relaxed interview.

There was a stand-up bar, always a media attraction. The only thing missing was a string quartet grinding out multiple choruses of "Getting to Know You," probably because since Rozelle took office, the league had been very sensitive about overkill.

If you are a working newsman, there is a value to this kind of gathering. In a relaxed atmosphere you can pick up all kinds of background information. It was at that gathering in New York that I first got the feeling that all was not peace and harmony among the troops at Camp Rozelle over how to conduct and, perhaps, even end the ferocious battle with Al Davis and his commandos.

The shoulder-to-shoulder, let-us-all-man-the-barricades image the NFL was projecting was apparently not as unanimous as it seemed. Until now all the yearning and whining for peace had come from the rebels. But now, for the first time, I was to hear a member of the establishment utter similar sentiments.

And what a member.

Vince Lombardi was seated on a couch with a huge poster on the wall behind him of Jim Taylor moving forward with an expression that seemed to indicate he was about to knock down the Great Wall of China. There was a drink on the low table in front of him. "Glad to see you," he said, which was a lie because the three things in his world that irritated him to his very core were fumbles in his offensive backfield, Packer fatigue of any kind in the fourth quarter, and obligatory sessions with the press anywhere and at any time.

We talked briefly about the draft and about the unsigned players and about the impact the new AFL commissioner, Al Davis, might have on this interleague war. And then we spoke about the suddenly elevated new role of player agents and the big money the Packers had to shell out to sign Texas Tech's Donny Anderson and Jim Grabowski of the University of Illinois. It was the most money the Pack had spent since this interfraternity battle had erupted.

"The way it's going now," I said, "it looks like this thing is never going to end."

His response was immediate and forceful in the manner that only Vince Lombardi could fire back. "Oh, it can end all right, mister." His jaw tightened and his eyes burned fiercely beneath his glasses like twin lasers. "It can end all right, if somebody does what he is supposed to do." Then he lapsed into a kind of Trappist-monk silence designed to drive a visitor away—which it did.

I didn't know it at the time, but he was already on the record with that in terms of his colleagues with a burst of outrage during the owners' Gogolak discussion. The "somebody" he was speaking about was Pete Rozelle. It was clear that he felt Rozelle had to take the steps needed to end this before both sides lost a franchise or two. He had good reason.

Lombardi did not personally know Al Davis, but he knew enough about him to understand the economic danger that an adversary like Davis could pose.

In order to pose such a threat, Davis had to make sure he had sufficient leverage. His first act, therefore, was to finalize his contract that paid something like sixty grand a year—a pretty good salary in those days—for five years. Of more importance was a clause within it that stipulated that if he was fired or if he quit because the owners ignored his advice, he would be paid in full.

And he had something else. Wayne Valley, the man who had hired Davis and the man who was then the Raiders' managing partner, had sent him off to lead the troops with a fail-safe weapon in his back pocket. It was an iron-clad legal document guaranteeing that if he left the commissioner's job for any reason whatsoever, he was guaranteed a return to Oakland as managing partner with equity in the ownership franchise.

With both commissioners rock solid in their authorizations and both league offices just a few city blocks apart in Manhattan, the great face-off began. One of the first things Davis did was to get his newly assembled PR staff moving to cut into the massive advantage the NFL had enjoyed. And inch by inch it began to earn respect in various sports departments around the country.

Davis was a quick learner in this area, but he was also a longtime grudge holder, so his PR staff had to walk a gossamer tightrope to squeeze concessions from him in that area—particularly in the matter of whom he would agree to sit down with for interviews.

Davis was approached by Mickey Herskowitz, who had used his old-boy Texas network to get Steve Perkins of the *Dallas Morning News* to agree to an in-depth interview with Davis. Mickey understood that this was a coup of major significance because Perkins was a major local writer in his city who was perceived as having a track record of closeness to Clint Murchison and the NFL Cowboys.

It was, indeed, an accomplishment, and when Mickey told Davis what he had scheduled, he had every right to expect an enthusiastic response. Davis sat silently for what seemed an eternity, and

then he said, "Don't you have any sense at all? Don't you know he is the enemy and Dallas is an enemy city?"

"Look," Herskowitz said. "In the first place, it doesn't work that way, and, second, if you get a favorable piece in an NFL city, that has to help."

"Okay," Davis said, still not convinced, "but if he crucifies me, I'll never take your advice again."

Perkins came and interviewed him. The piece was to run the following Sunday. On Monday morning Davis called him in and demanded: "What did he write about me?"

"Al, the piece ran yesterday in Dallas, Texas. We are in New York City. This is Monday. I can't get a Dallas paper until this afternoon, and neither can you."

"Davis said nothing," Mickey recalled. "He just sat there, and then he pulled a desk drawer open and yanked out a long piece of yellow Western Union paper. He had gotten a friend to wire the entire story to him."

"In the future," Davis told him, "I wanna know what's said about me before anyone else does. I wanna be ready to answer the next set of questions."

If Davis tested his PR soldiers intensely, there was one public relations—minded guy he did not have to challenge. He knew what Jets owner Sonny Werblin could do for the AFL with both his wallet and his imagination.

His MCA experience made him the most valuable television asset in either league. It also gave him a rare big-money negotiator's talent. As a case in point, I remember having dinner with Sonny in Houston on the eve of the 1965 All-Star Game.

Just before dessert, Jack Kemp, the Buffalo quarterback and later a highly respected member of Congress, approached the table. He was the AFL's first player representative. "I'm sorry to interrupt your meal, Mr. Werblin, but I wondered if we could talk about our player contract after dinner."

"Jack, I am with a very important guy doing a very important interview that will help this league. Let's do it tomorrow morning."

After Kemp left I said to Sonny, "You really sounded arrogant," and he said to me, "Arrogant? Hell, I just had three glasses of scotch. If he thinks I'm going to negotiate after that, he's out of his mind."

Nobody ever had an edge negotiating with him. And as a star maker in Hollywood or on Broadway or on the Jets' sidelines, nobody had an edge over him there, either.

A year earlier had changed the thrust of this battle for as long as it would last. When it happened, he locked up every front page in America for the American Football League. In the spring of 1965 Werblin, the old star maker, saw exactly what he was looking for in "Joe Willie" Namath, the University of Alabama quarterback.

Namath had also been drafted by the Cardinals, who then gave the rights to the Giants, who never made a bid. They already knew that Werblin was offering more than four hundred thousand dollars, the largest contract then in the history of pro football.

Werblin did, in fact, proceed to create a superstar, and the league's first media star . . . Broadway Joe Namath . . . Namath with a white llama rug and a plethora of airline stewardesses as his apartment decor . . . Namath, the darling of every New York gossip columnist . . . Namath, who spoke with a sexy Alabama drawl although he was raised in a small Pennsylvania town near Pittsburgh . . . Namath, from the playing field to Manhattan's glamorous nightlife, who fulfilled every criteria to qualify as a New York matinee idol.

Suddenly, his Jets began to leave large footprints all over the city's newsprint. The AFL had its first big-city headline grabber. It also now had its first genuine superstar player and its first commissioner who was not only willing but eager to engage in a street fight. With his own contract written in stone and with Namath as the first AFL attention getter already in place, Al Davis was leveraged to launch his battle plan.

It was known in the AFL office as the 50-50-50 plan. Davis would go after every NFL quarterback and superstar he could convince and give them a fifty-thousand-dollar signing bonus upon sign-

ing a postdated contract to the date of their free agency, another fifty thousand for the first season, and yet another fifty thousand for the second.

Davis did not let many in on the plan. Mickey Herskowitz found out about it like this:

> Davis calls me into his office and flatly asks, "Who do you know over in the NFL? I mean really know." I told him that John David Crowe and I had been close since he played for Texas A&M. He was established as a star and now was with the Cardinals.
>
> And Davis said, "Good, he's your man. Call him and tell him we will give him fifty grand to sign, another fifty for the first year, and a third fifty for the second."
>
> I called John David at his home in Arkansas, and I laid the deal out for him and he got very excited. I told him to sit tight. He is still sitting because two days later, a funny thing happened.
>
> Davis walked into my office, and he laid a piece of paper on my desk and told me to sign it. He laid the same paper on the desks of everyone in PR that he had brought in. It was a two-year contract. He said it was for our protection and to sign it with no questions asked. Looking back it was kind of typical. He was protecting us against a merger, but he wouldn't say so. Al always loved mystery and intrigue.

It was a side of Davis rarely written about. He knew a merger was coming. He was protecting those hires who had given up steady jobs to join him, ensuring that when the two leagues merged, his employees were guaranteed jobs with the new entity. It was a side of him all the more surprising in retrospect when you consider the number of others who were later fired by him when he returned to Oakland for offenses real, imagined, or exaggerated.

But the 50-50-50 plan still rolled on. He knew some signees would cost much more. Don Klosterman and Scotty Stirling, who had replaced Davis as general manger when he left Oakland to become the AFL commissioner, would be designated as the ones who would be the point men in the pursuit of the heaviest hitters.

It was Klosterman who would make football's first millionaire

out of John Brodie, the 49er quarterback who had never won a title. In the end there were others who were eager to sign and play for any AFL team for the right money: the Bears' Rudy Bukich, Cleveland's Jim Ninowski, Washington's Sonny Jurgensen, Detroit's Milt Plum, the Vikings' Fran Tarkenton, and the Rams' Roman Gabriel.

I knew this last because on a visit to the Raiders' office, Stirling showed me Gabriel's contract, just where Davis had left it. Technically, Brodie never formally signed, but he ultimately got his money after the merger because of a hastily written memo on a hotel bar cocktail napkin signed by Klosterman that would have killed the AFL in court.

As the merger drew nearer, Davis believed he had won. He believed his league would be the stronger one, and he believed he would emerge as commissioner of the newly united fraternity as soon as it happened.

And what was happening back at Pete's Place while all this was going on? Well, nobody had to leave a wake-up call for him. He knew exactly where he was headed and exactly what he had to do to get there. Later on, after the merger, Rozelle told me:

> I know Al was upset. I know it was out of pride and human nature because I am sure he means it when he says he honestly felt he had us beaten.
>
> But he didn't . . . not even close . . . believe me. He could have signed almost anyone he wanted, and it wouldn't have mattered because we were about to do the same thing to them—and, unlike them, we had all the money we needed. We were not out to steal the few stars they had. Beyond Namath, who even knew who they were? We were going to go after their soft underbelly.
>
> We were going to go straight through their rosters and denude them.

But having so little in star power, didn't it make sense that the AFL had far less to lose because the NFL had so many stars it could steal?

"No," Rozelle insisted, "because here was all you had to do, and we were ready to do it."

You simply go out and create chaos. You talk to so many players of all levels and skills that you trigger a bloodbath. And then every rookie that Bill Sullivan [Boston] talked to—and he was desperately concerned about money because he didn't have any—well, Billy would have to wonder if you had talked to him already and for how much.

And the player, of course, was going to leave the impression that we had whether it was true or not, because it gave him bargaining leverage.

We could have broken them without even thinking about quality. We would have gone after the quantity that they didn't have instead, and there would have been nothing with which they could fight back.

We didn't have to chase an E. J. Holub, the great Kansas City linebacker, for example. We could have signed a slew of lesser players, and they would have come because almost all the teams they played for were staggering financially.

If we hadn't achieved the merger through talks, we would have won anyway.

Clearly, public relations was not Mr. Rozelle's only forte.

Meanwhile, the secret Schramm-Hunt merger talks proceeded cautiously. In the beginning, they met in a parking lot at the old Dallas airport, appropriately called Love Field. There in the shadow of the Texas Ranger statue (an ironic twist because the Cowboys actually were named Rangers for the first two weeks of their existence), Schramm spoke to Hunt of the virtues of a 100-yard society where law and order and a common draft prevailed.

Why were the meetings held in Schramm's car? "Why was that?" I asked when Schramm and Rozelle and I had breakfast together the morning after the merger press conference. "Why not a hotel room?"

"Listen," Schramm said, "if anyone was going to be bugged for the record, it wasn't going to be me. After we got past that, we took to visiting late at night in each other's homes."

Schramm would report periodically to Rozelle, who would not share the information with other owners until he felt it was a done

Ain't Gonna Study No War No More 133

deal. The bombshell Schramm had dropped in Modell's suite the day of the Gogolak signing was rapidly becoming more than a notion.

Unlike Rozelle and Schramm, Hunt knew the time had come when he had to enlist allies and immediately set about forming an ad hoc committee, whose members would be the only owners consulted. After all, the AFL was winning the battle for fans and attention in the two markets of most importance to it—New York and the Bay Area as represented by Oakland.

The San Francisco 49ers were last at 6-6-2 in the NFL West. The Giants were last in the NFL East at 1-12-1. Clearly, the old guard was losing badly in those two areas. Given these facts it might seem strange to the devoted historian that neither the Jets' Sonny Werblin nor the Raiders' Wayne Valley was on the AFL's secret committee. On the committee? Hell, they weren't even told what was going on. And with good reason from Hunt's standpoint.

The terms of the final peace treaty were still in negotiations, but they would call for eighteen million dollars in "war crimes" reparations to be paid to the NFL. Given advance notice Werblin surely would have asked why he should pay that kind of money to a franchise that hadn't laid a glove on him. Ditto for Wayne Valley, who had brought new pride and dignity to Oakland and was instrumental in getting the city a new stadium that put that warehouse disguised as Kezar Stadium, where the 49ers played, to shame.

Clearly, the 49ers and the Giants had become toothless tigers against their immediate geographical enemies. Valley and Werblin were justified in the bitterness they expressed when they were merged against their will. They were the ones—that is, the only ones—to meet the enemy head-on ... They alone had carried the direct burden for their lodge brothers ... and now they would be asked to pay money to the two franchises whose rear ends they firmly believed they were kicking the hell out of.

When the agreement was finally reached, this last would become the stickiest diplomatic mess Rozelle had ever been asked to scrub clean. And the way he handled it hurt Werblin and Valley to their

very core. He was rewarding the two franchises the AFL had begun to dominate.

Werblin, at the time, was checking into a hospital for minor surgery. Had the ad hoc committee told him what they were doing, the Borough of Manhattan would have been treated to the sight of Mr. Show Biz in a hospital gown racing down Park Avenue with two orderlies in hot pursuit. So the ad hoc committee met secretly.

"It was bad luck for Al because," Herskowitz says, "Werblin was in the hospital. He never would have let them keep Al out of the loop. Al knew something was going on, but they never held any of their meetings in the office. I think Al believed he was winning. He believed they were nervous about his signings, and so the AFL could win on its terms and he would be the commissioner.

"This was like a heavyweight fight, and Al saw no reason we should lose it. I never said anything, but I was pretty sure we wouldn't win because they still had the big guns."

For his part, Davis knew the merger was near, although he was deliberately kept out of the negotiations. What he did not know was how much the sub rosa ad hoc committee was willing to concede.

Rozelle, meanwhile, by keeping matters pretty much between him and Schramm, had been able to distance himself enough so that had the deal fallen through, it would be bouncing off Schramm's shoulders and not his, leaving him to put Operation Soft Underbelly into practice.

At three on the morning of June 7, the telephone rang in Rozelle's apartment. It was Schramm, whose fatigue was evident in his voice. He had just gotten off the phone with Hunt, who, ironically, was holed up in a New York hotel just a few blocks away from Rozelle.

"It's all set," Schramm croaked.

"I'll call you," Rozelle said.

"Can I go to bed now?" Schramm said.

"Yes, but don't make a habit of it," Rozelle replied.

Rozelle showered, dressed, and checked the airline schedule; called his aide de camp, Jim Kensil; and then called Schramm back.

"Do you know it's 6:00 a.m. here?" Schramm grunted.

"Time difference," Rozelle said, "and daylight saving time as well. It's 8:00 a.m. up here, sleepy head. Call Hunt back and tell him we will meet him, in Washington."

Rozelle caught the noon shuttle out of LaGuardia to make sure he would not tip off the world by traveling with Hunt. As an extra precaution he wore sunglasses. Schramm had told Hunt to check into the Sheraton Carlton Hotel, just behind the White House, where Murchison, the oilman, kept a suite for his lobbyists under an assumed name. He was to stay in his room until they got there so as not to attract attention.

Schramm and Rozelle met at what was then Washington National Airport and took a cab to the hotel. When they pulled up, to their terror, there was Hunt on the sidewalk, waving to them.

"Hi, Pete. Hi, Tex," Hunt shouted.

They grabbed him. It is conceivable that over the distance between the front door and the elevator, Lamar's feet may not have touched the ground. They spent the rest of the day in cloistered communion.

The next morning the trio went over to the offices of Covington and Burling, the law firm that represents the NFL and, thanks to the complexities of the sports business in the modern world, has had an enormous practice in all kinds of things related to the Justice Department.

Next, Kensil, who had flown in with Rozelle, presented them with a long list of questions he anticipated would be asked at the merger press conference—and most of them were. They put Hunt through a dress rehearsal. Kensil said Lamar did just fine. What he didn't say was that he would have preferred to have the show get a ten-day trial in New Haven.

When they were done, Hunt left for New York to join Sullivan and Wilson. Schramm left in search of the nearest bed.

That night rumors had begun trickling over the AP and UPI wires. When they did, Ray Walsh, the president of the New York Football Giants, flatly said to anyone who asked, "There is no merger. The talks have broken down."

In midafternoon Herskowitz called me at my desk at the *Newark Star-Ledger*. "Can you do me a favor?"

"Sure."

"Can you find out what the hell is happening? Nobody in this office has a clue."

"I just got off the phone," I told him. "Don't send out for ice, friend. You are booked on the *Titanic*."

The press conference was called for late afternoon in the Warwick Hotel. There are some things in this business that you never forget . . . the sun rising off the Congo River behind Ali's villa in Zaire . . . the frosty collective breath of fifty thousand Packers fans at the game they call the Ice Bowl . . . the look on the faces of the flora and fauna of sports journalism when they were told that General William D. Eckert had been named the commissioner of baseball and they struggled not to yell out, "Who?"

And then there was the strange motif spilling across the wall of the Essex Room at the Warwick on the afternoon that Pete Rozelle walked away with the B'nai Hunt Brotherhood Award. The wall itself was a dandy end-to-end mural of an English garden . . . a sprightly blending of hedgerows and green grass that made you want to go out and roll Easter eggs, which was perfect because within the hour, we would learn how badly the AFL, itself, got rolled.

Clearly, it was the money. After all, neither side really won the battle of who could sign who and who could steal who. And for the AFL to pay more than $18 million, as it turned out, just to get a little love did not sit well with Werblin and Valley in view of the fact that each felt it was winning against the old guard in its own territory.

They also had agreed to cede another $7.5 million from the sale price the AFL was getting for its expansion franchise in Cincinnati. Davis, who was not there, was rightly furious. It was as though the progress he had made in signing NFL stars was meaningless. Now, instead of being the meaningless commissioner of the AFL until the final merger in 1970, he opted out, taking his 10 percent

Raiders ownership, vowing to be heard from again—a promise he made good on again and again from his new West Coast base.

The conference began on time. They filed into the room, the worried officials from NBC who had the AFL rights and the smiling gentlemen from CBS, who still had the rights to the old guard, part of the disenchanted office staff from the AFL and the gloating winners from NFL headquarters . . . You expected to hear a guy in a tuxedo advising the multitude: "Bride's family to the left . . . Groom's family to the right."

On a powder-blue couch, directly facing enough television cameras to film the Original Exodus, Schramm of the NFL, Hunt of the AFL, and Rozelle, now of the world, sat side by side, bathed in an invisible cloak of brotherhood.

Rozelle sat in the middle and held a portable microphone that he occasionally loaned to Hunt. He wore a dark-blue suit and occasionally leaned forward, which can happen with a man who just swallowed nine new franchises in a single bite.

The American Football League had migrated from Harry Wismer's kitchen to Pete Rozelle's dining room. They had the good sense not to ask, "What's for dinner?"—knowing full well it was them.

Rozelle was smooth as silk as he ran the press conference, and Lamar sat there grinning. Occasionally, when the reporters asked a question Rozelle did not particularly like, he smiled and said, "I'll let Lamar answer that one," and handed over temporary possession of the microphone.

As press conferences go, this one offered few surprises. The terms were not surprising when you consider that it had come about by throwing Davis under the American Football League's love bus.

In return for its money, the AFL would participate in a common collegiate draft. There would be a championship game. And guess who would emerge as the commissioner?

The next day Wilson, Hunt, and Sullivan showed up at the AFL headquarters, went into Davis's office, and closed the door. Then the shouting began.

"I was in the next office with a couple of guys," Herskowitz recalls. "As soon as we heard the shouting, we all pressed our ears against the wall so tightly it's a wonder our molecules didn't melt into the wood."

Above the raucous voices, they heard this:

SULLIVAN: We're pissed off that you publicly said we three sold you down the river.

DAVIS: I never said that.

WILSON: Yes, you did.

DAVIS: I never did and I can prove it. I'll call Sonny [Werblin], and he will verify what I said.

HUNT: He's in the hospital.

DAVIS: I don't care. I'll get him in his room right now, and I'll put it on speaker phone . . . [Sound of dialing] "Sonny, did I ever say Ralph, Lamar, and Billy sold me out? They are here with me in the room."

WERBLIN: No, you didn't. What you . . .

Davis hangs up.

DAVIS: So all three of you are wrong. Now I'll tell you what I really said. What I really said was that every one of you sons of bitches sold me down the river.

Point . . . set . . . match.

Later that day Davis walked into Herskowitz's office. He sat down in Joe Foss's old rocking chair and rocked in silence. Then he looked at Mickey and said in a soft, emotional voice: "Mickey, I hope someday, someplace, wherever you may be or I may be, you will have occasion to say something nice about me."

"I hope so, Al."

And then Davis exploded into laughter. "I was only kidding," he said.

"So was I, Al."

And then they both laughed and laughed and laughed.

It was the end of an era.

More properly, it was just the end of that particular era because Rozelle and Davis would clash again . . . and again . . . and again.

Pete Rozelle had won the most fiercely contested 100-yard war in the history of professional football. But now there was the matter of getting the mandatory antitrust approval to validate it. Without it, there could be no merger. And arrayed against Rozelle on this alien battlefield would be one of the most powerful men in the United States Congress.

1. Pete Rozelle and Jane Coupe at their 1949 wedding. Courtesy of
Anne Marie Rozelle Bratton

2. The young Rozelles and daughter Anne Marie. Courtesy of
Anne Marie Rozelle Bratton

3. Rozelle gets in some daddy time. Courtesy of Anne Marie Rozelle Bratton

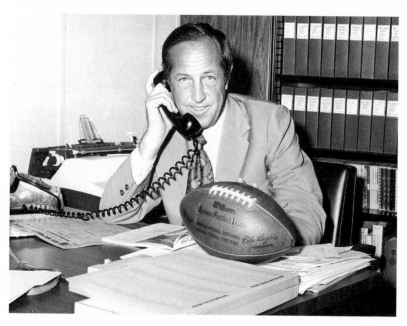

4. Even in the office, not far from football. Pro Football Hall of Fame

5. A fella in high places wishes Rozelle bon voyage after one of his many Washington lobby wars. White House photo

6. Rozelle (*left*) awards the Super Bowl XXI trophy to Giants co-owner Wellington Mara and coach Bill Parcells (*far right*). Jerry Pinkus, New York Giants Sports Photo

7. George Halas, who helped pro football through its infancy, and Pete Rozelle, who made it America's passion, share memories in the press lounge during Super Bowl Week. Pro Football Hall of Fame

8. The Hall of Fame committee meets with notables Lamar Hunt (*left*), Rozelle (*center*), and George Halas (*right front*). Pro Football Hall of Fame

9. Pete Rozelle cuts the ribbon and
opens Pro Football's Hall of Fame.
Pro Football Hall of Fame

10. And then along came Carrie Cooke, whom he married in 1974. Courtesy of Anne Marie Rozelle Bratton

11. The Rozelles and the Cookes merge. Courtesy of Anne Marie Rozelle Bratton

12. Pete's special friends at his surprise
birthday party at 21. *Standing, left to right*:
Jack Landry, Herb Siegel, Bob Tisch, and
Frank Gifford. Seated next to Rozelle is
David Mahoney. Courtesy of Anne Marie
Rozelle Bratton

13. Thelma Elkjer and Anne Marie Rozelle Bratton share a private moment at Anne Marie's wedding. Thelma was Rozelle's executive secretary with the Rams and with the NFL. For forty years she was the gatekeeper to the commissioner's office. She was also a much younger Anne Marie's shopping guide, confidante, and watchful adult companion. Courtesy of Anne Marie Rozelle Bratton

14. Rozelle and his Hall of Fame presenter and first boss, Tex Schramm, await the big moment. Pro Football Hall of Fame

15. Pete Rozelle at the Hall of Fame banquet in the Land of the Autograph Hunters. Pro Football Hall of Fame

16. The Hall of Fame
Class of 1985. *From the
left*: Frank Gatski, Joe
Willie Namath, Pete
Rozelle, O. J. Simpson,
and Roger Staubach. Pro
Football Hall of Fame

17. The commish:
Alvin Pete Rozelle.
Courtesy of Anne
Marie Rozelle Bratton

10

Bringing in the Sheaves

What do you mean, you don't know how to thank me? We have a deal.
　—Representative Hale Boggs, reminding Pete Rozelle of the merger
　approval's quid pro quo

What will I tell my little boy if he sees sixteen teams in one league and only
ten in the other?
　—Al Davis on realignment

And so it was over, the most bitter economic war in the history
of all professional sports. On the surface there was something in
it for everyone. Lamar Hunt got what he had always sought—the
soft, warm comfort blanket of acceptance. For Wellington Mara
and Lou Spadia there was eighteen million dollars guaranteed
them as "war crime reparations." And for all the owners, includ-
ing Al Davis, headed back to Oakland, there was a common draft
and an end to the dizzying spiral of incredible spending.

For the players it was something else. While John Brodie did,
indeed, get his hush money to keep that now famous cocktail-
napkin contract from winding up in the courts, the nightmare of
rival leagues trying to stone each other to death with their wal-
lets was over.

And for the influx of new college kids, there was the specter of
the dreaded common draft that emasculated much of their lever-
age. The babysitting army was out of business, or as Mel Farr, a
UCLA All-America, told me on the eve of the first common draft:
"When I was a junior, I couldn't walk two steps without scouts
coming around wanting to take me here or there or inquiring

about my welfare. Then they merged, and now nobody even offers me a cup of coffee."

Clearly, 100-yard peace in our time meant all things to all men. "All men" included the United States Congress and a willful, battle-tough senior citizen and constitutional scholar named Emanuel Celler.

The football people could say they were merged, could act as though they were merged, could share a drink or a dinner as though they were merged. But in no way could they substitute the wish for the deed. Until Congress said so, they were a long way away from their one-monopoly, one-commissioner dream.

Manny Celler never ran for the Senate. He didn't need it. Year after year the people in his Brooklyn district kept sending him back to the House of Representatives, and with each reelection he moved higher within the power structure, as the seniority of retired or defeated congressmen melted away.

Long before this merger, Celler was already chairman of the House Judiciary Committee and the powerful subcommittee on antitrust legislation. The prevailing wisdom was that he would not be a problem to Rozelle, since in 1961 he had gotten the NFL approval of its one-TV contract, one-payday-for-all antitrust exemption.

Celler steered it through only because it could in no way benefit Major League Baseball, and Major League Baseball was much on his mind. The Dodgers had abandoned "his Brooklyn" and moved to Los Angeles for the 1958 season and, in so doing, had stolen what was considered a birthright by the constituency he had served for so long. Its pain was reflected in the words of a Brooklyn doctor named Louis Lostfogel, who once diagnosed a patient as depressed. "It was something I thought about a lot because I saw so much of it in men of a certain age who were Dodgers fans."

It was as though Walter O'Malley had drilled a hole in the borough's soul. You do not get elected as often as Manny Celler did by the people of Brooklyn without understanding that. He was not going to cast a vote on anything that could be stretched into

a benefit for O'Malley, the man who had taken Brooklyn's beloved baseball team to the West Coast.

Rozelle, as pro football's savvy point man, had been down to Congress many times as the point man who defended all of professional sports during varied congressional hearings. But now he was caught in the cross fire between baseball and Manny. Anything that could benefit O'Malley in the slightest way was anathema to Celler, and too bad for pro football if it got caught in the middle.

Not that O'Malley could possibly benefit from an NFL merger approval, but old political feuds neither did nor would fade away. Once he and O'Malley went around and around over the Dodgers, Celler opposed anything and everything pertaining to professional sports: mergers, franchise moves, anything he thought might strengthen the highly questionable Supreme Court decision behind which baseball often hid.

Celler was not bashful in expressing that idea to Rozelle. Unlike other commissioners and influential sports franchise owners, Rozelle immediately understood that it was imperative for him to change Celler's mind or immediately find someone even more powerful in the Congress (not an easy task) and impress upon him the notion that football fans vote. What he next did, no commissioner of any sport before him had ever done.

There is no doubt in my mind that none of the other players in this coast-to-coast arena could have had the diplomatic skill to do it—not Al Davis, not Lamar Hunt, nobody. Rozelle was the best at this, and there was no number two. To launch his campaign, he zeroed in on the only public forum that could enable him to mount the pressure necessary for a campaign to save the merger.

The annual charity football game between the defending NFL champion and the college all-stars in Chicago was the perfect occasion. Here, where rival babysitters had once struggled to snatch eager young bodies in years past, all was now peace and harmony. This would be the first event where the old and new guards would gather as equals. It was, if you saw George Halas and Lamar Hunt in happy conversation there that week, the liv-

ing example of what pro football fans (who were sitting on a lot of votes) deeply wanted.

On August 5 Pete Rozelle addressed the Football Writers of America to launch that campaign. You couldn't have kept him away from a stage like that with a gun, a whip, and a chair. He told them that with any chance of a formal catchall sports bill he sought now in limbo because of Celler's fixation on the Dodgers, he had asked the congressman to consider a bill limited to approval of pro football's recent peace agreement. He told his eager and highly friendly audience: "This would allow us to implement the merger plan we have already set forth. This bill is important to us. If it fails to pass, it does not mean the merger is dead, but it does mean we will have to look at it again and be responsible for the future of the game.

"Time is our problem. It may be possible for us to get legislation this session of Congress, but now the importance of the Civil Right Bill and the airlines strike have occupied everyone's time."

That put Rozelle on the record before the most receptive audience at the best possible time. If Mr. Celler needed a favorable opinion to act, Rozelle had placed it in the typewriters of the only people who could generate that kind of impact in every corner of the country. And because of the way he always thought three moves ahead, he knew he had an untapped but potentially decisive hole card in his pocket.

It had been there for some time, placed there by a New Orleans antique dealer in the city's French Quarter named Dave Dixon. His goal was to get an NFL franchise for the city, and in 1964, with no expansion planned by the league, Dixon gambled and brought the Cardinals and the Packers to Tulane Stadium for a preseason game.

When a crowd of sixty-three thousand showed up, it was not lost on Rozelle or any of his owners that here was a genuine football town. Rozelle immediately made it his business to cultivate a friendship with the eager Dixon.

The afternoon of the game, Dixon had rented space at the New Orleans Country Club for a kickoff luncheon and invited every civic official he ever knew or would like to know to a reception

there. To his amazement Governor John McKeithen showed up and introduced himself. "I didn't know him, and I didn't expect he would come," Dixon told me.

> But he was a north Louisiana hillbilly guy who loved football. I told him about my plans for the largest completely domed football stadium in the country to house a football team for the city of New Orleans. Most folks were laughing at that idea. But not him. He knew I didn't have that kind of money, and he said he wanted to help with a bond issue when the time came on the condition that I call it the Louisiana Super Dome.

> Hell, I would have called it anything they wanted. And that was the beginning, because without the dome, we never would have had a team.

> Pete called me after he had this trouble with Congressman Celler and wondered if I could help with Senator Russell Long and Hale Boggs, who was the House whip. He knew I knew them both. He also went out of his way to infer that the prize would be our NFL franchise and a couple of Super Bowls.

Dixon had been active in state and local politics, and Rozelle knew that one of his biggest strengths was he never needed a scorecard to know the players up at the capitol in Baton Rouge. Dixon responded immediately. He hired a fellow named David Klack, a well-known local lobbyist who had often advised Long and Boggs on election matters. Dixon sent him up to Washington to help generate emotion for a deal that would save the merger and capture an NFL expansion franchise.

It was Rozelle's hope that with Long, chairman of the powerful Senate Finance Committee, and Boggs, the House majority leader, he could find a way to neutralize Celler. Both were facing the possibility of bitter reelection fights. Nobody had to tell either one of them that Louisiana football fans were Louisiana voters.

It was a powerful touchstone in a legacy that the commissioner was building that he dared to face down Emanuel Celler—one of the most powerful congressmen of all time. Nobody else in professional football or, for that matter, any professional sport could

have done it. Diplomacy was not the biggest strength of either Davis or Hunt. The stakes were the kind of big ones on which Rozelle had always thrived. He knew that if he failed, the entire merger would have collapsed and the two leagues as they were then structured would have lost a number of franchises and the ultimate preeminent position the NFL holds today.

The deal was simple. They would pass it in the Senate and then attach it as a rider to a tax investment bill and use the Democratic-controlled Ways and Means Committee to get it done. The battle would give the term *Mississippi riverboat gambler* a brand-new meaning. The 100-yard New Orleans poker game was under way.

"I invited Rozelle to my apartment at the Watergate and showed him how it could be easy because the Johnson administration wanted that tax bill," Senator Long told the *New Orleans Times-Picayune* years later. "I told him we had to have the New Orleans franchise in return."

"I spent quite a lot of time with Russell Long," Rozelle told me later in all candor. "I remember one night we sat up drinking in his apartment until 3:00 a.m., and he was fascinating. He told me fabulous stories about his uncle Huey and his father, Earl. Yes, although I hadn't consulted with my owners, I did vaguely make the New Orleans commitment that night. I remember I said, 'Well, I'm sure you know that we are eventually going to expand. Where the hell do you think we are going to go? Fort Wayne?'"

To hedge that bet, Rozelle made three appearances before Celler's House committee. The congressman told Rozelle that he would endorse a merger bill if it covered only the merger and nothing else and if he would publicly agree that the player draft, the awarding of new franchises, and pay television would be totally outside of that antitrust exemption.

Some chance. Would Attila the Hun turn in his sword? Would Henry Ford recruit somebody to organize a union? Rozelle respectfully declined.

"They are simply poor negotiators," Celler told the public that

day. "They are asking the House to rescue them from their own ineptitudes and follies."

Dixon sent Klack back up to Washington for a third time on the day of the Senate vote, which came first. This is what Dixon told me happened that day, according to Klack, adding:

> I believe it word for word. I was paying David, and he had no reason to lie to me. David said:
>
> "I was walking the rotunda with Hale and Pete on the way to the vote, and Pete said, 'I don't know how to thank you for this, Hale,' and Hale said, 'What do you mean, you don't know how to thank me? We have a deal . . . We do have a deal, don't we, for the New Orleans franchise?'
>
> "And Pete said he would give it his best effort, and Hale told him, 'Well, you better go back right now and find out whether you can or you can't deliver because until you do, there's no vote. The vote is officially off,' and he started walking away. He did not look back."

Dixon said next that "Klack told me Pete actually ran after him, and Hale wasn't lollygagging. He was moving pretty good when Pete finally caught up with him and said, 'Hale, you have it. I'm sure you have it.'"

Their dialogue was Rozelle's final deal in the World Championship of Liars Poker. Later Pete would tell me that not a single club owner knew about the deal. "I just did what I had to do," he said. Obviously, it was neither the first nor the last time.

The bill that left the Senate for the House involved taxes, and now appended to it as a rider was the NFL-AFL antitrust merger exemption. Long knew that the Johnson administration desperately wanted the tax bill passed. He was ready for Celler.

Now it was up to Boggs, who immediately enlisted fellow Democrat Wilbur Mills, chairman of the powerful Ways and Means Committee, and made it a matter of party loyalty at a time when Boggs's seat was in danger in the upcoming election. Together they orchestrated what followed.

It began when Celler demanded the House delete the rider and

pass the tax bill without it. At that point Representative Jackson E. Betts (R-OH) called for a motion that would have killed the entire bill. By a vote of 184–57 (few Democrats would risk the wrath of Lyndon Johnson), the motion was defeated. The bill and the rider then passed 161–76 over the protests of a badly shaken Celler.

After Johnson signed the bill, Celler raged to his colleagues: "I have lost the game but not the series. I am going to continue this inquiry, and I am sure that a great deal will become manifest that if you knew now you wouldn't have voted to pass it."

The lone House voice in Celler's defense came from Representative William Cahill, who said that Celler had "not been beaten by an end run. He had been clipped from behind and the House subjected to unnecessary roughness; the commissioner should be penalized half the distance to the goal and the game postponed until next year." He did not add that the brothers had lost the chance to finally win one for the Gipper, but with clichés like that, it is no wonder Cahill went on to become governor of New Jersey.

Rozelle had made a powerful enemy in Congress, but in typical fashion he immediately set about trying to repair the damage with a man who would surely have him back again as a witness. He sent him a personal handwritten note, explaining that he had indeed made an end run around the congressman, but he hoped he would understand. He cited the enormous pressure generated by the American public that had left him no choice. It is interesting to note that a few days later, Representative Celler showed Rozelle's letter to fellow committee members without rancor.

On November 1, 1966, Commissioner Pete Rozelle arrived in New Orleans to announce the formation of the New Orleans NFL franchise. Actually, it was set a few weeks earlier, but the public relations man in Pete Rozelle's soul could not pass up this kind of opportunity. He had delayed the announcement until this date, which was celebrated on the New Orleans calendar as All Saints' Day. The team, of course, would be named the Saints.

Now only two hurdles remained for Pete Rozelle to clear before

the end of this 100-yard junior-varsity Armageddon. There had to be a championship game, and there had to be a sorting out of twenty-six franchises into two one-world conferences.

While all of America's football public viewed the title game as the real showdown, who would eventually play where each year presented major problems that nobody had even considered. The first telephone call the switchboard operator at the NFL office took the morning after the war ended came from Denver:

"I want two hundred seats right now for the championship game."

"Well, sir, we don't know who will be in it, where it will be played, or how much tickets cost."

"I didn't ask you any of that. I just want to buy two hundred seats."

The telephones never stopped that day. But in all that jingle-jangle, there were only two bells Rozelle was waiting to hear. One would come from CBS, and the other would come from NBC. He did not have to wait long. But they did.

Between them Bill MacPhail of CBS (the old guard's network of record) and Carl Lindemann of NBC (the AFL network) would spend enough on calls to the commissioner to pay Uganda's phone bill for a year. This would be the ultimate prize in their network careers, and they knew it. Which one would get Rozelle's blessing?

CBS had been the NFL house outlet from the moment Rozelle negotiated the single-network deal for his teams in 1961. MacPhail would argue that CBS had spent millions for the NFL schedule and its title game . . . a game that had now been reduced to the status of a semifinal match. NBC had been shellacked in the ratings 2–1 that season, but if money could be the factor, it would spend it. It would come to these negotiations prepared to fight all the way down to the last Ivy League vest in its sales department. And Rozelle ignored both of them.

"What are you going to do about this?" I asked him.

"Well, I'm not exactly sure," but I knew he was.

"How long before you decide?"

"I'm not exactly sure," but I knew he was.

He had learned an awful lot about TV negotiations from two of his owners, Art Modell, the former ad exec who knew the business inside out, and Sonny Werblin, the old MCA king who just about invented it.

Rozelle had already rejected Ralph Wilson's suggestion that maybe they should go pay-per-view in the theaters where they could make possibly even more money. "As long as I am commissioner," he told me and others, "we will never, ever charge television viewers for a title game."

Rozelle let both networks stew until July. Then the talks began. They talked. He listened. They argued. He listened. They demanded. He lit up another cigarette and suggested they meet again. July melted into August. August dissolved into September.

One thing, however, remained chiseled in stone. There would indeed be a championship game involving the two league champions. It had been written into the legalese they had agreed upon in accepting the merger. The NFL insisted. The AFL insisted. But most of all Pete Rozelle sensed that before too many renewals, America would learn to love the weeks leading up to determining the last two teams standing.

The game would happen. But who would televise it? Rozelle was patient because he knew the Madison Avenue suits had to come to him.

And so it was that one day with absolutely no warning, he handed them the formula he had wanted all along. Both networks would carry the game in a simulcast, and each would pay $1 million. As a sop to MacPhail, CBS cameras would be responsible for the video, but NBC would have its own director pick and choose the pictures it would show. In phase two CBS would have two Super Bowls sandwiched around one for NBC. For phase two, each would pay $2.5 million per game.

It was Werblin who had come up with the simulcast idea. But even he did not understand that in so doing, the newly merged NFL had created a second drama that gripped America with unexpected interest.

CBS would throw its vast resources into the video buildup to attract viewers a month before the game. It planned to cash in on the enormous name recognition of its announcers and the population of its NFL cities. Its hype included announcements punctuated by kettle drum and staccato voice-overs. You could almost close your eyes and expect to hear the unseen announcer say as the drumbeats grew louder, "Patton crosses the Rhine."

NBC, with really only two nationally known TV faces of the AFL, Curt Gowdy and Paul Christman, opted to eschew the ruffles, flourishes, and cannon's roar and go for erudition. Their tack here was the two best who would give you insight instead of bombast.

So the video battle lines were drawn. It would be CBS versus NBC, the Ford Motor Company (the NFL's prime sponsor) versus Chrysler (their AFL counterpart), Jack Whitaker, Frank Gifford, and Pat Summerall (the CBS primary announcers) versus Gowdy, Christman, and Charlie Jones. Together the rival networks would give Rozelle the greatest hype in the history of sports. With this in mind and the expected huge media group anticipated to work both camps the week before the game, Rozelle's next order of business dealt with the volatile psyche of Vince Lombardi.

Approaching any game, Vincent generally had all the restraint of a falling safe. Competition of any kind was his emotional heartbeat. I remember his wife, Marie, telling me of a day he played marbles with his young grandson in the Lombardi living room. When the kid began to cry and Marie asked him why, he said, "Grandpa is winning all my marbles."

"Jesus, Vince," she whispered, "he's only a baby. Let him win once."

"Mind your business, Marie," he said.

Obviously, he did not need to be reminded of the pressure of this particular football game.

But he was—constantly. Wellington Mara, his former Fordham classmate, had written him a letter in which he said how important this game was to them and voiced his belief that "I would want no other general to carry the NFL flag into battle for us."

"I understood his feeling," Vince later told me, "but that letter made me even more uncomfortable."

The game would be in Los Angeles. The Chiefs would train in nearby Long Beach, and Lombardi wanted no distractions (translation: as few media interviews of the Packers as possible). He planned to train at a place called Ricky's in Palo Alto, 111 miles away.

If that plan held, writers attempting to cover both teams would log more miles in a week than Vasco de Gama did in a year. Told of Vince's intention by Jim Kensil, Rozelle said just seven words: "He is not going to Palo Alto."

Then he picked up the telephone, called Green Bay, and told Vince: "You are not going to Palo Alto."

After each of Vincent's arguments as to why he was, Rozelle repeated those same seven words, and when the conversation ended he said them again, which is how and why the Packers set up camp in Santa Barbara.

While the Packers and the Chiefs worked that week, the NFL staff with three new additions from the AFL office—Herskowitz, Pinchbeck, and Kaze—were following Rozelle's detailed instructions as to how to run something nobody had ever tried to run before. The group included the usual suspects: Kensil, the second in command; Weiss, who did a little of everything; Granholm, the onetime king of the Rams' locker room; and Duncan, now supervisor of officials. It was these last two who brought George Toma from Kansas City out to the Coliseum to take a chicken-shit turf and turned it into chicken salad. Toma was the Rembrandt of all groundskeepers and worked decades of Super Bowls.

"This is how well organized Pete was," Herskowitz will tell you. "Nobody had ever run a Super Bowl. None of us had any idea what a Super Bowl was. But Pete wanted to be ready. He actually sent me a twenty-two-page note of things he wanted us to do as soon as we got there."

The Super Bowl may have excited America's army of football fans, but Seymour Siwoff, the league's head statistician, ran into the one place that wasn't even mildly excited. He told me:

In no time we were out of everything—paper . . . staples . . . rubber bands—and Thelma Elkjer, Pete's executive secretary, told me to find a stationery store and get as much as I could of everything. I gave this guy a humongous order, and then I showed him my NFL ID and explained that Super Bowl headquarters was just around the block at the Statler-Hilton, and he told me, "Marvelous. I hope you like your room. But I don't know anyone associated with you, and you ain't gettin' no credit here."

I had to use my own personal credit card.

We were all so wrapped up in trying to please Pete by making it perfect. I don't think Duncan ever went to bed. He was so punchy from sleep deprivation that one day he said, "Seymour, this is almost as big as a championship game." And I said, "Mark, this IS the championship game."

The game did not sell out—the only Super bowl that did not. But historians forget that the Coliseum had eighty-five thousand seats, and when sixty-five thousand or so attended the huge sections of empties gave a misleading impression.

Years later, recalling that day, Rozelle told me:

I can still recall the way I felt. What I never said before was that I was still very much a football fan, and I was really curious to see how well the hype would hold up. I was anxious to see what the new kids on the block could do, and for a half I was pleased that they kept it close.

But I did have a rooting interest that was strictly triggered by what I knew was in the future. I have to tell you that I was rooting hard for Green Bay in that first game. The reason was that I was thinking about future TV contracts for the game. After all, it was a simulcast, and I was more concerned about the future money that would be coming from CBS, since it had two of the next three.

But I will tell you something that I never said before. Later on, when the Jets gave the AFL its first victory in Super Bowl III, I was quietly rooting for them—hard. We really needed an AFL victory to protect our product, and when the Jets gave it to us I was as relieved as I was happy.

Three years after that inaugural game in Los Angeles, the final bill of the merger came due. It was 1970, and under the terms of the agreement this was the year that the twenty-six franchises were to split into two conferences, with the winners meeting in the Super Bowl. When the process began they were no closer to that than they had been during their premerger vendetta.

As Rozelle prepared for that realignment battle, it would have been more helpful had he brought along a Ouija board, a set of thumb screws, the collected works of Sigmund Freud, the UN charter, and the unabridged version of *Mrs. Esther's Never Fail Lucky Number Dream Book*. It was going to be that kind of struggle.

The tip-off should have come from the NFL's interim restructuring plan. Working within the framework of the peace treaty's three-year grace period, the old guard had to keep some framework alive so it could come up with a way to have a Super Bowl the first two years. The AFL, of course, had remained intact over that span, and the NFL reorganized in what it knew would be a temporary alignment.

It elected to go with four divisions, which it named Century, Coastal, Capitol, and Central. For the record, it was agreed that the Century and the Capitol would last one whole entire year, with New Orleans and New York then switching divisions. The Coastal was a handy traveling unit with two teams on each coast with a mere three thousand miles in between them for commuting purposes. The Central, well, the Central was a quartet of four cities born to host December football because all of them were without noticeable sunlight between Arbor Day and Christmas. Right away you knew the structure could not last.

But the main thing it did was to provide something to keep the boat afloat until the Great Realignment Day was upon them three years later. Rozelle could and did a lot of things, but freezing the calendar was not among them. As far back as the new NFL divisional debut, it was clear that not only was there trouble in Eden, but Rozelle had not given them a road map to find the joint.

One of the most important things that marked Rozelle's style

was his ability to avoid surprises, as explained by Ernie Accorsi, who worked for him and also later served as general manager of both the Browns and the Giants. "It was hard to surprise him because he was one of the best listeners I ever knew. What he'd do is go around the table and ask for opinions and thank us for them and then tell us what he was going to do. He was a quick study and a great listener.

"With the owners, he would ask for straw votes and leave the room while they cast their temporary ballots. But friendly owners would tell him where everybody stood, and he was ready to come back and work the room."

It is clear, therefore, that as the calendar melted away, he knew that Wayne Valley, still in control of the Raiders, and the Jets' Werblin felt they were winning—their opposition, the 49ers and the Giants, was awful. The Jets and Raiders were now stealing headlines from their rivals. Valley believed the Bay Area was behind him. Werblin was sure Broadway Joe Namath would give Broadway lock, stock, and barrel.

Neither wanted to be merged, and they would be two of the main obstacles on the way to permanent realignment. In October 1966 Valley confirmed that for me. We were sitting in his San Leandro office, and he spared no invective to explain that he and Sonny voted against the merger and had not been informed it was in the works (as Davis, now back with Oakland as a minority owner, had not been), and both he and Werblin were enraged at having to pay reparations to a pair of franchises, to quote Valley, "whose asses we had kicked."

"Well, details seem to cloud a lot of AFL positions about realignment. When I asked a variety of owners who they want to be grouped with in 1970 and how they expected to be treated, I got blank looks and mumbles in return."

Valley smiled and nodded. "If there hadn't been a merger," he said, carefully choosing his words, "there might have been a murder. We were at the stage where this could have been a bitter battle." (One shudders to think what he considered bitter if what had

already happened did not qualify.) "In the long run we will all benefit. There are other things I better not say except for the fact that now that I have been merged, I expect to be treated accordingly by the commissioner and his group—and I better be."

"And do you think you will?"

"I think there are still some honorable people left in this world, and if we are full partners, we must . . . we must . . . be treated on equal footing."

"But they can outvote you 2–1."

"So you understand how I feel. They better understand as well. You come from the East. You know what a street fight is. In a street fight, I wouldn't be afraid of 15–9 odds against me [the way it was in 1966], but I don't know what I'll get here."

Clearly, by 1970 the Raiders and the Jets would not go into that last realignment meeting bearing the olive branch of peace, and if Rozelle permitted himself to think so, he might just wind up picking olive pits out of his forehead.

Additionally, there was tremendous pressure (or at least as much as they dared to apply) coming at him from NBC. The structure of the existing telecasts locked NBC out of home bases in Los Angeles and Chicago. Moreover, within the AFL-NBC structure, San Diego and Denver were not very lucrative markets. NBC was demanding a solution that fitted its obvious needs.

To complicate an acceptable solution even further, the AFL itself was split over its future identity. Lamar Hunt thought it would be nice to somehow retain the old gang's identity. Virtually all of the rest of the rebel group wanted the other side to ship them three viable teams from the NFL social set.

As for the old-guard NFL, it didn't want to get, give, or get up off of anything. As always in a league-wide difference of opinion, Rozelle cranked up his PR machine and took his case to a friendly audience. With the media in the room, he held a press conference in Dallas, a city with an old-guard franchise and the residential homes of Schramm and Hunt, his merger point men. "There are

certain areas of difficulty about switching leagues or conferences," he said, leaving the assembled media to test the waters. "For example, would Cleveland with an 80,000-seat stadium want to play in the same division as Denver with far less seating?"

And from the back of the room, in a voice calculated to shatter all the windows in the Dallas Mercantile Building, Art Modell could be clearly heard saying, "Over my dead body."

They met twice and failed to make progress. Then it came down to May and the spring meeting in New York. Now the unresolved makeup of the new realigned National Football League had dumped even more problems on Rozelle's plate. The urgency of both television networks' need to make plans, coupled with the need for a 1970 league schedule and the need for sanity, decided Rozelle. They would settle this thing now or pitch tents along the Hudson River and not leave until they did. Without a solution, he told his confidants, nobody was going anywhere.

At the previous meeting in March they had battled, they had huffed, they had puffed, and nobody had achieved a damned thing. The truth of that matter and the mechanics of the solution had been put forth by, of all people, Al Davis. Then a minority partner but knowing he could eventually become the majority leader of the Raiders, Davis put aside rancor, profanity, and his man-in-black pose and turned to the reasoning power of a visual aid.

Stepping to a blackboard, he wrote the names of all ten AFL franchises on one side and all existing NFL franchises on the other. Then he drew a vertical line between them. Then he spoke. "If you take three teams from the right side and move them to join the ten teams on the left side, there is an excellent chance that you will wind up with two thirteen-team leagues. And if you don't, what will I tell my little boy if he sees sixteen teams in one league and only ten in the other?"

It was first grade arithmetic and the ultimate solution, but nobody on the right side was killed or herniated trying to drag his franchise over to the left. They adjourned to think it over.

"I was thinking when we adjourned," Rozelle would later tell me, "that we had to find the least disruptive move. To me that meant St. Louis and two of our expansion franchises.

"The reason it made sense to me was that the Cardinals had spent so much time in Chicago before their relocation that they no longer had a geographical rival. Moreover, Kansas City, which shared Missouri with them, would make for an excellent natural rivalry, much like Washington and Baltimore or New York and Philadelphia."

But that got nowhere and they adjourned until May, and the commissioner had determined that this would be the final hour of decision. They would not meet as expected in a conference room at their usual home-away-from-home New York base. They could check into the St. Regis Hotel as usual, but they would meet at the league's Park Avenue offices. Those offices contained a lot of things, but they did not include superfluous items like beds. Rozelle was going to get a resolution by convincing them that sleep was overrated.

"NBC was pressing furiously for a 13–13 setup," Wellington Mara told me later, "and I couldn't blame them because they did have what at the time was a less attractive package. Personally, I didn't know who was going to be willing to move."

That night, on the eve of the final session, an emotional blood-bath during which Rozelle would hold them there for thirty-five fours and forty-five minutes, Rozelle, Schramm, and Modell agreed to have dinner together. On the way to the restaurant, Modell told his two old friends, "In case you are interested, there's something I want you to know I am considering. I would be willing to move the Browns to the AFL under certain conditions," I recall he told me.

Pete's reaction was negative. He wanted to move the Cardinals, and he was right because they had no traditional rivalry. But I had spoken to the Bidwill brothers [who then owned the team], and they made it clear they did not agree on the proposed move [actually on that or

anything else because later they dissolved their partnership]. So then I told Pete that if I did go, I had to go with the Steelers in my division. I'd want them because of our great rivalry, and I wanted Paul Brown in Cincinnati with his Bengals because the inter-Ohio rivalry made sense. "What about Rosenbloom?" Pete asked. "Don't ask me. Who knows what he thinks?"

The subject did not come up again at dinner,

The next morning, just as it looked as though there may be some daylight here, Art Modell showered, shaved, dressed, came down to the St. Regis lobby, and collapsed. He was taken by ambulance to Doctors Hospital on the Upper East Side of Manhattan with a bleeding ulcer. "I told Rooney that morning what Art had said," Mara told me, "and he wondered what I would do, so I said it could work because we could always preserve the Giants-Browns rivalry, which was one of the best we had, with an annual preseason game, and he agreed. Then we heard about Art and drove up to the hospital with Art's son Dan to see him. Our league meeting wasn't until the afternoon."

"I know Rosenbloom likes to tell it differently, but this is exactly what happened," Modell told me years later.

I'm in bed propped up, with Wellington to my right and Art to my left, and I'm facing Dan. I told them that this issue had gone on far too long, and I wanted to stop it. If I can keep the Giants-Browns deal alive and you guarantee that the Steelers go with me, I will move. The two conditions are each of you must approve.

I recall Danny interrupting and telling me, "Mr. Modell, the Pittsburgh Steelers are going nowhere. We are staying in the National Conference, so you will have to get somebody else." And then Rooney put his arm around his son's shoulder and said, "Dan, you can do what you want, but I'm leaving with Art." And then we all laughed.

So Mara and the Rooneys left to attend the meeting, and immediately yet another problem arose. There would be debates. A third team had to be found, and each involved owner had to agree or

disagree. Then the lawyers said, "No, you can't tape another person's voice. It has to be heard here."

And then Pete Rozelle came up with a solution. "We used to have this ancient squawk box," he said, addressing his staff. "I think it will work. Go find it and get it here, and Art can listen and speak from his hospital telephone."

"It was unbelievable," Rozelle later told me.

> Here we are cutting a deal worth maybe a billion dollars over the years to come, and we are gathered around this silly-looking box, and over on the Upper East Side Art is gulping medicine and trying to listen and talk at the same time, and the damned box sounds like it has frogs living in it. It's going "Beep . . . beep . . . beep."
>
> And then someone says to ask him for the exact divisional lineup he would like. It sounded like this: "Beep . . . beep . . . Cincinnati . . . squawk . . . beep . . . beep . . . beep."

They finally got it figured out, and thus the Great 100-Yard Migration was accomplished not with a whimper, not with a bang, but with a beep . . . beep . . . beep and a round of applause for good old Arthur.

"Rosenbloom made it three," Modell says, "when he agreed to take his Baltimore Colts to the AFL, but you know he did it for the money and not to save the league, as he sometimes said. You know the three teams would be paid."

All that remained was to sift through five different plans and set up the new divisions for the National Conference. Again Rozelle knew his people who were travel weary, half starving, and more than a little groggy. Rozelle placed five envelopes in a crystal bowl. "Here's the deal," the commissioner said. "Thelma, please."

Thelma Elkjer, Rozelle's executive secretary for twenty years, stepped forward. She had been with Rozelle since his Rams days. She was the gatekeeper to his office, the companion of Pete's daughter, Anne Marie, even the keeper of the hat Reeves had told him to buy on his election as commissioner in deference to New York City fashions but which he had never worn. She fielded calls from

irate team owners, congressmen, and reporters. She even reminded him of dinner dates he may have forgotten.

But now she was about to rewrite the geography of the National Football League. She picked out the envelope that became the new thirteen-team National Football Conference. Nobody applauded this end to the marathon session. What they did was head for the airport before they collapsed.

The big job was back home for the nomadic three. They had to convince constituencies and sell ads and tickets. Their job was not easy.

Rozelle, meanwhile, did the expected. He flew to Cleveland, one of three towns that had to be sold on their new place in the NFL alignment. He met the local press. He visited local radio and television stations. And the last day of his whirlwind appearance he was saluted at a luncheon by the International Council of Marketing. The award they gave him was named "Marketing Executive of the Year."

11

The Failed Coups

Why in the world would you write a book about him? . . . I am the man who saved the National Football League.

—Carroll Rosenbloom when he learned I was writing this book, talking to the author poolside at his Beverly Hills home

He loved me once, and I hope he will come to love me again.

—Pete Rozelle, explaining his "high noon at 410 Park Avenue" with Carroll Rosenbloom

They were strong men with huge egos, these NFL club owners. Quick to anger and slow to compromise. The older ones had been through hard times and empty stadiums. The newer ones had the kind of bankrolls they equated with power.

For Pete Rozelle, they continued to present a constant test of wills even after "peace in our time." For openers, there was George Preston Marshall. For the first quarter century after he moved his Boston Braves to Washington, where he renamed them the Redskins, no African American had earned a spot on his roster. If it were up to George, none ever would.

After all, his fight song, "Hail to the Redskins," originally included the line "fight on for old Dixie," the residue of the days when his team owned the entire South, from the nation's capital all the way down to the Texas-Florida Panhandle. His love of that radio-TV income and desire to appeal to southern markets put him at least a decade behind *Brown v. Board of Education.*

Additionally, he made no secret of his feelings about racial matters even after his death when his will proclaimed the six million

dollars in assets he would leave to charity had only one qualification: none of it could be used "for any purpose which supports or employs the principle of racial integration." He fought Rozelle on signing as much as a single black player until 1962, when the commissioner made an end run around the whole Redskin franchise and brought in the federal government to generate the necessary heat.

When it came to Washington DC, Marshall might have owned the football team, but from the moment that the NFL got its limited antitrust legislation for a single TV contract, Pete Rozelle could have given Marshall six points and still beaten him in any game with the federal establishment.

Rozelle learned that the DC Armory Board controlled District of Columbia Stadium, where the Redskins played. And the Armory was controlled by the Department of the Interior.

Enter Stewart Udall, secretary of the interior, along with Attorney General Robert Kennedy. After a talk with Rozelle, Udall sent a letter to Marshall, reminding him who held his stadium lease. "Unless you sign an African-American player," Udall told him, "we will negate your 30-year lease as being in violation of federal law."

With no options left and no place to go, Marshall drafted Syracuse running back Ernie Davis. When Davis said, "I won't play for the son of a bitch," he traded him to Cleveland for Bobby Mitchell, another Afro-American.

On the day Marshall surrendered, Udall made the following statement: "I should like to thank Mr. Rozelle for his constructive action. He has performed a distinct service to American sports for his willingness to mediate this dispute."

Rozelle had jammed a whole new way of life down Marshall's throat. The Redskins' owner was bitter and angry and still extremely influential within league circles. But never once did he mount an attack upon Rozelle.

It was clear that Rozelle's statements about the integrity of the game and its social impact on the public were not just empty words. In 1974, as America first began to discuss openly the impact of

drugs in the locker room, he announced he had fined Gene Klein, owner of the San Diego Chargers, twenty thousand dollars for laxity in controlling drug problems on his team. Other clubs had similar problems. The Chargers felt that because they were a losing franchise, they were being made a scapegoat for the league. But never once did Klein mount a public attack on the commissioner.

Over the years Al Davis had fought Rozelle, had sued Rozelle, had never made peace with Rozelle. He often implied to his players that they were penalized more because of Rozelle's feelings about him than their conduct on the field. But never did he ask for Rozelle's resignation as commissioner.

Outside of the emotional meeting over the Pete Gogolak signing, nobody had ever gone that far with Rozelle. George Halas blistered the air with his language and with his tirades in which the devil and the incompetence of game officials were conspiring to deprive the Bears of their rightful place in the standings. But every time it counted for as long as he lived, Halas supported Rozelle.

Edward Bennett Williams, who once owned the Redskins, was forced to go to what he had announced as a major press conference, and when the media arrived he was compelled to say he had nothing to say—the result of a single telephone call from Rozelle.

Actually, the media had been invited to learn of the signing of Vince Lombardi as the Skins' new coach, but Rozelle told him the contract had yet to be approved. "That was the most embarrassing moment of my time as an NFL owner," Williams would later say. This was man of serious power and clout and enormous prestige as one of America's most famous trial lawyers. But even after the humiliation of a moment like that, he remained a Rozelle supporter in critical situations.

Through the years they sniped and they grumbled, and a few like Davis struck hard in interviews far distanced from league meetings, but nobody ever walked through the doors of the old headquarters at 410 Park Avenue with the avowed purpose of taking the youthful commissioner to the mat over the way he ran the league. Nobody.

That is, until Carroll Rosenbloom turned on the man he had nominated for the job and demanded his removal. Looking back on the long history of Rosenbloom's relationship with pro football (he was an owner seven years before Rozelle became commissioner, and at the time only he, Art Rooney, Paul Brown, Wellington Mara, and Lou Spadia predated his stewardship), it would be hard to find a less likely candidate to attempt a palace coup.

He often took credit for ending the logjam in Miami Beach that finally broke free and elected Rozelle. In happier times he had often publicly said that pro football had the best commissioner in all of sports. During the war between the AFL and NFL, he had been an outspoken supporter of Rozelle.

When, oh, when, it is logical to wonder, did the magic leave this marriage? To wade through that minefield of confusion, it is first necessary to know the mind of Carroll Rosenbloom.

"I know they were close when Carroll had the Colts in Baltimore," says Ernie Accorsi, who had worked for both men. "So whatever happened between them was after Rosenbloom had swapped the Colts with Bob Irsay for the Rams and moved to California."

In regard to the genius of that swap, Carroll openly proclaimed that "we avoided capital gains taxes by doing it this way. It was the kind of deal only I could put together."

Why did he turn against Rozelle so violently? "Frankly," Accorsi said, "I don't think you are going to actually find a reason, because Carroll was the kind of man who had to go through life with an ally and an enemy, and they could be interchangeable. Reasons never really mattered, or else he forgot them. He could wake up one day and think, 'I don't like this guy.' And then he would look for the reasons."

A case in point was his vitriolic feud with John Steadman, a revered Baltimore newspaperman who loved the town and who first drew Rosenbloom's wrath when he attacked him for including the Colts' preseason games in the overall season-ticket package at full regular-season prices. From a single-issue feud, it went viral. Steadman made his attacks on Carroll a defense of munici-

pal pride. Rosenbloom made Steadman's name anathema anywhere near his office. Then one day Carroll screamed at Accorsi, his PR man, "If you don't pull Steadman's credentials, I'll fire you. And if you give him a parking pass, I *really* will fire you."

Accorsi paid no attention but told Steadman, "John, listen to me. My job is really on the line. See if you can find a parking space near the Eastern Shore of Maryland."

The controversy over Carroll's "extended" season-ticket scam rolled on. Steadman aroused the community. "In my opinion," said Bert Bell Jr., a Rosenbloom employee and the son of the commissioner who had brought Rosenbloom into football in the first place, "that exhibition thing was highway robbery."

But for Carroll it was nothing personal, just business. And he had been about business for a long, long time. As a young man he was determined to escape the dominance of his father's successful economic shadow and forge one of his own.

When, at age twenty-four, he was sent to Roanoke, Virginia, by him to liquidate the Blue Ridge Overalls Company, a small factory that his father had owned, he saw his escape route. Returning to Baltimore, he convinced his mother to loan him the money to buy Blue Ridge for himself without telling his father who the buyer was. He believed it was worth the gamble. But then there never was a gamble that Carroll could pass up.

The country was in the throes of the Great Depression. When President Roosevelt signed the newly authorized Civilian Conservation Corps into law as a youth employment service and a developer of the American West, Rosenbloom sought and got a lucrative contract for Blue Ridge to manufacture their denim work uniforms. Ironically, roughly ten years later, after the Japanese bombed Pearl Harbor, Rosenbloom went after and got one of the most significant textile contracts of his career, a deal to manufacture military fatigues. Textiles were the pebble that grew into the huge rock upon which he founded his millionaire's future, but it was a rock that reached into all kinds of investments and industries.

The fuel that drove him in all aspects of his life—business, rec-

reational, and social—was, pure and simple, his unabated passion. As a case in point, he had been known to cry after his football team's emotional victories or defeats. This was a man who either won or lost but rarely—if ever—compromised.

He was also man who collected friendships with celebrities on both sides of the social street. He played golf with Joe Kennedy. During the 1964 Democratic National Convention in Atlantic City, President Lyndon Johnson did not stay in the hotel where he was registered. He stayed in Rosenbloom's home in Margate City, New Jersey.

And he was a gambler of no small reputation—whether it was sports betting or card games. As a result of this last and his home away from home in Margate, he was active in the neon nightlife of Atlantic City.

One person with whom he socialized (and to whom he lost a good bit of gin rummy money) was a local mafioso named Skinny D'Amato, an ex-con, member of the resort city's dark-side social set, and the front man for the infamous 500 Club at 6 Missouri Avenue. In its showroom, the 500 Club featured entertainers such as Frank Sinatra (who performed for free in deference to his close ties to D'Amato and stayed at Rosenbloom's home when he was in town), Joey Bishop, Dean Martin, Jerry Lewis, and Sammy Davis Jr. In the rear there was gambling. And at the bar there were generally a few ladies of the evening.

It was D'Amato who encouraged Rosenbloom to buy a half interest in Havana's Nacional Hotel and Casino. Unfortunately, it was an investment that cost him dearly. The ink was hardly dry on the bill of sale when Castro marched into Havana and shut down the gambling and nationalized the hotel at a major financial loss to Carroll.

But in a strange sense this setback actually reinforced the public perception of the man as the ultimate high roller. After all, despite his father's money and business acumen, it was a series of personal gambles that made Carroll's fortune, starting with his turnaround of the dying company he had bought out from under his father.

He lived for challenges both business and recreational, and there were no secrets about Carroll's love of high-stakes gambling.

There had been rumors for years that Rosenbloom had needed his Colts to beat the Giants in the historic sudden-death title game of 1958 by more than three points so that he could cash a bet. They were fed by the fact that the Colts had not tried to kick a field goal in the shadow of the Giants' goal line and instead had finally had Alan Ameche run the ball in for the winning score.

They persisted even though they were absolutely false. Rozelle was not even the commissioner when the Colts played that game. But innuendo and gossip survived, and so in 1963 Rozelle launched a six-month investigation by Jim Hamilton, the league's chief of security, because that was the same year in which he suspended Horning and Karras for gambling. What made it worse in Carroll's eyes was that at the same media conference in which Rozelle barred the two players, he was asked about his investigation of Rosenbloom and replied, "No comment."

The probe finally cleared Rosenbloom. But as always happens with newspapers in such cases, the possibility drew the headlines, but the exoneration was barely mentioned. Rosenbloom remained furious.

In truth, Wellington Mara once logically speculated for me that Rosenbloom felt that because the league had made it to the top of America's popularity charts through the long reach of Rozelle's high-powered public relations staff, Rosenbloom felt the commissioner could have and should have done more to trumpet his innocence to the general public. Mara, knowing Rosenbloom as he did, believed Carroll never forgot or forgave that, and it further fueled his ever-lasting anger.

In 1975 with Rosenbloom's animosity toward the commissioner steadily growing, the commissioner used the rarely employed so-called Rozelle Rule against the Rams in what came to be known as the Cullen Bryant case.

Carroll had signed the Lions' Ron Jessie, who had played out his option. As a means of loosely enforcing the league's reserve clause, the commissioner had been granted the right to arbitrarily designate compensation to the team that had lost its player.

Because of the growing sensitivity involving anything between the league and Rosenbloom, Rozelle called in two NFL employees, Joe Kuharich, his old USF football coach, and Ernie Accorsi, whose previous employment by Rosenbloom the commissioner felt might be useful. "He told us," Accorsi said, "to figure out what would be fair compensation to the Lions. We talked it over, and Bryant was logical because he was not a starter but clearly had a bright future ahead of him." It led to a major Rozelle defeat. Bryant won a court case. Rosenbloom silently financed the action.

So by the summer of 1975, Rosenbloom, the man who always needed an ally and an enemy, was obsessed with putting the youthful commissioner in his place. It was the summer in which I had begun serious research on this book. The Rams were about to play a preseason game against the Raiders at the Coliseum on September 21. When I told Rosenbloom what I was doing, he invited me to meet him at his Beverly Hills home and attend the game with him.

Before the game I saw Al Davis in the tunnel leading to the field, and I told him what I was working on. He declined to be interviewed. He said, "That's all in the past, and I'd rather not talk about it." Then he wished me luck with the book and walked away. (Of course, he later sued the NFL—Rozelle in his view—twice and testified against it in the USFL antitrust trial.)

After the game I went back to Beverly Hills with Carroll. We were sitting in his family room with Georgia, his wife, and Jonathan Winters, his friend, when Carroll suddenly turned to me and said, "Young Jerry, step outside onto the patio with me. We need to talk."

So there we stood. As I recall, we were facing the swimming pool, and Carroll was silent for a moment, as though he were about to reveal a great truth of some sort. Then he spoke in that deep, resonating voice that he always used when he knew he was right and you were wrong:

Why in the world would you write a book about him [Rozelle]? You should be writing about me. I am the man who saved the National Football League. Without my agreement to move to the AFL . . . which I never did for the money [although he pocketed a reported three million dollars] . . . I did it to protect the National Football League. And I will tell you now that I will not sit idly by and tolerate his arrogance, his usurpation of powers that belong to the owners, and his extravagant waste of our funds. He has built a palace on Park Avenue and made himself an emperor. Bert Bell ran this league out of his back pocket, his kitchen table, and a little office in Philadelphia, and we did all right under him.

"Well, it was you who nominated Rozelle to be commissioner," I replied.

"Yes, I voted for him back then only because I thought he was just another harmless ass-kisser. Who really knew him? I didn't. But listen, I pay 1/26th of his salary [based on the size of the league at that time]. He has an army of people in New York. Why should they be responsible only to him and not to the owners, and nobody knows what the hell is going on until something goes wrong?"

He did not offer to fight him on the beaches and in the streets, but then he was never one to tip off his strategy. But he was itching to give a small hint. "Can you come back tomorrow? If you can, I'll give you a serious idea of what I'm about to do."

Would I come back for that? The Chinese Eighth Route Army couldn't have kept me away.

The following morning he took me into his den, turned on his speakerphone, and called Thelma Elkjer, Rozelle's secretary and doorkeeper.

"This is Carroll Rosenbloom," he boomed into the phone in a voice loud enough to shatter all the stained-glass windows in the real Notre Dame. "I am calling to speak to Mr. Rozelle."

"I'm sorry, Mr. Rosenbloom, but the commissioner is very busy right now. He is not taking calls. Shall I have him return your call at this number when he can?"

I don't recall exactly what Rosenbloom said, but I do recall that his facial coloring changed from millionaire's tan to apoplectic scarlet. As he walked me to my rental car, he put his arm around my shoulder and said, "Everything I told you last night, I told you because I trust you. It is exclusively for your information. We should talk again before you do the book."

Some exclusive. That was in mid-September.

The following January 1 Rosenbloom gave out an "exclusive interview" to the *San Bernardino Sun-Telegram* that was immediately picked up (he knew it would be) by the Associated Press and sent nationwide. In it he referred to Rozelle as "His Majesty," pointed to lost court decisions, and punctuated it with the charge that "the NFL has been beaten on all fronts."

He then added: "The commissioner is supposed to act in the best interests of the owners and the players. Because of Ed Garvey [the director of the NFL Players Association, or NFLPA] the players don't consider him as the commissioner. And because of the lawyers he's been listening to, Rozelle hasn't been helping the owners. He's in limbo."

In regards to the five-thousand-dollar fine Rozelle had slapped him with for publicly criticizing game officials, Rosenbloom fired one more salvo when he volunteered that "there have been a lot of social changes lately that passed the commissioner by and freedom of speech is one of them." That was January.

In February Accorsi got a call from an old friend and former coworker, Steve Rosenbloom, Carroll's son and executive assistant. He wanted a lot of specific information about how the league office operated. He had twenty questions to get answered by going into the files and wanted Accorsi to telecopy the answers to him as soon as possible. Accorsi recalled:

> There was this squawk box behind all our desks, and when we first came Pete told each of us that if something comes up you feel urgently needs my attention, use it and you will get it—always.
>
> I used it as soon as that call ended. Pete and Kensil told me to get

him everything they wanted. So I did and I call back, and they don't take the call because obviously Carroll isn't there and even I know he has to be on the other extension.

I call back and tell Steve that I got everything, and what I didn't get, Pete and Kensil filled in for me. And then this booming voice comes on and shouts, "WHAT??? . . . YOU TOLD ROZELLE AND KENSIL???" . . . Of course it was Carroll, so I said, "Mr. Rosenbloom, I am as loyal to Pete as I was to you."

Later that month Rosenbloom rehashed his charges, and then obviously not to alienate whatever mysterious support he was counting on he tempered his charges with: "I'm not trying to destroy the commissioner, I just want him back doing his job."

And the commissioner? Well, when I asked him about the simmering war, he just smiled and said, "He loved me once, and I hope he will come to love me again."

So the battle was definitely coming. I wondered about what support Carroll could hope to muster. Well, there was Davis, of course. Al Davis, like Rosenbloom, remained a tough competitor and in many respects a brilliant tactician whatever the battle.

When it came to Rozelle he would drop a word here . . . a phrase there . . . and the message was always clear but never put together in a way calculated to get headlines attributable to Al Davis. But what it came down to, therefore, in terms of support for Rosenbloom was more under the heading of aid and comfort as opposed to bomb-throwing revolution. Rosenbloom was about to take on the role of self-appointed field marshal of what he incorrectly believed to be signs of growing dissatisfaction among other owners, starting with the Patriots' Billy Sullivan.

A West Coast writer had somehow been fed the information that Sullivan would take an active part in the revolt. Not so. Sullivan made sure the writer understood that. He personally contacted him.

Max Winter of the Vikings? Max had once been miffed at Rozelle in the early days of the Vikings, before he had an office. Rozelle

had forbidden him from selling tickers out of his bar. But Max wasn't that miffed.

Who then? Surely not Gene Klein, he of the twenty-thousand-dollar fine, or Leonard Tose of the Eagles or Herman Sarkowsky of the newly minted Seattle team. They were the committee chosen to sit down with Rozelle and negotiate a new contract rumored to be in excess of three hundred thousand dollars a year.

Now it was March 1976, and the lodge brothers had assembled at the post Del Coronado Hotel in San Diego to talk business. It was Rosenbloom's first chance to go on the offensive. He offered a plan of rule by committee that would have heavily undercut the commissioner's power.

The owners called for a voice vote as to whether they should vote at all on the plan. From Oakland Rosenbloom got mild support. From the rest of the room he got nothing but silence. As Jay Moyer, the NFL in-house counsel back then, recalls, no vote was taken.

The next morning Rosenbloom returned to the meeting for an all-out assault. "I knew it was going to be a big thing," Modell told me. "He was wearing that beautifully tailored blue suit he saved for special occasions, and he was all tanned and he had this damned speech he wanted to give. He even asked for a microphone, and he goes, 'One . . . two . . . three . . . testing.'"

"Then he gave this long, rambling speech," Wellington Mara recalled. "The longer he spoke, the more emotional he got, and everyone was getting more and more upset."

"Wellington actually saved the day," Modell said later. "Everyone was furious, and I don't know what would have happened if Wellington hadn't called for a lunch break."

After lunch George Halas called for the floor and delivered an impassioned speech in Rozelle's defense. He was followed by Lamar Hunt, who did the same. Both men received standing ovations. Admittedly, a standing ovation by two dozen people is hardly a replay of Frank Sinatra at Madison Square Garden, but it was all the noise Rozelle needed to hear.

Rosenbloom heard none of it. He had stalked out of the room at the lunch break and did not return. In the months that followed, he continued to bang away.

In early October of that year, he fired off his most vocal public assault. One can only assume it was calculated to pick up support from the handful of Jewish owners.

The Rams had been scheduled for a 4:00 p.m. game in Miami on October 3, which was also the eve of Yom Kippur, known to Jews around the world as the Day of Atonement. It is the holiest day in the Jewish religion. The holiday begins at sundown, and, with its late start, the game could not be finished before then. "This is a thing that was done with malice aforethought," Rosenbloom told anyone within earshot. "They say 'let's put the Jew in Miami for Yom Kippur and see how he likes it.' I just know Rozelle and his stooges were giggling about it the day they released the schedule."

Actually, the day they released the schedule had been back in April. The day Rosenbloom complained was more than five months later and almost on the eve of the game itself. His comments were picked up by newspapers around the country.

Six years earlier when Rosenbloom owned the Colts, they had been scheduled to play on Rosh Hashanah, the Jewish New Year. He did not complain. He did not ask for an alternate date. He played the game without comment.

Now it was October 1976 and the owners were back in New York for a second league meeting, and while they did not expect Rosenbloom to drop the matter without comment, they never expected the explosion that followed.

They had assembled at league headquarters in what the staff had come to call the "fish room." The first time you hear it described that way, you visualize a posh meeting room with a large and well-stocked aquarium built into the wall. But this had become the room the interior decorator never visualized. What happened was that during one of his deep-sea fishing trips Rozelle so enjoyed, he won a long, tough decision over a very large marlin that he immediately had stuffed and mounted.

When the commissioner's fish arrived at 410 Park Avenue, Thelma Elkjer, holder of the keys to the kingdom, was adamant: "Not in this office."

Hell hath no fury like a determined executive secretary. The fish was mounted instead in Pete's conference room. Now, when this thing started, it looked as though Rosenbloom wanted to mount the commissioner himself.

For the meeting he had brought with him the Rams' general counsel, a prestigious entertainment lawyer named Ed Hookstratten, known at times in show-biz circles as "the Hook."

Rosenbloom sat next to him with arms folded and snow-white hair, neatly coiffed. The attorney read aloud from a large yellow legal pad outlining Carroll's charges against Rozelle. They ran the gamut from financial irresponsibility to abuse of power and so on, and so on. One man who was in the room said he seemed to recall a charge of anti-Semitism based on the infamous Yom Kippur game in Miami.

In conclusion, Hookstratten said to paraphrase, "Mr. Rosenbloom wants you to know that he will not set foot in this building again until Mr. Rozelle is removed as commissioner."

Then Rozelle stepped to the microphone, showing absolutely no emotion, and said before Rosenbloom and Hookstratten could leave the building, "Uh, if that's about it, perhaps we should break for lunch."

NFL counsel Jay Moyer recalled that as he marched to the door with Hookstratten, Rosenbloom looked back over his shoulder and shouted, "If I can't get you in here, I'll get you out there." Within a year the Internal Revenue Service (IRS) had demanded to look at the NFL's books. It was generally felt among the top NFL brass that Rosenbloom had used his well-known political contacts to force the investigation.

During that lunch break George Halas, Lamar Hunt, Leon Hess, Wellington Mara, and one or two others crowded into Rozelle's office and expressed their anger at the Rams' owner.

Halas said, "Somebody find out what plane Rosenbloom is on

today, and we will get on the one after it, go out to his house at Beverly Hills, and tell him that if he can't abide by the rules, we'll throw him out."

Rozelle did not tell them to go. He did not tell them to stay. He didn't comment at all.

History does not record what Halas & Co. did, but it is a fact that Rosenbloom never reopened the subject.

At long last he finally had the answer to the question he asked Paul Brown more than a decade earlier when he had agreed to nominate Rozelle for the commissioner's job. His question had been "Who the hell is Pete Rozelle?" He never had to ask it again.

12

Power to the Tackles

They [NFL owners] will stick together and work together . . . [and] punish anybody who won't do it their way.
 —Ed Garvey, NFLPA executive director, 1971–83

I think Marvin Miller [baseball] is clearly the best labor leader in sports. Marvin is not looking for a new career. He knows what he wants to be. Who knows about Ed?
 —Pete Rozelle, laying down the gauntlet

In 1947 the Pittsburgh Steelers, a franchise that had lived through more tough years than Cassandra, staggered toward a meeting with the Philadelphia Eagles that could have brought them their first-ever divisional title. The losing of football games had been developed into an art form by the Steelers, but suddenly these orphans of the storm found themselves in the unaccustomed role of flirting with destiny.

Their season had ended at 8-4. Philadelphia was 8-3 with one left to play. Should Philly win, they would break the ensuing tie with an extra playoff game against the Steelers the following week. So the Steelers waited, and while they waited, they practiced. Well, not exactly. Jock Sutherland, their coach, had made it clear that under no circumstances would they be paid for the extra week. When the owner, Art Rooney, reminded his coach that the players just might need money for frivolities like food and lodging, Sutherland replied, "Those who need money are also those who need the practice." And the owners at the time actually wondered why the players might like to have a union of their own.

Eight years later players representing every team except the Chicago Bears (who were painfully reminded that George "don't allow no union playin' 'round here") presented to then commissioner Bert Bell what the owners considered a lot of arrogant demands, including a request they no longer be required to buy their own shoes. And the owners still wondered why the players might like a union of their own.

Paul Brown, owner of the Cleveland franchise, later recalled that "they didn't realize it was an interlude in their lives . . . the good old days . . . a time when it wasn't a career and they were young and fresh with a zest to play the game [for the fun of it]." And the owners wondered why the players might like a union of their own.

Like all sports unions, the history of the goals, the struggles, and, yes, later the ultimate excesses of the NFLPA were rooted in the past sins of management. Football was not alone. The very same year that NFL players were trying to get the owners to buy their shoes, a lawyer named Robert Murphy set out to organize the Pittsburgh Pirates of the National Baseball League and led them to the brink of a strike.

But then a pitcher named Rip Sewell killed the union in a locker room speech that pointed out the difference between real baseball players and union members. He might have been right if you measured that in the volume of alcohol consumed and the poorly treated social diseases of those who opposed collective action. The strikes never happened, and when he retired Sewell got a gold watch from management—but no pension.

In any event it was the threat of a Mexican millionaire named Jorge Pasquel, who, in the 1940s, offered large sums of money for Americans to jump to his outlaw Mexican League, that began to awaken the players slowly toward the action that created the greatest labor leader in sports history—Marvin Miller. And a fellow named Larry Fleisher did the same for the NBA, creating previ-

ously unheard-of average salaries of one hundred thousand dollars. "I consider much of our success was due to the owners' stupidity," he once told me. And through all of this, pro football players lumbered along.

From the small informal group that petitioned Bell, nothing much happened. Of necessity it was more social than activist. They were told over and over, "You are professionals, not time-clock punchers. Don't let them ruin your game." It was both flattering and effective until March 18, 1968, when John Gordy, an offensive lineman with the Detroit Lions, presented Art Modell, representing the owners, with a twenty-five-page document that set forth the neophyte NFLPA's demands.

By the standards of what later followed, these demands were hardly Emma Goldman at the oratorical barricades shouting, "Let the bosses take the losses." Among the major demands were no discrimination against players because of race, religion, or national origin; a fifteen-thousand-dollar minimum salary; an annual owners' donation of five million dollars to a pension fund; and a review of the option clause. "As with any union," Gordy said, "these demands are negotiable." Clearly, this group was not preparing to launch anther bloody Harlan County, Kentucky, coal strike.

Moreover, the owners were far ahead in this game, and they knew it. Several months earlier Harold Gibbons, a power in the Teamsters Union operating out of St. Louis, had formed an alliance with a disgruntled Cleveland Browns player named Bernie Parrish. Together they had made a serious run at organizing pro football players. At one point he claimed to have ninety of them who had expressed a desire to join that union.

Somebody—nobody ever really established the identity—had put up a lot of money for Parrish to go on a whirlwind tour around the country to enlist the help of the media. When I talked with him in New York one day, he showed me a copy of a legal brief filed by Jim Ninowski, a journeyman quarterback with the Browns, that, had it ever come to court, would have put the league's standard contract under massive fire.

He was extremely vocal over what he called "the owners' blackball policies." He attacked the league's most vulnerable area, the league's unwritten racial discrimination. Parrish was making progress.

But then on January 27, 1968—eight years into Rozelle's commissionership—the Lions' Gordy delivered an impassioned speech at the Hollywood Beach Hotel in Hollywood, Florida, to the members of both the NFLPA and the AFLPA, at the time still separate groups. The room was packed.

Without naming either the Teamsters or Parrish, Gordy said that "four or five teams have indicated a willingness to sign with an outside union. But I don't want my family to be associated with the type of people who are trying to get into pro football."

Then to forestall what he saw as an attempt at a Teamster take-over of the NFL's collective bargaining, Gordy passed out sign-up sheets designed to get enough proxies and now combined members from both leagues to petition the National Labor Relations Board (NLRB) for official union status.

He had entered the room as the president of a loosely organized social club. He left as the head of a newly empowered group of players that would change the entire labor structure of professional football.

When Gordy beat back the Teamsters' charge, NFL owners were thrilled—until Gordy realized that he had to show his own members something in the way of progress. As Gordy's twenty-five-page manifesto remained untouched by ownership, he asked for and received a strike-authorization vote—the first in the history of the game. They called it to start on preseason camp.

Soon after it began many players expressed doubt as to whether they needed or could manage a strike. Others seemed to come closer together.

In Green Bay a twenty-eight-year-old sometime starter with the Green Bay Packers spoke to me with the promise of anonymity. That was long ago, and today that need is obviously gone. His name was Doug Hart. This is what he told me:

The salary has nothing to do with it. It's the pension plan. They [the owners] are getting all that punitive-damage money from the AFL. They could throw some of it in our direction. We are willing to cut our demands to seventy-five thousand dollars per club. Half of that becomes a write-off for them. So it costs them what? Forty grand?

When they called me on the strike vote, I was shocked. I never thought it would get that far. Then I thought about guys who get paid what I do on other clubs and never are lucky enough to be with teams good enough to earn playoff money. I had to think beyond myself. I had to be loyal to them.

I don't want a strike, but don't get me wrong. I won't back away. If they lock us out, it would be tough, but I could sit for a year. Hell, it would be a piece of my life. By July you know you are looking ahead because you played in high school, you played in college, you played here. It's the way your life has been laid out.

I think a shutdown or a sit-out would be stupid.

For the view from the other end of the spectrum—the super-star—I went to John Unitas.

"Right from the start the owners have tried everything not to recognize us. They worried that someday we would quit squabbling among ourselves, and they knew that when that day came, they would be afraid they would be in for some hard bargaining, Well, they were right. All you have to do is read the standard player's contract. It's an owner's contract. Only a jerk wouldn't recognize that."

On July 14 the strike ended. Through the negotiations Rozelle had been very quiet, although we know he did, in fact, meet with both Modell and Gordy. When the strike threat was first raised, Modell asked me, "What do they want? Do they want to reduce 40-yard sprints to 25 yards? This has no merit." Gordy, conversely, was the first successful player to organize, even though his results were modest.

Rozelle's "soft-line," back-door approach, even though he met them without the knowledge of the management council, was effective. His low-key, unpublicized approach quietly put together

a temporary peace. But he knew what waited just around the corner. Actually, it had been out there all the time.

In 1938 a guard named William Radovich joined the Lions after a distinguished college career at USC. He played five years for them and left for military service in World War II. Upon his return he jumped to the Los Angeles Dons of the All-America Football Conference. When the league folded, his desire to return to the NFL was impeded, he claimed by an owners' blackball.

Nobody remembers the All-America Football Conference. Nobody remembers the Los Angeles Dons, and almost nobody remembers William Radovich. Nobody except every lawyer who ever worked on an NFL antitrust case—particularly if they were employed by the NFL.

Because of him the United States Supreme Court voted 6–3 that pro football did indeed come under the federal antitrust laws.

It was the Radovich case that sent Rozelle to Representative Manny Celler of New York to get approval for the NFL television contract. It was the Radovich case that sent Rozelle to Russell Long and Hale Boggs to get consent for the NFL-AFL merger. It was the Radovich case that leaves the specter of antitrust action hanging over the NFL even now.

And, perhaps, its greatest impact was on a Baltimore tight end, the late John Mackey, who was a driving force in the NFLPA and hired the Minneapolis law firm of Lindquist & Vennum. The NFL had been beaten by Radovich in the courts, Mackey reasoned, so maybe that's where the players needed to go more often.

His new legal firm assigned a young lawyer named Ed Garvey to advise him. It didn't take long for Garvey to go from adviser to executive director. Now, the battle lines were drawn, and they would have warmed the heart of John L. Lewis. If Garvey needed to design a playbook, he couldn't have come up with a better model than the NFL standard player's contract. The labor problems laid out within it would function as a giant buffet table for the union.

Labor historians refer to them as the freedom issues. They

included management's right to deal with every player's personal life on a certain level, its right to fine him, its right to bind him to management for a year after his contract runs out, and then to make it difficult for him to find other football employment.

In the battle to come, the other side (management) would say with some justification, among the freedoms the players sought was to do whatever they wanted to whomever they wanted and in any manner they wanted to do it. Ironically, the college draft system (the first infringement on any player's rights) got no attention at all until a judge dropped it right in the players' laps.

In the matter of free agency, this is the way it was. Management kept a firm hold on the employee with something it called the modified reserve clause plan. Under it a player was then bound to his employers until trade or retirement did they part.

At the conclusion of his contract he could (for a 10 percent pay cut) elect to play one year without a contract and then be free to sign with another team. Like hell he could.

First, he had to find a team that would be willing to take on the burden of the league's compensation clause—known colloquially as the Rozelle Rule. The commissioner was empowered—indeed, mandated—to decide what should be taken away from the new employer and assigned to the old one to serve as balm for his monumental and unexpected loss.

Its genesis could be found in 1967, just one year before Gordy's liberty-or-death speech to the troops. A highly gifted wide receiver named Dave Parks became disenchanted with his employer—the San Francisco 49ers. He played out his option and signed a contract with the New Orleans Saints for the 1968 season.

It was then, as they used to say in Asia, that the fit hit the chan.

To understand the strict action Rozelle was about to take, you need to know the difference between the old baseball player contract that bound him to one club until death or trade did they part. Pro football never had that kind of hold on its players. Technically, they could play out their contracts and become free agents, hoping someone would sign them.

For a very long time that's the way it was. The player could re-sign with his team or go pump gas at a local filling station.

But then other owners, one by one, suddenly felt, why not sign these guys if they could help? Who would stop them or set a price on their actions?

Enter Pete Rozelle.

Rozelle was determined to make a point, and he came down hard. He set up a method of compensation to be paid by owners who signed a player under those circumstances.

At the time it was a reasonable strategy because to keep the house in order was part of the commissioner's job. He set a high price for Parks. He reached into the Saints' camp and grabbed a great prospect from Notre Dame named Kevin Hardy, who had been the Saints' first draft choice, and sent him to San Francisco. He also gave the Niners the Saints' number-one pick for the following year.

"I simply tried to figure out," Rozelle explained, "what the Niners would have received had they traded Parks to New Orleans."

This was followed by loud screams from New Orleans and a standing ovation from the other NFL owners. Garvey would later say, "They [the owners] got the message. They will stick together and work together for as long as they can. They are going to punish anybody who won't do it their way. The compensation rule has got to go."

When it was successfully challenged a few years later, compromise finally won the day. In 1974, with Mackey as the president and Ed Garvey as their counsel, the players struck just before the preseason games over what they called the "freedom issues." It was doomed from the start. It was a disaster.

To be honest about it, Rozelle's only input was public relations. But it was the deciding factor. The NFLPA had about as much chance to beat Rozelle at that specialty as a mouse crawling up an ele-phant's leg with carnal intentions. The players worked out of the Squire Midtown Hotel in Manhattan where Mackey did his best to answer the media's telephone inquiries. Press releases were writ-ten out of an all-night delicatessen down the block. The Rozelle

Rule remained in effect, a new general contract was signed, and a few fringe benefits were granted.

As a strike it was a washout, but as a harbinger of the future, it was all things to all men. Rozelle knew they would be back with litigation to spare. But they had better bring enough provisions (read: money here) to last out a series of monumental sieges. The NFL attorneys planned to pile up four after hours of testimony, writs, and arguments. That cost money. As Napoleon warned, "God is on the side with the best artillery." And Rozelle knew he had most of the guns.

The failed strike proved that the union job was too complex and time-consuming to be handled by an active player. A new approach was needed. To Garvey's credit he seized the opportunity. In 1971 he was appointed the first executive director of the NFLPA.

Garvey was a quick, nervous kind of fellow. If the match were for the world's personality championship, Rozelle would have won by TKO on the way to the ring. An objective interviewer had to come to the opinion that he came across as a man motivated by style rather than compassionate conviction. As an orator he was as exciting as watching a tree form its annual ring. But as an opponent, he was very much in the game.

He was born in Burlington, Wisconsin, and went off to the University of Wisconsin, where he fashioned a career in student politics. The National Students Association of which he was president was bursting at the seams from both the political left and the right. Later it would be accepted rumor that the Central Intelligence Agency's money played a role in settling that dispute. Garvey would emerge as a favored son, and his connection with the winning side would take him overseas to run at least one international conference.

His brilliant career in law school is still remembered with awe by many, and Nate Feinsinger, later professor emeritus at Wisconsin Law, once called him "wise beyond his years. He's going to be a Congressman or a Senator one of these days."

On October 3, 1970, the Associated Press sports wire carried a brief article, announcing that quarterback Joe Kapp, who had

played out his option while leading the Vikings to the Super Bowl, had signed with the New England Patriots. Then, as the Pats went to camp, owner Billy Sullivan alerted Rozelle that Kapp was having some problems with what form the contract with the Pats should take. No big deal, he told Rozelle, "just a few problems." The commissioner promised to look into it.

"Sullivan called again," Rozelle told me, "and said that Kapp's financial advisers wanted to review the contract. I said fine. You can always make modifications. I didn't believe he would throw away six hundred thousand dollars."

> Finally, preseason camp opened and still no contract. I told Billy I couldn't let Kapp go in. I mean, I was not going to let him into camp without a contract. If we permitted that, nobody would have a contract, and we would have chaos. Looking back now that it's over, I still feel that way.
>
> Anyway, I later got another call from Sullivan. They were in camp and Kapp wanted me to talk to his lawyer, and I suggested he talk to one of ours because we weren't getting anywhere. One last phone call, he hadn't signed, and I told him Kapp was out. Nobody ever mentioned this, but the collective bargaining agreement that the NFLPA had signed clearly stated every player would sign a contract before preseason camp. And then Kapp went home.

He sued, and before the Kapp affair ran its course, the owners, the players, and the American jurisprudence system were all going to have his name forever in their memories.

Kapp went to court and claimed the contract was unconstitutional and in restraint of trade. He won a summary judgment after four years. But two years later (April 1, 1976) in the trial for damages, the jury ruled he was not damaged.

Nevertheless, the original verdict ultimately led the NFL to the wisdom of devising the rules on free agency and culminated in a multimillion-dollar settlement between the NFL and the NFLPA. It was an enormous setback for the league, although Kapp never played another game. Now Rozelle and the league's version of sta-

tus quo would be tested as never before. It took a long time for revisions, but it was the Kapp case that opened the door.

"The Rozelle Rule," the commissioner said to me one day and then shook his head. "God, how I hate that name. It was Kapp's lawyer who hung it on the compensation clause, and I wish to hell he never had. It just put my name on something I didn't decide all by myself in the first place."

Rozelle, as almost always, understood the wisdom of compromise. Not everyone agreed.

Rosenbloom, for example, who would have blamed Rozelle for the French and Indian War if he could have, jumped on the Kapp case. "He should have let it slide," he told me.

He should have done what any smart businessman would have done. He should have looked the other way instead of jeopardizing our business over nothing. Hell, here was a guy who really didn't want to play any more football, and in a year he would have been gone.

All Rozelle had to do was nothing. Instead, he takes this guy who probably couldn't have made any team a year later, hands him a suit, and now we have a hell of a lot of trouble. He relies too much on lawyers. When I want to do something in my business, I do it and then tell my lawyers to justify it. Instead, he asks his lawyer, who says nothing and then sends us a bill.

When I told Rozelle what Rosenbloom had said, the commissioner seemed to struggle to straddle a fine line between anger and rage.

Beautiful. "Let it go by." That's fine. But my contract says I must . . . not I should or I can . . . but must . . . enforce the league constitution. You will find a hell of a lot of owners who would have been more than a little upset if I had just "let it go by."

With no contract a player would not be subject to discipline. He could even have openly bet on games, and I couldn't do a damned thing about it. My job—unless it changed five minutes ago—is to enforce the league constitution.

Meanwhile, Garvey was not idle. He would decry the merger between the NFL and AFL, move the NFLPA offices to Washington, and say: "I admit this was like buying a fire extinguisher after the Great Chicago Fire. We should have been there earlier. The merger that they slipped over on us never should have happened.

"The old Association [pre-Garvey] didn't fight it, didn't lobby, didn't use the players the way the NBA did to block an NBA-ABA [American Basketball Association] merger. We got licked and we got hurt. It was a fact before I even got this job. We've had to work to put things together since."

Garvey unleashed a fusillade of legal actions. Complaint upon complaint were shoveled onto the agenda of the National Labor Relations Board by him. Mackey and a coterie of other players filed a class-action suit against Rozelle, the league, and the owners.

Meanwhile, Garvey hit upon the one strategy never tried in professional football. It was brilliant. If Rozelle was the Big Bopper of all previous negotiations, then, Garvey reasoned, the players would not fight him. Instead, they would neutralize him.

"Who is Pete Rozelle?" he demanded.

Is he the neutral guardian of the sport as the public thinks and the owners would be pleased to have us all think? Or is he, as the players think, a man with quasi-governmental powers, who is the primary spokesman for the owners in their effort to preserves the present system?

Look, we consider his whole function is to keep costs and salaries down. We consider that he cannot be a neutral arbiter. How can he mediate anything about player-owner relationships when he is part of ownership? Let him go down (to Washington) and speak on the TV blackout and other things that deal with the owners' business. But don't say he's neutral and don't say he can mediate labor-management debates because that doesn't make sense.

Suddenly, the shrewdest and most powerful man in sports was put on the defensive. It was a role that he was locked into by the very nature of the owners' past history. But when I asked him about that, he came out swinging.

"The commissioner, in my view, represents the players, the owners, and the fans. But when he doesn't, then the unique self-government of sports will have had it.

"If any one of the three groups doesn't get a fair shake, then your self-government is in trouble. When they talk about the owners paying me," he said with controlled but mounting anger, "then Garvey squawks, but that's a crock. I wouldn't care if the players paid part of my salary.

"Listen, I have always demanded long contracts so that I can be free to do what I think is right. Everyone talks a lot about theory, but in practice, what happens?

"I fine owners. I would say that about half of the player-owner disputes that I've settled have gone in favor of the players."

It was obvious that there was little affection between commissioner and labor union chief. Garvey once told Steve Guback of the *Washington Star* that "this is nothing against Rozelle but I find that as an attorney the whole struggle of civilization is to move away from arbitrary power invested in one man. No matter how good the man is, he still has his weak spots."

To the best of my knowledge, Rozelle never said publicly what he thought of Garvey or for that matter what he thought Garvey really wanted. Privately, in the commissioner's view, he believed that Garvey wanted a world wherein the owners could make no moves without his permission. He believed that confrontation instead of negotiation would give him that. It was then that the owners finally took the bait.

Garvey continued to hammer away at Rozelle publicly. He angered the owners when he publicly cited a Labor Relations Board case involving a taxi cab company in which the board ruled that by virtue of who paid his salary, the company's dispatcher could not possibly be considered neutral. The board had ruled he was management and not impartial. "I consider Rozelle to be no more neutral than that taxi cab dispatcher," Garvey said.

Recalling that, Paul Tagliabue, then a senior legal counsel to Rozelle and later his successor as commissioner, told me:

Wellington [Mara] and Tex [Schramm] went crazy when they heard that and considered it a major insult to Pete's integrity. They told Pete not to get involved, to stay out of the room and from now on they would take care of it.

What they did was to create the NFL Management Council and after several false starts hired a man named Jack Donlan in 1980, whose career was built around negotiating opposite unions, tracing back to his prior employment at National Airlines. In the beginning its purpose was to protect Pete, but as years went by its purpose became to isolate him.

It made sense in the beginning, and it worked in the beginning, but later on Tex and Tampa Bay owner Hugh Culverhouse felt Pete was too soft on the players. It created a split. So then instead of the management council being in place to protect him, they used it to exclude him. It led to two strikes; the second one in 1987 led to the use of replacement players—which Pete definitely did not want—fifty-seven lost games and what had seemed a good idea at the start turned into a tragic mistake. They felt he was too soft—too willing to make concessions—but actually Pete was still interested in solving problems rather than confronting them.

The power bloc among the owners clearly had a different agenda than the commissioner. The late Bob Oates of the *LA Times*, who had exceptional contacts around the league, explained the sidetracking of Rozelle like this in a 1987 column: "Donlan, the man who heads the Management Council's negotiating team, gets his instructions in strike committee meetings or directly from Culverhouse. Donlan is the extension of Culverhouse, who is the extension of a majority of NFL owners. It was at an owners' executive session that this year's most radical policy measure was adopted. The proposal: Continue the regular season with nonunion players." It was strategy to which Rozelle was fiercely opposed, but he was powerless under the authority granted the management council.

History would prove Rozelle right. When Tagliabue succeeded him, one of his preconditions was that the owners agree he be

given full control over the management council. Without that he would not have accepted. "It was the first thing we did when I took over," Tagliabue told me.

There are still a lot of folks who truly believe the strikes of 1982 and 1987 never would have happened and, certainly, there never would have been "replacement football" if Rozelle had not been pushed aside by the management council.

Even before Donlan was hired, Rozelle had suspected that unlike the old civilian blood-and-thunder unions, "solidarity forever" was more rhetoric than belief among the majority of NFLPA members with whom he wanted to be able to deal. A lot of them were looking for solutions other than a strike. Some of Garvey's concepts were not necessarily theirs. As a case in point, he knew all about the "Anderson Letter." In 1976 a new president, Dick Anderson of the Dolphins, released a letter he had written to all twenty-eight of his player reps in which he said: "I really believe that we will never be able to achieve an agreement that will be acceptable to Ed Garvey. He wants too many things that management will never give up." Then Anderson made a courageous move. He met secretly with Dan Rooney of the Steelers management. The management council did not know. Garvey did not know. But one suspects that Rozelle, who had been legislated off the management council, had to know. He and Rooney and Rooney's father, Art, were extremely close. And how else would Rozelle have been able to take advantage of the bitter union meeting that followed with a shrewd maneuver of his own?

Anderson had authored a document that included a modified acceptance of the Rozelle Rule. But Anderson was no match for his union's executive director. Garvey's response was to tell the players that if they accepted a modified Rozelle Rule, they (read: the NFLPA), could ultimately be sued along with the league by a disgruntled player. To prove that point, he brought in five lawyers to back him up.

The meeting in Chicago lasted ten hours and produced the most bitter internal warfare the union had ever engaged in. Garvey shrewdly beat back the challenge by employing a parliamentary

maneuver that forestalled any vote, pending a future clarification of the legal aspects. He had won a stalemate.

But at Super Bowl XI in January 1977, Rozelle took center stage in the debate by casually saying during his traditional mass press conference that the owners were highly receptive to any agreement that would yield some kind of assurance from the players about the college draft. Without the voice or lead of the management council, he had put a fertile ground for negotiation on the table, knowing the NFLPA membership would have professional reasons to accept.

The very next day Garvey, battling to get back in control of his union, said the players would be agreeable, providing the legal hurdles could be worked out. Well, you can bet your Field Turf they were, because here was a pool of tough, young kids coming into their league with the express purpose of stealing some of the members' jobs. Screw them. Let them deal with management any way management wanted.

After Rozelle won that concession I asked him how it was legally possible for NFL owners to deal with a union to which the college kids had not yet joined to mutually decide their employment fate.

"There is a legal precedent," he said.

"I find that hard to believe," I told him.

"Go check out the seamen's union," he said.

And, holy anchors aweigh, the lion lay down with the lamb on this one, keeping Garvey solid with his members and Rozelle one jump ahead.

But under the surface the war between management and labor continued to boil. Garvey knew his tenure was at stake. Things reached a disastrous turning point in 1982.

All of the court cases seemed to be going the union's way. The NLRB even ordered the league to pay back twenty thousand dollars in fines. But Garvey knew he was still in trouble. The players were winning court cases and losing their pension fund. The owners, bound by no contract, had simply stopped contributing to it and could not be legally forced to do so. Garvey had to do something.

Despite the fact that he did not have an adequate strike fund

to back him up, he still went ahead and induced his members to strike. It was both a ferocious and a devastating battle that lasted fifty-seven days. Among the demands, the NFLPA was seeking what proved to be a flawed wage scale based only on seniority and not position or achievement.

To finance his hurting members Garvey scheduled a series of all-star games. They ought to be remembered as the Disaster Bowls. Only two were actually played, the first at RFK Stadium in Washington and the second in the Los Angeles Memorial Coliseum. Garvey claimed an attendance of roughly 20,000 in each. Objective sources put the RFK attendance at 8,760 fans in Washington and 5,331 in LA.

Very few stars showed up to play in either. It was no surprise because there was no money for personal injury insurance. In that matter each player would be on his own. They knew the strike would ultimately end. They needed to be ambulatory when it did. Playing a football game without medical coverage was not calculated to keep them that way.

The "showcase" games were badly promoted and sold on the cheap to the Turner Network. Officials were recruited from high school and college football leagues.

Garvey, a highly skilled labor lawyer, had reduced himself to the role of a sandlot football promoter. The strike ended with a player revolt against its own union. Garvey had no choice but to resign. The consequences of bargained-away leverage also set back player free agency.

The final NFL work stoppage under Rozelle's tenure occurred in 1987. Rozelle, of course, was still barred from negotiations through his own management council, but this one had a profound impact on his sense of how the league's business should be conducted.

The strike in 1987 put tremendous pressure on him but not from the source you would expect. It came from his own management council. There had been a short period after Garvey's "taxi

cab dispatcher" description when Rozelle felt the creation of the council was a good idea because it served to insulate him from the public perception that he could not be neutral.

But the aggressive stance of the Schramm-Culverhouse faction was not meant to negotiate; it was meant to crush. And the most powerful owner in that strategy was Tampa Bay's Hugh Culverhouse. He had become a power in the management council during the 1982 strike and was so forceful now that NFLPA president Gene Upshaw said that "at times, the whole league seemed to flow from this one guy."

Over Rozelle's private but heated objection, the management council got approval to use replacement players once the NFLPA players walked out in the second week of the season. Rozelle was incensed. From a public relations standpoint, the greatest PR man in the history of sports commissioners knew the three weeks of "scab football" would be a disaster. From a labor-management standpoint, however, the move eventually split the union. A large number of picketing veterans discarded their signs and joined their teams. The biggest defection was in Dallas, where Schramm, in a right-to-work state, wrote personal letters to Cowboys who had negotiated annuities with the team, warning them they might never get them.

Rozelle held his public silence, but early during the negotiations Upshaw did not. Surprisingly, he told the media, "There is a 'mystery person' who could bring the strike to a quick end." Shortly afterward, a union spokesman said that Upshaw had met with this "mystery person" in New York City. The "mystery man" was Pete Rozelle. The strike went on, but the reason for the meeting was for the union to try to bring the commissioner into the situation as a moderating force with the management council.

That represented the polar opposite of the view Garvey had sold them in 1982. And Rozelle did manage to do one thing with that secret meeting. He brought both sides back into larger-scale bargaining talks. When the strike ended in major victory for management, he did not gloat. Part of that was because it was not in his nature, and part of that rarely discussed was a symptom of his

subliminal anger at how the management council had emasculated his effectiveness in labor negotiations.

He never forgot how some in the media had criticized him for not taking a more forceful role in negotiations without doing enough homework to understand why his own management council had isolated him from doing so. For the record, six years later in 1993, the NFL and the union concluded another negotiation that brought the players free agency and management a hard salary cap.

Instead, he spoke of how the strike had damaged both sides and how a strike always does. Rozelle retired on November 5, 1989. Tagliabue, the new commissioner apparent, got the owners to approve a change that put him totally in charge of the management council in 1990. Without that agreement he would not have accepted the job. Jack Donlan resigned within a year.

The terms of Donlan's severance package were never clear. There were some in the league office who believe the reason for that was the fact that Hugh Culverhouse deliberately misled the bulk of the other owners on the numbers. For the record, Donlan's management council severance after ten years with the league was actually larger than Rozelle's after twenty-nine. Later, Donlan served as a trustee of the Hugh Culverhouse Foundation. You may draw your own conclusion about the relationship between Dolan and one of the men who was supposed to have supervised his every move on behalf of the league.

Meanwhile, Rozelle remained bitter over being pushed out of labor negotiations. Culverhouse and his group believed more and more in strong-arm tactics. Rozelle's success in creating trust between union and negotiating team became an empty thought.

He confided in Paul Tagliabue, who would eventually succeed him, that the owners had created the perfect mess. The lesson was not lost on Tagliabue, who when elected commissioner would demand full authority in labor negotiations and got it.

13

Another Day, Another Dragon to Slay

"You know, commissioner, my mother was really down on you these past
few weeks."

"Well, Joe, my mother wasn't too thrilled with you either."

—Dialogue just before Joe Namath and Pete Rozelle announced the
end of the Bachelors III dispute

[The owners] don't even understand what the hell you are doing—thank
God.

—Rozelle to NFL Films' Steve Sabol

It was 1969. It was the time of Vietnam. It was a time when the very
soul of the country was torn apart, as it had not been for decades.
In a real sense the unrest that shook American campuses and the
tension between the country's youth and its middle-aged, the emo-
tional gaps between hard hats and radicals and between long hairs
and crew cuts, were the unavoidable fallouts from what at the time
was the most unpopular war in America's history.

Incredibly, the division even swirled around a controversy
between the commissioner of professional football and the quar-
terback who was fresh off engineering the Super Bowl upset that
shocked both their worlds. The fact that a football player and the
football establishment were caught in these emotions was more a
comment on what professional football had become to too many
Americans than what was, in reality, a commonsense business deci-
sion. What made Pete Rozelle's role even more difficult was the
fact that "Joe Willie" Namath had come to mean all things to all
men—and all women.

It is fair to say that as a youngster living in a family dealing with hard economic times and in a town of limited horizons, Namath was hardly the stereotypical boy next door. The real shaping of much of what he would become was done on the campus of the University of Alabama under the influence of his coach, Paul Bryant.

The football and leadership skills he learned there set the stage for what followed far beyond the football field once Sonny Werblin signed him for four hundred thousand dollars for the New York Jets. In the beginning it catapulted him into a lifestyle far beyond his maturity at the time.

It has been said that his signing helped save the AFL—and it did. It also was said by no less an authority than Vince Lombardi that stylistically, he was one of the greatest pure throwers of a football who ever played the game.

There were the Manhattan bachelor pad, the items in the gossip columns, the groupies on the road and at home. Then he beat the Colts and the NFL old-guard establishment in the Super Bowl.

A jock hero with long hair? Young America had fallen in love.

At the same time, the echoes of discord rocked the country: Vietnam, campus riots, the Students for a Democratic Society and the Weathermen, hard hats marching down Wall Street singing "God Bless America," the clubbing of America's youth from Chicago's Grant Park who protested outside the Democratic National Convention.

All of this, light-years removed from the playing fields but part of the backdrop as the infamous Bachelors III Affair took shape. In the middle of the cross fire stood Pete Rozelle.

Perhaps no issue moved him so often and so intensely as his belief in the need to keep the league's integrity totally above reproach or innuendo. He was not some kind of Frank Merriwell at play in a field of dreams. His role was born of intelligent business decisions based on the shrewd knowledge that once a product like professional football loses its credibility, the entire structure would come tumbling down. Rozelle always saw his job as commissioner as central to that notion.

It was the rationale behind his Karras-Horning gambling probe. It was the reason he brought in Jim Hamilton, the LA supercop to set up his security program. It was the reason for his close ties to law enforcement agencies across the country. Next to the standards Rozelle set for the league's image, Caesar's wife might as well have been an Eighth Avenue hooker.

It began with a tip, typical of the many tips that find their way to the NFL offices just about every week. The word was that some law enforcement agency had put a tap on the pay telephones at Bachelors III, an East Side Manhattan watering hole that Namath had an ownership piece of and which his nightly appearances had turned into one of the most popular singles joints in an area of the city famous for its boy-looks-for-girl-and-girl-looks-back nightspots.

At the same time other rumbles began to drift into the league's Park Avenue command post. As a case in point there were disquieting reports about the joint's liquor license. Both Namath and his former Alabama teammate Ray Abruzzese each conceded he was not the principal owner, although theirs were the only names on the license.

Now the league's security people began to call in old favors and offer new ones to their contacts to find out exactly what the hell was going on here. The more they learned, the more acid ingestion began to spread across their tummies.

What they learned was that the joint had become a special gathering place for a large number of questionable characters. Among them was John William DiGiovanni, an ex-boxer, convicted bank robber, and much-sought-after bail jumper of whom the post office posters read: "Likely to be armed and extremely dangerous."

Other frequent attendees included Carmine Persico (alias Carmine the Snake) and Thomas Mancuso (alias T-Balls), both of whom were said to be intimate members of the Colombo Cosa Nostra family. The lawmen also turned over the names of four other regulars who were hardly strangers to the FBI.

The story began to leak out into the streets. The very week that the Pro Football Writers of America were to hold their annual din-

ner in New York, a former main-event boxer sat in another East Side place with a visiting NFL general manager and nearly knocked him off his seat when he told him, "They're going to knock over your superstar's joint, you know. If you don't know it, you are the only one in this bar who doesn't." The reason it jolted the football guy so hard was that here was a total outsider who knew it.

The standard NFL player contract gave the commissioner the responsibility of seeing that players do not patronize such places—let alone own them. Rozelle realized by then that the weight of evidence indicated that the moment of truth was fast approaching. He also knew Namath and the way he relished the role that hero worshippers had assigned him. He also knew, based on that, that there was no way he could anticipate the way the quarterback would react when the pressure was applied.

But in truth it was Joe Willie who he felt was his biggest hurdle. He was deeply concerned that any illegal activity—if made public—would immediately catapult Namath's name into the headlines.

And it was even more of a real fear that too many of the wrong people in a place that would naturally be patronized by football players could turn it into a clearinghouse of casual but significant information for gamblers. Football players, like everyone else, have been known to talk too much when they drink.

Rozelle made a brief but stunning statement. Joe Willie Namath would give up his ownership in Bachelors III or be suspended.

Teammates would rally to the quarterback's defense. "If it was that kind of place," charged Gerry Philbin, the Jets' all-pro defensive end, "then why wasn't it off limits to us? I took my wife there. We could have been raided."

What Philbin had no way of knowing was that for months, Rozelle had desperately tried to induce Namath to sell the joint. First, he spoke directly to him, but that conversation achieved nothing. Then he prevailed upon Phil Iselin, the president of the team, and Arnold Grant, its treasurer, to intervene. Each had Namath's respect, but again Namath declined.

There followed several negotiating sessions with Mike Bite,

the young Alabama lawyer who had handled Namath's original Jets contract but who apparently did not handle the legal work for Bachelors III. Once again, the word came back that Namath would not sell.

And then the suggestion became an edict. The commissioner's security people had been fed the most disturbing leak of all. They were told that law enforcement people had enough evidence to strike at any moment against people using the telephones at Bachelors III for bookmaking purposes.

Namath was totally innocent, but the mess that could follow such a situation could play hell with his image and that of the league. Rozelle was also informed by his people that the arrests could come in one of two ways. The joint itself would be raided, or the arrests would come elsewhere in the city, but the charges would cite illegal acts that took place in the bar owned by football's most visible superstar. To make it even worse, Rozelle was told that a paid informer had been working in the bar for some time. All the ingredients for a scandal that would rock the NFL were in place.

On June 6, 1969, Joe Willie Namath held a press conference. He wept unashamedly. He spoke about loyalty and friendship and being his own man. In his words, "rather than sell out, I will quit pro football forever." He said this even after he had identified photos of known criminals for the police, men known to patronize his bar. Yet within a month he traveled to Boston and announced plans to set up additional Bachelor III clubs and said, "I will continue my interest in Bachelors III until somebody shows me where there is something wrong."

Exactly how much more he needed in the way of evidence puzzled logical people. Rozelle never hesitated at this point. He did the smartest thing he could possibly do. He had offered a choice. The door was open, but there would be no more public statements. In his mind he had already decided that should Namath elect to sell, there would be no punishment or further embarrassment. A way would be found to give him the best of it publicly.

Then from the West Coast came a familiar voice. It belonged

to Al Davis, and he was quoted copiously by the wire services and television commentators. Surely, somebody would be willing to help this fine young man . . . surely, somebody who was not a bureaucrat but a football man who understood football players. Yes, if asked to mediate, Al would pay any price and travel to any battlefield to save this young man for the game both he and the young man loved.

Rozelle didn't even bother to say thanks but no thanks. Does the keeper of the henhouse invite the fox in to do the census?

The mail from the public was staggering in size—not only in the league office but in newspaper sports departments all over the country, the battle lines were clearly drawn. In their view Joe Willie Namath was either a spoiled brat or a freedom fighter.

And then, as quickly as it began, it ended. Namath held a joint press conference with the commissioner of football to announce his return from limbo. All of the previous week, Joe Willie had met with teammates in secret and had indicated that it would soon be settled.

Rozelle's handling of what followed was superb. To begin with, he stayed in the background and let Namath have center stage. It wasn't easy. With a style and a charm and a soft Alabama accent by way of western Pennsylvania that had morphed into his verbal trademark, Namath said that "so much was written and so many people were involved that it just got out of hand."

He implied that mysterious forces such as the press, the magazines, and the commissioner's office were responsible for the confusion. About one thing he was right. It had been blown out of proportion, and the kid with the bicycle pump who did it was Broadway Joe himself. It ended with the exact result that Rozelle had sought in the first place. But in between Joe Willie had behaved like an eighteen-month-old Onassis demanding a solid-gold pacifier.

It was, indeed, Joe Willie who created the impression that he was fighting for the right of anyone who ever wore a jock strap to own his own bar. It made you wonder how all the teammates

who bought that claim squared it with his announcement that he would sell the bar.

In the end Rozelle—aware of the value of the man who brought the notion that the Super Bowl would now be competitive front and center—made Namath a winner by the way the surrender was orchestrated. Consider that the way it worked out, it must have taken more than a few mantras and some heavy breathing exercises to enable Rozelle to keep his temper as the only adult in the debate.

He permitted Namath to recover gracefully after the boorish way in which he and his designated speakers handled their mess. For openers, he wanted the press conference on Friday, and that's what he maneuvered. Understand that with no Internet back then and newspapers as the main source, the stories would run on Saturday—the day of the smallest paper of the week. For decades politicians had used that technique to underplay breaking stories.

Tested as he was, Rozelle never lost his sense of humor. He could still laugh at himself, as witnessed by this anecdote he told me about one of those meetings with Namath:

"He came to my apartment, and my teenaged daughter kept staring at him in a kind of awe, and I said, 'Well, Anne Marie, I think you better go to your room.' So we talked, but when it came time for him to leave, she rushed out and got close to him out and said, 'I just want you to know, Mr. Namath, that not every Rozelle hates you.'

"So much for parental discipline," Pete recalled, and then he broke out laughing.

Not everyone agreed with the pressure he put on Namath during negotiations. Steve Sabol, the president of NFL Films, stopped by his office one day when Pete was going through the mail his staff had scanned for him. "This is interesting," he told Sabol, holding up the letter. All it had was one word on a blank page. The word was *asshole*. "People," he said, "often forget to sign their names. Now, here's a guy who signed his name but forgot to put in a letter."

In truth the battle of Bachelors III was easily settled with no major impact on the league itself. But a family feud that damn

near tore apart the league's showcase franchises would require the intervention of Rozelle, the statesman, at his best.

You cannot underestimate the importance of old Tim Mara, the bookmaker turned pro football pioneer who brought the game to New York in 1925 for a franchise fee of five hundred dollars. He didn't understand football, but he understood New York City. "Hell," he once said, "even an empty store in this town is worth five hundred dollars."

He called the team the New York Football Giants, and it became a linchpin for the NFL. Later, he passed it on to his two sons, Wellington and Jack. But he made a terrible mistake when he gave each of them 50 percent ownership.

It would bring the franchise to the brink of implosion in the 1970s. By then Jack had died, leaving his 50 percent to his widow and children. His son, Timothy J. Mara (Timmy), then became part owner. When the team's performance plummeted as never before, Timmy challenged his uncle for control. Their feud grew so volatile that even the other owners took sides. Fan burned tickets in the parking lot.

On November 19, 1978, with twenty-six seconds left and the Giants about to upset the Eagles, the fans' disgust reached a white-hot zenith. Instead of falling down and killing the clock, Giants quarterback Joe Pisarcik tried to hand it off to Larry Csonka. There was a fumble on the exchange, and the Eagles' Herman Edwards scooped up the ball and ran it in for a touchdown and Philadelphia won.

It was the ultimate indignity for a furious constituency. On December 10 a small plane flew over Giants Stadium trailing a banner that read, "Fifteen years of lousy football."

The Mara family feud seemed to explode, capturing all the headlines and all the speculation in the newspaper columns. At season's end both Tim and Wellington agreed on just one thing, the firing of head coach John McVay.

Now there was no coach. There was no general manager. When Wellington announced that he alone would now hire a coach, all hell broke loose.

Each contacted Rozelle, who suggested they hire Jan Van Duser, who worked in the league office, to be the GM. He immediately declined.

"What I think happened," Timmy later told me, "was that he worked in the city, and every day the newspapers were filled with the Giants' mess, and he must have said, 'The hell with this. I don't need it.'"

Timmy had his own version of what followed. So did Wellington. But this is what really happened, according to Rozelle. To understand what he did, you have to understand that too many high-profile people, including former Giants, were voicing their opinions publicly. Rozelle understood that the league's image was headed for hell in a handbasket if the prestige franchise went down the tubes.

Art Modell, who had been Wellington's close friend from the day he bought the Browns, told me at the time, "This is a disgrace. Who the hell does that kid [Tim] think he is? Did you know that under our bylaws we could break the deadlock by seizing the franchise? I'd be for that, and then I'd propose we sell it back to Wellington for a dollar."

It was becoming the kind of nightmare every league commissioner dreads. Rozelle called the old Notre Dame coach Ara Parseghian and told him he could have the job if he wanted it. He declined in about ten seconds. It was now the end of January, and the Giants had become a late-night television joke. Without a coach or a GM, their organization lay dead in the water.

Now Pete put his own underground network to work. Bobby Beathard, the Redskins' GM, and Frank Gifford, Rozelle's close friend, each recommended George Young, who worked for Don Shula in Miami.

Rozelle called Tim and told him he needed five names but to make sure George Young was on his list, along with Frank Ryan, the former Browns quarterback who was the athletic director at

Yale. Then he told Wellington to make a list of five names, put George Young on it, and make him last choice. Rozelle knew that as long as each man felt Young was not the other guy's choice, they would each pick him.

They both pushed Young as the solution. That was on Friday. The following Wednesday Rozelle took them over to the Drake Hotel, where Young was waiting, and they interviewed him for two hours and then moved over to Rozelle's office on Park Avenue. George wanted to fly back home and talk to his wife. Pete said no. He wanted it settled now. So Pete and Tim and Wellington were in one room crossing *t*'s and dotting *i*'s on a contract, and George was in another one on the phone with his wife.

The two Maras showed the contract to Pete. It was for three years. Pete said the money just wasn't good enough. He did not want to take a chance on another rejection. Now it was seven o'clock, and George finally said yes.

Meanwhile, I was on the other side of Manhattan with a gaggle of reporters and columnists and photographers, who were advised to go to the second floor at Gallagher's Restaurant and wait for somebody to announce that somebody was going to be named either coach or general manager or something, anything, of the Giants.

Back at league headquarters the trio had just come out of the lobby elevator when Rozelle suddenly said, "Damn, I can't believe this. Wait here."

In this, the most public relations—minded office in all of sports, nobody had written a press release and nobody had called the Associated Press. So there was Pete Rozelle in the darkened offices of his empire, sitting down to write the first press release he had written in roughly two decades. "I remember I looked up," he told me, "and I thought, 'I can't believe this. Here I am doing this on Valentine's Day, and it just also happens to be my wedding anniversary.'"

And if you understand the intensity of anger a family feud can generate, then you are aware that he had just finished presiding successfully over negotiations worthy of the Nobel Peace Prize. It was typical of Rozelle's style that he knew that by making each

man think he was getting the better of the other that the problem would disappear. The operative word here was *think*.

Frank Gifford put it better than anyone else. To understand this you begin with how close they were and the times Gifford saw someone try to change Rozelle's mind—and fail. They shared serious personal problems. They ultimately reached a point when there was very little each would not tell the other. Frank understood his style and, therefore, his power of persuasion. "His ability to 'listen on his feet' gave him a tremendous edge. It was the key to his ability as a negotiator. Guys would come away saying, 'Wow, that was a great conversation we had,' and then they'd think, 'What the hell did he say?' and then they'd suddenly realize that they had walked out of the meeting with their pants around their ankles.

"He could read people one-on-one or read the thrust of critical public opinion even as it was forming. His ability to put his fingers on an idea whose time had come was uncanny."

A classic example was his creation of NFL Properties. Originally formulated with all licensing fees designated to go to charity (it would and still does fund NFL Charities), it grew to the point where the owners could get revenues and still support worthy causes. But there was a time when such an idea was laughable—until Rozelle seized the opportunity and put it into practice. When I asked him about what triggered the notion, he explained that he had been disturbed for some time about what could happen to the league's public image with the wrong commercial exposure. It had bothered him for some time that as pro football's popularity exploded, so did the efforts of what seemed like every manufacturer on the planet to create a product they could tie to the game.

The league's limited licensing procedures were left in the dust. "It occurred to me," he explained one day, "that someday I would walk into a supermarket and see NFL toilet paper or into a drugstore and find an NFL jock-itch remedy. Enough was enough."

Back in 1963 NFL Properties was born. "Properties," as it calls itself today, was so effective that today in Super Bowl host cities, NFL "deputies" roam the streets (often with local police sup-

port) and confiscate nonlicensed NFL apparel with team names or league logos. They are policing what has grown into a billion-dollar licensing company here and abroad.

Rozelle's next move was the stepping-stone to the kind of national and international visibility that no other sport or business could even have imagined. A company named Telra had filmed the 1961 NFL Championship Game between the Packers and the Giants for a rights fee of fifteen hundred dollars. There had been no other bidders.

Down in Philadelphia the following spring, a man named Ed Sabol was mired in a career selling overcoats for his father-in-law. It was a job of virtually no appeal for a man who had once been in vaudeville and films and a play with a limited run on Broadway.

Deep within each of us there is a Walter Mitty, yearning to break free. Most of us never hear his voice or listen to his voice. But Ed Sabol was not most of us. Sabol was forty-five years old, but roughly two decades earlier he had received a Bell and Howell film camera as a wedding present from his mother-in-law. It was that same camera that would ultimately give life to Sabol's dream. He had used it to film the boyhood of his son, Steve: the first haircut, the high school football practices, and family excursions in between.

When Sabol read how little Telra had paid for the rights to the 1961 game, he thought, "Hell, I can beat that," which is why Thelma Elkjer, executive secretary to Pete Rozelle and official gatekeeper to the Rozelle appointment book, got the telephone call. "I had nothing to lose," Sabol told me. "I called and said I wanted to make a bid for the film rights to the 1962 game. She told me to come on up."

Sabol went to lunch with Pete and offered more than double what Telra had paid. Logic dictated that Pete used the bid to get more from someone else rather than give what he considered the NFL showcase to a man whose portfolio was basically the kind of home movies that make visitors get down on their hands and knees and crawl out of the room once the lights go out.

But he saw something in Sabol. It was something you couldn't put your finger on, but the Rozelle instincts knew it was there. He

sold Sabol the game rights. The result was a film called *Pro Football's Longest Day*. For the next two years. Sabol retained the rights to the title game. Then he came back to Rozelle with a proposal that the NFL form its own film company.

When the owners agreed, he produced his first film for them. It was named *They Call It Pro Football*, and the press premiere was set for Toots Shor's restaurant and saloon on West Fifty-First Street in Manhattan. The venue itself ensured an impressive and influential audience. For years it had been the magnet for every sports columnist in the Great Megalopolis. When the clock was ticking and you still needed a column, you went to Shor's. Everyone from Joe DiMaggio to Alex Webster could happen to be there and solve your problem.

Rozelle felt that Shor's was the ideal place to showcase the new baby. At the time pro football trailed baseball and college football in the television ratings. Rozelle had seen the film, and he was impressed that the company he had put in business had made it without marching band music and with incredible use of montages that broke down the emotions of the crowd and the piece-by-piece anatomy of the big plays. It was easy for the Rozelle propaganda mill to produce a gaggle of writers for the event.

"That was the day I decided that Pete Rozelle might just be the coolest man in the world," Steve Sabol, who would later take NFL Films far beyond his dad's expectations, told me.

They were all there . . . the biggest writers in town . . . the ones with national audiences . . . even some players from the Giants. So the lights go out and the music comes up, and the title is there big as life. We are just ten minutes into the film, and then crash . . . bang . . . oh, crap.

A waiter trips over the projector, and it goes down into the hors d'oeuvres. The lights come up, my dad says, "Uh . . . uh, well, just give us a moment," and before he says anything else, Pete is up and he is addressing the room.

He never skips a beat, while he brings up Frank Gifford and Del Shofner and Alex Webster, and he's holding a press conference about

their thoughts on the game they are about to see in film while we're cleaning up the mess and getting the film out of the crab legs. By the time the film is ready again, we have a fascinated audience. I think only Pete could have done that. It could have been disaster.

Rozelle knew he had taken a major gamble on what films could do for the game that was his product. Today, the experiment that the Sabols began has become the greatest propaganda and merchandizing tool in sports history.

There was a moment when much of this could have been lost. NFL Properties, noting the commercial success of NFL Films, tried to get the Sabols to move into Manhattan under the NFL Properties umbrella. Rozelle refused to let that happen. It was his opinion that "Films" was not like selling jerseys. He did not want the "suits" to muscle in where they had no background.

He believed Films might be a kind of country cousin to Properties but never under its editorial control. He felt that left down in Philly, away from Properties' influence, Films could remain pure to the public relations purpose he and Sabol had agreed was the right direction for it. "He understood even better than we did," the elder Sabol said, "how we were remaking the game of football."

> I remember when this issue came up, he said he wanted us to stay down in Philly. He said to me, "This is no deodorant you are selling. You don't need to be up here with the ad guys and the lawyers. You need to be left alone, and remember that you are not making films for the owners or the coaches or the players. You are making them for the fans. And you will continue to see that a lot clearer down there instead of here with people looking over your shoulder.
>
> "Don't worry about the owners. They don't even understand what the hell you are doing—thank God."

It was not an idle boast when, speaking of NFL Films' early success, Steve once said, "The only other human endeavor more thoroughly captured on 16-mm film than the National Football League is World War II."

14

At War with the Counterculture

I think the [social] drug thing really hit him hard. He was worried that we could be headed to where the NBA was at the time in the matter of so-called social drug use. Even before Len Bias and Don Rodgers died from cocaine overdoses, he had been trying to formulate a disciplinary plan he hoped to get past the players union.

—Jay Moyer, former NFL in-house counsel

The trouble was that the men went crazy for steroids. They figured if one pill was good, three or four of them would be better, and they were eating them like candy. I began seeing prostate trouble and atrophied testes.

—Dr. John Ziegler, father of synthetic anabolic steroids, who later regretted introducing them to athletes

Pete Rozelle knew what was coming, and he was desperate to derail its runaway course. In 1986 during an interview in his office he told me, "We have a huge drug problem in this country here and now. We have it in the culture and on the campuses of our colleges, and it's naive to think you can look away because the young men coming into our league are shaped by that culture and come off of those campuses."

He never mentioned the single biggest trigger for his concern that day. He didn't have to. We were coming off a summer that ate away at Rozelle's worst fears. During an eight-day span in June, twenty-two-year-old Len Bias, an enormously gifted basketball forward out of the University of Maryland and the number-two choice in the overall NBA draft, died of a cocaine overdose just two days after his selection. A week later the Browns' Don Rod-

gers, a former rookie of the year at safety and an all-pro, died the same way.

This wasn't something whose impact had sneaked up on the commissioner. Cocaine and pot were a growing problem around the NFL. He had already commissioned Don Weiss, a top aide, to work with a team of outside lawyers to get some kind of drug policy in place.

How long had the problem nagged at him? He had made a serious personal decision to do something about marijuana years earlier after an unplanned experiment had given him firsthand knowledge about marijuana, which he knew had already been smoked in NFL locker rooms and preceded cocaine in terms of popularity.

In the early 1970s Acapulco was still at the zenith of its popularity as a vacation magnet for celebrities, jet-setters, and moneyed people. Its growth had begun in the 1950s in the northern part of the city, where celebrities such as Errol Flynn, Clark Gable, John Wayne, Hedy Lamarr, and Roy Rogers, to name just a few, flocked there for fun in the sun. Small wonder that in 1957 the attraction inspired Frank Sinatra to sing "flying down Acapulco way." And they did.

Elvis Presley made a highly forgettable movie there called *Fun in Acapulco*. Luxury hotels began to sprout in the southern part of town. Travel agencies spread the word that now LA secretaries, college kids, et al. could share that fun in the sun with the stars at affordable prices.

But the beach houses to the north continued to be popular with old-guard snowbirds. One of them was Ed Sabol, who spent a lot of winters in the old beach settlement with his closest friends. One of those regular houseguests was Pete Rozelle, who loved the sun, the easy life, and, most of all, the fishing in the Gulf of Mexico for which Sabol was the perfect companion.

Blair Sabol, Ed's daughter, who knew the commissioner well, told me this version of a night circa 1970 when the commissioner expressed an interest in learning exactly what the big deal was

about pot because it had already been detected in at least one NFL locker room. This is what she recounted:

> I was so much younger than him, and he knew that pot was a big thing with my generation. That afternoon a friend and I scored some Acapulco gold on the beach and brought it home. There was a big drinking scene at dinner that night, but here I must tell you that for all the years my family and I were around Pete, I never saw him drunk and he wasn't that night.
>
> He loved Acapulco. He loved to fish, and every time I saw him down there he was tanned and totally relaxed because he was away from the tremendous stress of the commissioner's job.
>
> So it was late at night and my mom and dad had gone to bed, and it was just me and Pete, and my brother Steve, and his houseguest. It was a beautiful night, and we were sitting on the porch when Pete asked me what the big deal was about pot because he knew I smoked it.
>
> As I recall he had said, "Someday I am going to have to deal with a lot of players over this." He was a cigarette chain-smoker anyway, as we all knew, and I said if he wanted to find out, he ought to try it and see for himself. I remember laughing and telling him that since he was so stoic, it probably wouldn't have any effect on him anyway.
>
> So he did. He kept puffing and exhaling and saying over and over, "This does nothing for me . . . I don't feel a thing . . . nothing at all . . . absolutely nothing," and then he started to laugh and we started to laugh and it went on that way for a while, and then he got very quiet. Thinking back, he probably was stoned.
>
> The next day, I recall he said something like, "I still don't know what the big deal is, but I feel like this [pot] could be a problem for my guys."

And in terms of public image it would be.

In the matters of both pot and cocaine, Gene Upshaw, the executive director of the NFL Players Association (1983–2008), felt that any attempt to test the players would be an invasion of privacy. He repeatedly fought Rozelle's attempt to get a joint agreement about policing drugs.

This was a battle that exasperated Rozelle for years because the standard player contract and the league constitution both seemed to give the commissioner power to protect the image of the game. In 1973 and again in 1975 he notified the players that the league would test for marijuana and cocaine. Disciplinary action would follow, he told them, but for the most part there was little or no progress because he had no green light from the NFL Players Association.

But even the Players Association began to feel the weight of public opinion when *Sports Illustrated* ran a cover story in June 1982 about cocaine and marijuana problems in the NFL. To compound the image problem, the entry of two players, Chuck Muncie and Rick Upchurch, into rehab about that time became public knowledge.

That same year a new collective bargaining agreement gave Rozelle the right to test only in preseason camp for drugs and further confidential testing of those whom the league had suspicions as a result of the first set of tests. But an NLRB arbiter ruled out spot-testing because it was not covered by the CBA.

Rozelle had the mechanism he wanted but no ability to enforce it. And, as expected, one voice emerged to blame him for that. Al Davis, who despite his later claims never liked or accepted Rozelle, returned to his ongoing vendetta, telling *Sports Illustrated* that Rozelle's attempt to control drug abuse had failed, and the league still needed "a strong program and someone with the guts to enforce it."

Having fired that personal broadside against the man he forever viewed as a public relations specialist who never should have survived the war between the leagues at the expense of a football man like him, he neglected to point out that the union, led by one of his former players, Gene Upshaw, had derailed every single attempt at an enforceable agreement.

In 1991, two years after his retirement, looking back over the difficulty he had in trying to do what he felt was right in relation to cocaine and marijuana, Rozelle said in an interview later run by the Academy of Achievement:

It's tough when you're supposed to be the guardian of the sport. You're repulsed by that [drug abuse], you know, you hate it. But people are people, and you just do the best you can.

I wanted to be sure that we were clean, so I set up a testing program. Their union took it to arbitration, and got it softened a great deal. So now I will be criticized in the future for drug incidents, yet I was unable to execute a testing program that could stop it.

I personally feel that drugs constitute the biggest major problem we have in this country, forgetting sports, because drugs create the medical problems that cause the increase in all our medical costs. They contribute to the homeless, that's a big problem many people see today, and a lot of that stems from drugs.

Unfortunately, during the period that I attempted to develop a stronger program, the players protested, and they felt that should be individual rights and so forth, and they wanted to slow it down. And they were able to get an arbitrator to rule that there was only so many things you could do.

But in 1987 and 1988 when negotiations with the players' union for a new collective bargaining agreement bogged down, Rozelle's determination to slow down drugs in the NFL caught a break. During negotiations for a new CBA, the players decertified their union in order to institute a tidal wave of individual suits against the league and its owners. Now there was no agreement for a mediator to cite, and Rozelle stepped in. He imposed the best drug-testing program in all sports. The NBA had one that protected secrecy at the time, but it contained forgiveness clause after forgiveness clause, according to George Young, then GM of the Giants. "Read the damned thing," he told me, "and then read ours. The NBA rule is based on hand-holding and encouragement. Ours is genuine tough love . . . a kind of crime-and-punishment type of thing."

"I think the drug thing really hurt Rozelle," Jay Moyer, the former in-house NFL counsel, told me. "It wore him down over and over because we were constantly catching people, and it really hurt him deep down."

Rozelle did, in fact, make serious inroads into the problem. But there already was yet another chemical challenge, and that one struck at the heart of Rozelle's obsession with public perception. Before he got it under reasonable control, it almost branded the league as a band of cheaters. It began with pills and then morphed into a full-blown national steroid scandal.

On October 11, 1969, a man named Houston Ridge of the San Diego Chargers played what would be his last game of professional football against the Miami Dolphins. Ridge, coached by Sid Gillman, was in his fifth season with San Diego.

Injured earlier in the season and treated by team doctors before that game, he later insisted that he had so many drugs inside him that he thought he was seeing visions. He said that in one game he had played while under the influence of nine separate drugs, including three different amphetamines and three different muscle relaxers.

The drugs he was given for that game by a doctor associated with that team included amphetamines and pain killers. He tore the inside of his kneecap into chopped liver and never even felt it. His injuries were career ending. When the doctor's name became public in the media, an interesting thing happened—which is to say nothing at all. Neither the county nor the state medical association investigated the doctor.

It was a national scandal. Sworn affidavits by the players that were never repudiated talked of the delivery system where "uppers" and "downers" were actually delivered to the right players' lockers. The Chargers settled with Ridge for $265,000. Back in New York there was both a sigh of relief at the settlement and an element of horror at the revelation that the Chargers had been ordering as many as ten thousand pills a year. Almost overlooked in the media coverage, the league office and in the public perception was the emergence of anabolic steroids in that very case. Since the early 1960s, the Chargers had been handing out steroids to players in training camp.

Nobody seemed to understand that there was something a lot more damaging than "uppers" and "downers" already finding a home in the Chargers' dressing room. It would later spread to a league-wide head-on potential disaster that Rozelle would soon have to fight like hell to bring under control. It began as anabolic steroids, a label with which few in the NFL headquarters, including the commissioner, back then were familiar.

A man who was, however, was named Dr. John Ziegler. As a doctor for the U.S. weightlifting team, he was well aware of why the Russian state-controlled national athlete machine was successfully kicking ass worldwide.

In pursuit of an insight into that, he met for drinks with a Soviet team doctor after a 1954 world championship meet in Vienna that was dominated by the Soviets. The doctor confided in him that their athletes were using various forms of testosterone to become bigger, stronger, and possibly even faster. He did not mention any side effects, in all probability because the Soviets, like the East Germans who followed in their wake, didn't care about the individual athletes. They cared about winning as an effective publicity tool in the political and cultural Cold War. Later, this is why they kept the subjects of their experiments in isolation between competitions.

The anonymous Soviet official had no trouble sharing a "state secret" with a man he considered a colleague. Ziegler returned home, determined to do something to help the American team. He developed an anabolic steroid called Dianabol with the financing and assistance of a Swiss medicinal chemical firm then known as Ciba (later Ciba-Geigy).

He had been motivated to level the international playing fields for America's international athletes out of patriotism. In so doing, he had set up what would be the only perfect control group for testing. Off medical examinations of the group, he would discover that a large number of athletes were taking five and ten times the dosage he wanted them to take. He was horrified to learn two critical things.

First, there were doctors out there (and, as we know, still are) who would write dangerous prescription dosages under the table for money. Second, those who availed themselves of this black market were prime candidates to wind up with testicular cancer; liver, kidney, or heart failure; and various forms of terminal cancer.

He preached against these deadly dangers for years right up until his death. Unfortunately, there were few voices in his army. The loudest and most knowledgeable among them was Dr. Robert Goldman, a medical doctor, a PhD, an athlete, and Ziegler's protégé.

The day before he died in 1983, Ziegler told Goldman: "I wish to God now I'd never invented it. I'd like to go back and take that whole chapter out of my life." Then he charged Goldman with continuing the battle to shine a light on what had become a Pandora's box of danger.

"There were so few of us who understood the danger at the time," Goldman told me. "So much of the criticism Rozelle received for being slow to act was unfair. It was easy to look back in hindsight and ask why it took him so long, but he was like most people who were just beginning to learn what this was all about. There is no question in my mind that among the major sports [baseball, football, basketball, and hockey], he was the first to act."

But back in 1963, not only were steroids not illegal, but the effects of taking them were completely unknown. Without warning the genie slithered out of the bottle and into the locker room of the San Diego Chargers. It would be more than a decade before enough facts were on the table to trigger a strong reaction from the commissioner.

In 1962 the Chargers were an embarrassment to their coach, Sid Gillman. After a 2-12 finish the previous season, the coach vowed a new order of discipline would emerge for 1963. This was his twenty-ninth season in the game. He had long been recognized as a brilliant tactician and an architect of innovation in the passing game. He was a slave to perfection and an admirer of those of like personality.

Gillman wanted to change the order starting with training camp, and he found it in Rough Acres, a failed dude ranch seventy miles east of San Diego, down a dirt road from the tiny town of Boulevard, California. It featured ninety-degree heat and some interesting forms of wildlife.

Each morning workmen swept the playing field for rattlesnakes. There, his players underwent the most physical drills they had ever experienced. And it was there that Gillman had introduced them to a man who would become pro football's first strength coach. His name was Alvin Roy, and he brought with him a special "strength builder." "This stuff is called Dianabol," he told them, shaking a bottle of pink pills, "and it's going to help assimilate protein and you'll be taking it every day." He distributed them at breakfast every morning. And when the team broke after practice sessions, the assistant coaches would remind them as they left the field to be sure and take their pink pills.

They became the first steroid-fueled football team to win a championship, beating the Patriots, 51–10, for the AFL title. Ron Mix, a Chargers offensive lineman, would later tell *Sports Illustrated*: "I still remember what the bottle said. It was in big red letters. It said, 'Dangerous. Not to be taken over extended periods of time, will cause permanent bone damage, liver damage, heart damage, testicle shrinkage.'"

Gillman is alleged to have told Walt Sweeney, "What do these guys know? They don't know anything about football. They're doctors."

"That [Houston Ridge] lawsuit may have been the triggering thing that told the vast majority of athletes that there might be something out there that is useful to you," Mix also told *Sports Illustrated*. Still, it would take almost twenty years before the NFL could formalize a steroid policy.

The more he heard about steroids, the more Rozelle was determined to act. And unlike his fight against player usage of cocaine

and other illegal drugs, the commissioner welcomed a powerful ally into the battle. As hard as Gene Upshaw, head of the NFL Players Association, had fought against the commissioner's efforts to fight cocaine and marijuana use by the players (a goal that Upshaw saw as an invasion of privacy), he was four-square in the commissioner's camp in the battle against steroid.

Upshaw had been a player. Hell, he had been a positively great player, and he saw steroids as a form of blatant cheating in order to gain an advantage. "Upshaw was very good on steroids as opposed to social drugs. And what he didn't do was as important to Pete as what he did do," says Jay Moyer, the league's former in-house counsel. "After two years of testing he still did not raise hell. And that was a huge help. He and Gene shared the exact same feelings on that subject. The union didn't fully cooperate but they absolutely never challenged us, and that was because both Gene and Pete were on the same page."

Finally, in 1989 with the players' union temporarily decertified by its members as a bargaining ploy in player-management negotiations, Rozelle took advantage of the opening to act. At a league meeting in Palm Desert, California, he announced he would unilaterally institute an antisteroid policy.

The mechanism provided for game suspensions without pay for players found to use steroids, starting with the 1989 season. His remarks that day made him the first of all professional sports commissioners to speak out publicly against the use of steroids by athletes. His concerns over the long-range dangers of steroid even surpassed his feeling about competitive advantages. "I'm convinced it's bad for players. A lot of things can happen to them to keep them from enjoying the quality of life after football," Rozelle said. That stamped him as the first sports official to understand that players had embarked on a regimen that might kill them in early retirement. "With that in mind," he added, "we will immediately get into educating players while advising them they could be suspended beginning in 1989."

It is worth noting that he had personally tried to ban steroids

in 1983, but until the union's temporary decertification, he had no chance to put teeth into the ultimatum. There had always been the union's threat to use the issue as a bargaining chip in negotiations over the collective bargaining agreement that got in the way.

But when he had first acted six years earlier, he had set a significant tone by banning anabolic steroids before professional basketball, before professional hockey, well before Major League Baseball, and a full nine years before the U.S. government had declared it a Category 3 controlled substance, a drug known to have legitimate medical uses but one that has the potential for physical or psychological addiction.

Rozelle's change on steroid punishment was not subject to vote by the NFL owners. How did Rozelle get the program through so quickly? "I just told them," Rozelle said.

The following year he announced that thirteen players from eight teams were suspended for flunking that first official testing under the new program. Upshaw's official response was to claim that just thirteen positives out of all those players indicated that the NFL had greatly exaggerated the extent of steroid use.

Rozelle's response as reported by the *New York Times* was a genuine restatement of why he had been so vocal on the subject: "We tried to educate the players for the past two years and at the same time learn more ourselves about [the dangers] of steroids. We now know that it gives a strong competitive advantage and has severe medical side effects. This is not a program designed simply to try to catch people but to get them off this harmful drug."

There was controversy both among the guilty and among the media, many of whom knew nothing or very little about the long-range effects of the drug. Not only were most of them ignorant about the dangerous long-term effects of it, but they failed to recognize the primitive stage in which the testing was still mired.

The one most prominent among the offenders who was caught in that first web was the Eagles' Ron Solt, whose only explanation was "I would do whatever it takes to make a million dollars a year. Most people would."

Of course, he had no idea what the physical risks were. None of them did because there was still so much research to be done. But the bottom line with which Rozelle had to deal was best described by the Packers' Mike Ariey, who said when he was suspended, "I think the league decided to pull these 13 guys as scapegoats because they had to come up with names to validate this big witch hunt for steroid users. Maybe I was naive, I'm not blaming anybody but myself but those other guys should have been accountable also. C'mon [just] 13 guys. It was ludicrous."

You have to wonder what they might have said twenty years later when they looked around and saw so many of them dying young, those who died before their time at forty-five and fifty and sixty.

It remains an ongoing battle, but at least Rozelle, during his tenure, like Tagliabue who followed, was willing to fight it. A full decade after Rozelle's retirement, Bud Selig and Major League Baseball were still afraid to ban the steroid Mark McGwire was using while he was attempting to break baseball's home run record and bring back fans still angry over a players' strike.

Of course, Rozelle might have made more progress if he had adopted George Young's antisteroid plan. Young, then general manager of the New York Football Giants, said when I asked how his club dealt with warning players of steroids: "We did pretty well. I really respect Pete, but he might have done better if he did what I did. Whenever the subject came up, I would tell them that what they did would be entirely up to them, but, personally, I wouldn't like it if my dick fell off." Rest assured his analysis did not fall on deaf ears that day.

15

Davis Again: Feud without End

One day he asked me if I had a choice did I want money, love, respect, or power, and I told him respect, and he said, "Wrong choice. With power, you get all the others."

—Writer Ron Borges, recalling a conversation with Al Davis

Think of Tunney and Dempsey. Pete Rozelle was Tunney, boxing your head off, and Al Davis was Dempsey, throwing bombs from every angle. Pete wanted to fight you in the boardroom. Al wanted to fight you in the street.

—Writer Dave Newhouse on the Rozelle-Davis 100-yard vendetta

They were as different as champagne and malt liquor—the urbane commissioner who wanted to be respected more than feared and the renegade who wanted to be feared more than respected. They fought from coast to coast all through the NFL-AFL wars and beyond. When Davis became AFL commissioner, they fought from separate but equal Park Avenue command posts. They fought in the media. They fought to gain favor with twenty-one-year-old linebackers on campuses all across the continental landmass.

Year after year they continued to battle. They were, in every aspect, Ali and Frazier at high noon in Manila, and the word *armistice* was not in their vocabulary. Eventually, their endless feud would take them to their final battlegrounds before judges and juries.

But never before in the history of professional sports—not even in Baseball's Curt Flood Supreme Court case—was the authority of a commissioner challenged as relentlessly and at times as successfully as in the personal crusade continually mounted by Al

Davis. Even after his Raiders-to—Los Angeles move was upheld by the courts, Al Davis persisted. Incredibly, he would actually testify against his own league in the USFL antitrust suit.

Money was not the overriding fuel in this strange vendetta. Nor was it public animosity. The strongest thing Rozelle had ever publicly said about Davis was to call him "a charming rogue." Much later, in private, of course, he would use other adjectives.

And to my knowledge, outside of testifying for the plaintiff (USFL) against the league Rozelle ran, Davis never publicly resorted to name-calling. Sporadic sniping was more his public style. But the intensity of what each man felt about the other never abated.

"I think," Frank Gifford says, "each man lost a lot physically by what he had to put into this personal battle. It was like watching two gladiators, and it took a toll on all the owners. It made them have to choose, and they didn't want that. There was no neutrality. Al wouldn't permit it. Davis made you take sides. You heard him say, 'Just win, baby, win,' but what he meant was just win for Al. They were both powerful men in their own way, but it was Al who kept the feud alive."

There was no doubt on whose side most of the league's old-timers came down. Looking back years later when I asked him his feelings about Davis, Art Modell said with great emotion: "Al Davis . . . don't ask . . . For me, the day I learned about Al Davis was a day that will live forever in infamy. There were things about him I admired, like his love for his ailing wife, but when it came to football wheeling and dealing . . . forget about it. When it comes to football and Al Davis and the good of the league, I don't even want to talk about it."

The split between Rozelle and Davis dealt primarily with an irreconcilable difference in agendas. "There was a reason that my father stood with Pete in those battles," John Mara, the president and co-owner of the Giants, says. "Like Pete, he believed that what was good for the league was more important than what was good for us or any one team. Al saw it the other way around."

"There was no mystery about Al Davis," said Paul Tagliabue,

Rozelle's major legal adviser and the man who succeeded him as commissioner. "I don't think Pete had any expectations about Al being loyal to anyone except Al Davis. He showed his colors when he stole the [Oakland] franchise from Wayne Valley."

Valley had been the owner who first brought order out of chaos to a franchise that had been a disaster. And he was the man who gave Al Davis his big chance, according to Dave Newhouse, a respected Bay Area columnist.

> Valley was an old-school, tough construction guy out of San Leandro. Out here he was to construction millionaires what Bill Walsh was to future NFL head coaches. They personally mentored a hell of a lot of them. Valley was a tough guy who hated to lose, and in Davis he saw the tough guy who could finally make his franchise a winner. Valley was solely responsible for his coming to Oakland. So Davis goes 10-4 and is coach of the year. But wins no championship. And he never did win one when Wayne was in control, and that rankled Valley.
>
> He nicknamed Davis "my genius," but from a compliment that nickname turned into a needle. The Raiders lost five AFL title games in six years when Valley was there. After the fourth one Valley saw him in the Pittsburgh airport and shouted in a voice that could have shattered all the stained windows in St. Patrick's Cathedral: "There's my genius. Hey, genius, when you gonna finally get us a championship?"
>
> Wayne was acerbic, to put it mildly, and Al hated that. He often criticized his coach in public and to his face, and Davis hated that. I think Wayne may have been the only guy Al ever actually hated. He didn't hate Rozelle. That was business. But Valley really got to him.

And what did Davis do about that? Well, wasn't he the guy who preached "Just win, baby, win"? So he went out and won. In old-fashioned football terms, he went out and mouse-trapped him.

There were three general partners in the Oakland Raiders—Davis, Valley, and Ed McGah. While Valley was off in Germany at the 1972 Olympics, Davis wooed McGah and got him to sign an agreement that made Davis the controlling general partner in perpetuity. Under corporate law at the time, he was able to launch

a palace coup. Since there were only three eligible voters in the corporation, Davis welcomed Valley home with the news that he was no longer in control. "Well, around that time Pete and I had to fly out to the Bay Area for a labor arbitration session," Jay Moyer, then the in-house counsel to Rozelle, recalls. "After that meeting, Pete said we had to go over to Oakland to meet with Al and Wayne, but he didn't explain why."

> So we walk into their conference room, and Davis is sitting at one end of the table and Wayne at the other, and nobody is saying anything. After we sit down, Wayne opens his briefcase and pulls out a newspaper and fires it the length of the table to Davis. Then he says, "Is this true?"
>
> Davis looks up and he says, "Yeah, it's true."
>
> And Wayne shouts back that he can't do that, and Davis shouts back, "Well, I damned well did."
>
> My recollection after that was that Wayne sued, and he asked for two things. He wanted the agreement invalidated, and he wanted Davis kicked out of the Raiders. The judge gave him the first but not the second. Wayne said he couldn't ever work with Al again. Pete tried to talk some sense into him, but Wayne was adamant. He sold out and walked away.

Later, when the 49ers became available, Valley tried to buy them. If successful, he planned to install Monte Clark, the former San Francisco player who had been spectacularly successful as an assistant coach with the Dolphins, as his head coach.

But the late Morabito brothers who had owned the team had a clause in their agreement that upon the deaths of both of them, ownership would pass to their widows, and the existing minority stockholders would then have first crack at raising the money to buy the team, should they sell.

One of those stockholders was Franklin Mieuli, who owned the NBA Warriors and had a piece of the San Francisco Giants. Mieuli and another minority stockholder, a prominent Bay Area attorney named Joe Alioto (who ironically would later represent Davis

on many occasions), tried to raise the money between them. As they struggled to put together the funds, they used their place in line to stall other buyers and keep their hopes alive. Meanwhile, the surviving Morabito widows grew impatient with the lack of serious bidding.

Confirmed details are hazy over exactly what followed, but this much is clear. Their representative contacted Davis to ask if he knew anyone who might be interested. Soon after, according to Newhouse, who was then covering the 49ers, Franklin Mieuli returned from a day on his boat and was handed an urgent message from the harbor master. "He was told it was imperative," Newhouse recalled, "for him to immediately call his office. When he did there was a message from Alioto waiting that read: 'The widows have decided to sell the 49ers to Eddie DeBartolo Jr.'"

The DeBartolo family had an interesting history. The father, Ed DeBartolo Sr., had built major shopping malls, owned racetracks, and unsuccessfully attempted to buy the Chicago White Sox (twice), Boston Red Sox, Cleveland Indians, and Seattle Mariners. The prevailing wisdom concerning those rejections is that, rightly or wrongly, baseball was influenced by various U.S. Justice Department reports that the elder DeBartolo had ties to organized crime. The official excuse was their ownership of racetracks.

But in a memo, made public years later, Bowie Kuhn, the commissioner of baseball, wrote to a select few that the DeBartolos were not the "R.P." Those who knew his shorthand said the initials stood for "right people."

The DeBartolos, originally from Youngstown, Ohio, were a cause of belated concern to Rozelle's security people. The father was said to have had friendships with several well-known mafiosos, which he explained like this when the league sent Moyer to vet him: "Of course I know the people on your list. I grew up with them in Youngstown. Hell, it was Youngstown. Most of the people I grew up with wound up with those ties."

But there was another aspect of the DeBartolo sale that boggles the imagination. Al Davis was at the very heart of it. It is

well known that he had been contacted by the Morabito widows in their quest for a buyer. As subsequent events proved, he had to know the DeBartolos.

It was Joe Thomas, a former NFL general manager, who brokered the deal between the Morabito widows and DeBartolo, and in return Thomas was named the Niners' new GM. Thomas and Davis had known each other since Al had been a scout for the Colts (then in Baltimore) and Thomas was their general manager.

Much of the talk about the elder DeBartolo and organized crime dealt with a bank in which he was a majority stockholder. The bank, whose loans were investigated by the State of Florida, was the Metropolitan Bank and Trust Company of Tampa. Metropolitan collapsed in 1982. It was thought to be the largest bank failure in the history of Florida. It was tied to a number of mafiosos, including their longtime elder statesman and adviser, Meyer Lansky.

It is interesting to note here that many years later, Al Davis was a featured speaker at the Fred Biletnikoff Award Dinner. The toastmaster that night was Dave Newhouse. He was the only newspaperman in the room, but he vividly recalls the strange anecdote Al Davis told the audience that night about an event during the week of Super Bowl II in Miami:

> I got to my room the Sunday before the game and I was unpacking when the telephone rang and a fellow on the other line said he was calling me because there was a national undertakers convention in town and [Meyer] Lansky wanted me to speak that Saturday night. I explained to him that I had the Super Bowl game on Sunday night and I had to concentrate on that, so as much as I would like to speak for him, it would be impossible.
>
> Then on Friday the telephone rang and it was the same guy, and he said that Mr. Lansky insists you speak. There would be a limo in front of my hotel at 6:30, so I went and I spoke.

"I was the only newspaperman at that dinner about ten years later when he recounted that story," Newhouse said, "but obviously he did know Lansky."

But an even stranger part of the sale of the 49ers came to light when Valley, bitter over the way the 49ers cut him out of a chance to buy in, called George Ross, the sports editor of the *Oakland Tribune*, and insisted that Davis had, in fact, received a six-figure finder's fee for bringing in DeBartolo (through Thomas). "There was a league meeting in Phoenix at the time," Newhouse remembered, "and Ross, who was my boss, told me to call Davis there and get him to confirm or deny. I did. I got him on the telephone and I explained who I was and told him what I wanted, and without saying another word, he hung up.

"So I called back and tried to explain, and he hung up again. Ross insisted I try one last time, and I did. When he heard my voice, he hung up for the third time."

I don't think Rozelle could or would have done much about Davis's finder's fee. The league could hardly have benefited from the public airing of a possible conflict of interest leading to a new challenge to DeBartolo's ownership. By the time Rozelle learned of the problem, it was far too late to do anything except let the matter drop.

But lawyers are, after all, still lawyers, and it is evident that the more the tension between Davis and Rozelle escalated, the more the lawyers most closely associated with Rozelle were sensitive to the need for vigilance to the nuances of almost everything David did. But nobody, absolutely nobody, expected the emotional artillery shell that Davis was about to fire at the establishment.

There are those who insist that the original germ of the idea that resulted in what followed was born not in Oakland but 371 miles to the South, where the late Carroll Rosenbloom lived in Beverly Hills luxury. There was a closeness between the owner of the Rams and Davis dating back to his pre-pro-coaching days as a scout for Carroll's Baltimore Colts.

In 1972, in a deal brokered by Hugh Culverhouse, who later bought the Tampa Bay Buccaneers, Robert Irsay purchased the Rams franchise for a reported nineteen million dollars and, then,

with Rozelle's approval, swapped the franchise to Rosenbloom in return for the Colts.

With both Rosenbloom and Davis on the West Coast, their friendship grew. I well remember a night in Los Angeles when their teams met in an exhibition game. Davis visited Carroll's box at halftime. They were joking about the terrible play of one of Carroll's running backs, and Davis said, "He's not worth the money. Dump him. Leonard will take him."

He was referring to the Eagles' owner, Leonard Tose, and Carroll responded with "Good idea. But the way the two of us have screwed him over and over, I better throw in a tube of KY Jelly."

And they both roared. Rosenbloom had always been an owner that Davis respected, and the bond between them was clear. That same night Carroll told me that he was going to put intense pressure on the LA Coliseum Commission and the city itself to get new facilities, possibly a new stadium, and a much better deal. "If they don't do what they should, I have spoken to people in Anaheim," he said, "and I'll do whatever I have to do." Because of their friendship, it is not unfair to assume that he had confided in Davis. Had he stayed in Los Angeles, the chaos that followed with the Raiders' move to LA never would have occurred.

For years, with San Francisco casting its magical shadow from just across the Bay, Oakland had been a second-class city in terms of image. As far back as 1937, Gertrude Stein had written of the city of Oakland that "there is no there there."

But that suddenly changed. It began with the building of an indoor arena and an outdoor multipurpose stadium that in concert were known as the Oakland—Alameda County Coliseum. Now Oakland had major league baseball and major league football and major league basketball. Starting in 1973 the Athletics won three straight World Series. The Raiders were perennial contenders and won their first Super Bowl in 1976. The Warriors moved over from San Francisco in 1971. To the outside world, Oakland had come of age.

Davis felt the Raiders' contribution to that wasn't properly appreciated. After all, the ballpark had been built in the era of multiuse stadiums that were fast becoming obsolete around the league. Davis wanted a new park.

As a counterbalance to his claim, Doug McAllister, a city councilman and member of the Oakland—Alameda County Commission, countered with the fact that the complex had turned a profit every year with the Athletics and the Raiders. Nobody in town felt Davis had any leverage to threaten. Where the hell could he go? "He never would have thought of Los Angeles if Carroll hadn't had a deal with Anaheim in the works," Newhouse contended.

So while the Alameda County Commission talked of its profits, Al Davis said nothing and planned a lot. "Find me a man like him," Newhouse continued. "He stayed to the very end even when he was terminally ill and still had an impact on his franchise. You can't figure people like him, and when you finally do, you realize he's ten jumps ahead of you. You go to a press conference ready to unload on him, and when it's over, you realize you didn't lay a glove on him."

The reason the scenario finally played out the way it did was that Al Davis was who *he* was and Pete Rozelle was who *he* was. For all his good qualities (remember, he hired the first African American head coach in pro football's modern era, and John Madden will tell you that if he was your friend, there was no greater friend to have), the fact is that he always operated from an "us against them" mentality.

He ran his team that way, and he ran his life that way. His feud with Rozelle was deeply rooted in his belief that he was the football man and Pete was the PR man. He was real, and for him Pete was just a fortunate spinmeister. He was damned if would lose any battle to him.

He believed that Rozelle was a product of privilege—which was totally incorrect. In Al's mind he, himself, had come up the hard way—which he did not. But for him, like most of us, perception perceived long enough that it became truth. He always saw their feud as he, the street kid, battling Pete, the silver-spoon kid.

Newspaper writer Ron Borges, who covered Al for the Oakland paper for a few years and covered Rozelle for decades in Boston, offers the most insightful analysis of everything that followed in this feud. "I really think that if Al had gone to Pete and laid out the rational part of his desire to move, Rozelle would have studied a million angles but in the end he would have worked it out, which was Pete's way. And if that happened he would have been in LA without a court case. But Al was Al, and he could never have sought Pete out. And Pete was Pete, and he never could have permitted himself to initiate that conversation." So all hell broke loose.

The Irsay-Rosenbloom swap was not relevant because owners and not franchises moved. Rosenbloom's move to Anaheim didn't count because technically his team was still the Los Angeles Rams in name and theory. The last obvious abandonment of a territory had been the negotiated move by Rozelle and approved by the NFL in 1960 of the Chicago Cardinals to St. Louis. "If you look in the dictionary," Newhouse joked, "you will probably see Al's picture next to the word *calculating*. Davis leaked his case to the media in increments. One day he would tell a reporter that the dressing room was a disgrace. The next he would tell another that the parking lots were a nightmare. A third guy would be reminded that the stadium's sightlines were bad and there were no luxury boxes."

So it was drip . . . drip . . . drip.

Then, before the 1980 season, he suddenly announced that he had signed a memorandum of agreement to move the Raiders from Oakland into the Los Angeles Coliseum. Under the NFL constitution a 75 percent approval of all owners was required. Using his intimidating style, Davis said he would move with approval or without it. Some owners were angered by his refusal to abide by the league constitution. Rozelle quietly made it known that he was of that same opinion.

Others decided to abstain because they themselves were thinking they might like to move their franchises one day and were quietly willing to see how this thing played out. The move, which

required three-fourths approval by league owners, was defeated 22–0 with five owners abstaining.

When Davis followed through on his threat, the NFL prevented it with an injunction. It was at that point that Davis joined an antitrust suit previously filed by the LA Coliseum and also filed an antitrust lawsuit of his own. He sued and later he debated, and later sued again, and later, well, on and on and on.

In all Davis sued and fought his own league what seemed to be as many times as most folks see doctors for their annual physicals. In 1982 a federal judge finally gave him the right to move his helmets, his shoulder pads, and football team to play in the aging Los Angeles Coliseum.

"We knew," Moyer recalls, "that we were in deep trouble. We were in a city where the hostile *Los Angeles Examiner* and the local TV and radio hammered away at how Los Angeles, a great town, had been deprived of professional football. We tried and failed to get a change of venue because it was clear that in the minds of the jurors, the only issue would be why this great team shouldn't come to their city."

So Davis won. It was settled. Right.

The NFL should have known better, and so should the City of Los Angeles. Historically, in the convoluted mind-set of Al Davis, nothing was ever over. In his mind he never heard a fat lady sing.

In 1987 Davis, as though he had suddenly realized all the disadvantages at the Coliseum itself, which were apparent before he even moved in, signed a good-faith stadium agreement with Irwindale, California. When the town could not deliver, he pocketed a nonrefundable $10 million.

Then in 1995, after failing to get a new Los Angeles Stadium, he went before the league's owners and asked permission to move back to Oakland, where he had been promised major improvements. Although as a result of his court decision other teams either planned to move or had moved, he was still Al Davis, and he won the right to return to Oakland by a wafer-thin margin of a single vote.

He immediately sued the league again, for $1.8 billion, claiming it had conspired to sabotage his efforts to stay in Los Angeles by failing to exert its influence to get him a new stadium there. This case was eventually thrown out by the California Supreme Court in 2007.

And in the middle of all of the above, he filed an almost Gilbert and Sullivan—style suit against the NFL, claiming that his franchise, now based in Oakland, still had the right to the Los Angeles territory. Once again, he lost.

You can make a ton of cases over why he sued to move to LA in the first place. You could say he tried to help the USFL because he had once been in that spot when he was the commissioner of the AFL. You could say this, but his efforts to help the upstart league were generated far more by his never-ending personal agenda concerning Rozelle than any possible form of altruism.

When Rozelle could be put at risk, Al Davis was never one to look a potential gift horse in the mouth, claiming that his franchise, now based in Oakland, still had the right to the Los Angeles territory. Once again, he lost.

Here came Donald Trump, bearing the gift of opportunity.

And again, when Rozelle could be put at risk, Al Davis was never one to look a potential gift horse in the mouth.

Rozelle, the great compromiser, on the other hand, could forgive Hornung and Karras for their gambling. He could forgive the lawsuits against the NFL for which Hunt was responsible.

But when it came to Al Davis and total forgiveness, for Rozelle, no penance and no span of time would be long enough for the emperor of the team Davis called the Raiduhs.

16

Never Take a Knife to a Gunfight

Mr. Rozelle and I were friends prior to my involvement in the (USFL) league. I just say after my involvement it was like I had the plague but before my involvement we were friends and I would see Mr. Rozelle quite a few times at various dinners and charitable functions.

—Donald Trump's response to direct questioning by USFL attorney Harvey Myerson, June 23, 1986

He was an acquaintance. He was not a friend. He was not even on my Christmas Card list.

—Pete Rozelle's response to Myerson on cross-examination, July 17, 1986

There were twelve of them . . . apostles of a brave new world as outlined by a dreamer named Dave Dixon, the man who had built the Superdome, brought the NFL to New Orleans without sharing in the glory of the profits, designed the master plan for the League of World Championship Tennis, and then had simply run out of projects.

With nothing else left on his drawing board, he had conceived and then midwifed the least likely of all professional sports projects—professional football in the spring . . . football in the middle of the NBA playoffs . . . football in the heat of baseball's summer . . . in terms of the calendar, football as a fish out of water.

And he had gathered his newly enlisted angels at a swank watering hole in midtown Manhattan called the 21 Club for the launching party. On that day in 1982 the most vibrant emotion it had triggered among the general public was a coast-to-coast yawn.

But on Park Avenue at Pete Rozelle's command post, the memories were still too fresh from the war with the AFL and from the brief but costly battle with Gary Davidson's ill-fated World Football League (WFL) to take the new league lightly.

Rozelle and his lieutenants figured all along that the USFL would try to move to the fall. But even at the start there was alarm when the commissioner saw that the new league's management was spending serious money on its new college draftees.

As a case in point there were the signings of Reggie White, Doug Flutie, Jim Kelly, Steve Young, and other marquee players. In addition, the NFL had yet to make players whose class had not graduated eligible for its draft. The USFL announced it would have no such restriction.

The impact of that decision was swift and, to the NFL, alarming. J. Walter Duncan, the Oklahoma oilman who owned the New Jersey Generals, immediately stunned the NFL when he was able to induce All-America running back Herschel Walker to leave the University of Georgia early to play for the Generals.

That signing caused major reaction not only within the NFL but through all of big-time college football. According to Gordon Forbes, writing a fascinating obit for the USFL in USA Today after the league went out of business, Georgia coach Vince Dooley knew all about Walker's contract well in advance.

But Steve Ehrhart, the Memphis Showboats general manager, told Forbes: "Dooley feigned innocence at a news conference. I was in his car driving in downtown Atlanta and I said you knew Herschel called us but that's the opposite of what you told the press. You said we were going to destroy college football.

"Then he slammed on the brakes and ordered me out of the car."

And that's how it began—coaches and agents playing both sides of the street.

The rebels signed NFL draft choices. They spent big money (money that in some cases they didn't have) to get them. Jim Gould, the president of the USFL's Washington Federals, threw down an unmistakable gauntlet with the NFL, saying, "There are two types of

(football) war. One where you go out and beat the NFL and another type, a psychological war where you get them (by upping the bidding costs) to start beating themselves."

It was a battle cry born of fantasy and self-hypnosis. The NFL owned the traditional football calendar. The NFL did, indeed, have the big money that television was capable of paying, all locked up. Rozelle understood he held all the cards, but he also understood that if these novices persisted in funding what should be a one-sided, hopeless battle, it would still cost the old guard an outrageous amount of money even in victory.

And then, without warning, the velocity of the gathering storm picked up speed in the USFL's second season when a new player entered the game. Donald Trump, Manhattan and Palm Beach man about town, real estate mogul, later the face of three Atlantic City casinos, and ultimately self-anointed presidential pretender, purchased the New Jersey Generals.

Long before he bought the Generals, he had made himself both a legitimate brand name and a legend in his own mind. His Atlantic City venue was the scene of major championship fights. His people made sure he made all the right gossip columns. He hosted successful and well-reported charity affairs.

He obtained a one-of-a-kind real estate variance in Manhattan to build his signature Trump Tower. He needed the variance because of its unique height in such a narrow space in that coveted part of the city's real estate. Few developers—if any at all—had the political muscle to get it.

He was a mogul who knew how to play that headline game.

The reasons he bought the Jersey Generals were simple:

First, there was the obvious spate of headlines it would generate for him, and he was sure that such ownership would eventually afford him the vehicle to shoot his way into an NFL franchise. On top of all that, he never met a headline he didn't covet.

Like much of what he did, it was enveloped in sound and fury signifying just one thing: it kept his name in the newspapers and on the airwaves.

Put many of his quotes together over the decades that followed his USFL involvement, and he comes across as a screaming, self-anointed caricature of the words written by Edmond Rostand in his play *Chantecler*: "I fall back dazzled at beholdng myself all rosy red, at having I, myself, caused the sun to rise."

Clearly, he did not buy the Jersey Generals to be part of a springtime novelty act on the edge of the New Jersey swamplands. Donald Trump lusted after a place in New York's autumn football firmament . . . a place where the elite among his friends did not have to (ugh) cross the Hudson to see if Donald really had a team. He immediately proved that theory.

Once he became an owner in this league whose payrolls outdistanced its television income, Donald Trump demanded to call the shots that would get him the exposure and the ego massage he craved and take his 100-yard act across the river to New York's golden mountain in a stadium that he would cause to happen.

His subsequent testimony when the USFL brought a $1.67 billion antitrust suit against the NFL made it clear he did not buy the Generals to participate in a springtime experiment. During direct testimony on June 23, 1986, he responded to his league's lead attorney, Harvey Myerson: "Following my decision (to buy the Generals) I spoke to people over in the networks and I based my premise on the idea that this could be a viable operation if we could get a network contract in the fall." And later in his testimony: "I felt that I would be successful in convincing the owners to move to the fall because they were losing too much money to stay in the spring."

The first thing he told his new partners was they had to move the schedule to autumn. It was true if they wanted better TV money and better crowds. But it was not true if they didn't want to go to war with the NFL.

One man who didn't was the late John F. Bassett, who owned the Memphis Southmen of the defunct WFL. Years earlier he had tried to get an NFL franchise and failed. He had been a charter member of the World Football League with the Toronto Northmen,

who were then legislated out of Canada when Parliament sought to protect the homegrown Canadian Football League.

He took them across the border, and they remained in the short-lived WFL as the Memphis Southmen until the league folded. When Dixon announced the formation of the USFL, John Bassett, son of a Toronto news media mogul and CEO on his own, came into the new game as the owner of the Tampa Bay Bandits. He had been burned by the WFL's overreaching and understood that the Davids had no chance against the battle-tested Goliaths.

He knew more about football than Trump. He knew more about the NFL than Trump. And he loved the game and wanted to stay in it. He was one of the leaders of the opposition to Trump's obsession with moving the operation to the fall. After that he believed he could keep his league in the spring, make a little money, and enjoy life.

This was totally unacceptable to Trump, which came to light when the transcripts of a USFL meeting picked up idle conversation between owners. Unlike the NFL, the USFL used a professional transcript company, and the reports recorded everything from coughs to side conversations. In one meeting, discussing a potential antitrust suit against the NFL, Basset rhetorically asked the group why it was doing this when he believed that Trump was the only one who wanted it.

Trump desperately needed an argument to win over those reluctant owners so the league could sue. He had discovered—although his testimony during the trial reaffirmed his ability to overlook the fact—that his self-styled charisma was not enough to win his intramural argument.

His intentions were strengthened by the strangest alliance in the history of sports litigation. The hard-core employees and senior officials at the NFL were not surprised. It may well have been that what happened next was the trigger that led to Rozelle calling the USFL's lawsuit "black mail litigation."

There is no doubt that Trump got some private advice from

Al Davis, who was for just about anything that would embarrass Rozelle. Subsequent events would support this.

In truth, some of Trump's renewed appeal to the significant group of holdouts was a battle plan that sounded strangely like some of the factors that had led to the settlement of the old AFL-NFL controversy back when Davis was the commissioner of the about-to-be-merged rebel league.

But the AFL model was actually something out of a time warp. The AFL and NFL settled in 1966, and conditions were not the same because the AFL had for years had its own lucrative national TV contract. It was bankrolling its war with that network's money. All the USFL had were spring games and spring TV money. Why had Donald Trump been so sure he was right?

Certainly, his co-owners were not all on the same page. It was Tad Taube, then owner of the Oakland Invaders, who insisted in 1984 that "if we are not successful in establishing player [salary] caps I can guarantee you that there will not be a USFL within three years, irrespective of improved revenue [from] television. . . . We have sighted the enemy and they are us!"

A year later Myles Tanenbaum, the owner of the Philadelphia Stars, came to a Chicago meeting believing he had enough votes to head off Trump on a fall schedule. He had, after all, won league titles, and Trump had none. He wanted to stay in the spring.

But Trump won enough votes, as he believed he would. He overpowered the opposition with dazzling self-confidence that stemmed from the notion that he would win. It was a conviction that sprang from the notion that in fact he was "the Donald," years before his first wife, Ivana, bestowed that title on him in several predivorce television interviews.

In support of that theory, Carl Peterson, an NFL veteran administrator with the Eagles before he moved to the USFL and built another winner in Tanenbaum's Philadelphia Stars, has been quoted as saying, "Donald was always about Donald. When he first bought the Generals, at the first meeting he was like a panther in the back of

the room. He got up and showed everyone at the meeting all the press coverage he got from buying the Generals. He said it would have cost him a million dollars to get this kind of coverage in the real estate industry and added, 'this is the greatest thing that has ever happened to me.'"

So there was that factor, and there is little doubt he received private encouragement from a strange source—Al Davis. He emerged in the days leading up to the actual antitrust trial as a kind of 100-yard version of *Nightmare on Elm Street*'s Freddy Krueger. All that was missing was an a capella chorus of poltergeists chanting, "He's baaaack."

Incredibly, Davis even agreed to testify against his own league in the antitrust lawsuit. Rozelle was not surprised. Tagliabue, who would join the outside counsel in this suit, was not surprised. Davis, after all, was still Davis, and despite his constant protestations his animus toward Rozelle never abated. In this case there came a moment a couple of days before he was sworn in as a witness in which he reached into his traditional arsenal to use the two weapons that were his stock in trade—intimidation and evasion. Shep Goldfein, the attorney who was closest to Frank Rothman, the NFL's lead attorney, recalls a meeting in which Davis played his traditional intimidation card:

> It was around July 4 while the trial was going on. We knew, of course, that he was coming to testify, so we called his lawyer Joe Alioto and told him he owed us the courtesy to speak for us to speak to Al about what he was planning to say and then we would set up a joint meeting at the Regency Hotel [in Manhattan].
>
> There was Frank [Rothman], Paul [Tagliabue], and myself. Bob Fitch [another outside counsel] was supposed to be there, but he had car trouble. We were in Joe's suite, and he explained that Al would join us. Joe told us that Al felt he needed to testify because he believed

in the free-enterprise system and he felt because of that belief he was obliged to testify, and Joe added, "Well, it won't be so bad."

Then Al walks in, and he is screaming the minute he crossed the threshold. He looked at Tagliabue, and he shouts, "I will sue you for malpractice and giving bad advice to the league for years." Then he looks at Frank and yells, "You have an undisclosed ownership interest in the Chargers with Gene Klein. You are a liar, and I'm gonna get you, too." He looked at me like "Who the hell are you?" and then he turned back to Frank and raises his voice even higher and screamed, "You ask me a question on cross-examination, and I'll drill you a new asshole."

Joe got up and he said, "Al, Al, calm down," and Al said, "Don't you ever tell me to calm down. You work for me."

And then he walked right out of the room, and that was the entire meeting. We just sat there and looked at each other, trying to figure out what had just happened. Then, as we were walking to the door, Joe stood up, and he said that Al didn't want us to cross-examine him after his direct testimony. I remember he told us that it would be okay and we wouldn't need to, because "Al isn't going to hurt you."

I knew why he didn't want us to ask him anything on cross— because there was so much we had about him, he knew he would be in big trouble. But Frank really surprised me. He said not to plan to cross Davis until he heard from me. He was going to talk to Cosell, who desperately wanted to testify for the USFL, because he knew him [and had once even been his lawyer], and he would call me after that conversation and tell me what we were going to do.

The NFL legal team knew that the other side thought it had discovered a "smoking gun," probably planted in private conversation by Davis. It was based on the notion that Rozelle had talked the other owners into keeping New York City open in the event Leon Hess decided to bring the Jets back from New Jersey.

If this were true, it would effectively keep the USFL (read: Donald Trump) out of New York and could have been a serious factor in making the USFL's case.

While the NFL lawyers were trying to figure out how to handle that without a blistering cross-examination of Davis, Rothman called Goldfein with a stunning decision: "We won't do much of a cross on Davis, if at all. I just spoke to Cosell, and this is what we are going to do . . ."

He had decided that he could take the pomposity of both Cosell and Trump and let them self-destruct during cross-examination, and he felt that would be all the jury had to see and hear.

Davis's testimony centered around the fact that he believed the USFL's Oakland team's future existence was threatened by what he believed to be a conspiracy between the NFL and the municipal government of Oakland. His "proof" seemed to convince nobody, but during his testimony Myerson went in search of what he thought was the smoking gun that could win the case.

Myerson's questioning of him was constructed to allege that the NFL and the Jets conspired to mislead New York City and state officials into believing that the Jets were willing to return from New Jersey. The purpose was to block the USFL's New Jersey team from moving to a new domed stadium (never built) in New York.

Davis, in response, modified the original idea that it had been openly discussed, backtracking to say he believed there was an "understanding" implied at a 1983 NFL owners' meeting to keep a USFL team out of New York. He could not say the strong words for which Myerson was looking. Every other person in that meeting emphatically denied it ever happened. And good-bye, smoking gun.

At one point Davis, who always portrayed himself as a man with a great and dangerous (to you) secret, innocently indicated that a set of minutes from an owners' meeting was not the same set he had received. A page or pages were missing, he claimed, from what the NFL had put in evidence. He was directed by the court to call his office and have the mysterious missing minutes faxed for reading the next day. When it was submitted it simply contained a single page that included a financial report and an agreement to recess the meeting. There was nothing there about a request from Hess to keep New York without another team . . . nothing about

a TV conspiracy to keep the USFL away . . . nothing much of anything. And not a hint of a smoking gun.

But his fear of cross-examination was real. Bob Ley of ESPN was quoted as saying: "During a brief recess in his cross-examination, Davis was heard to tell NFL executives, 'Be careful questioning me here because there is a lot I'm *not* saying.'"

It was a panic-driven threat. Deep down he knew there was a lot more that Rothman *could* be saying. Consequently, his testimony had not really hurt the NFL. Just as Alioto had hinted after Al left the room at that crazy meeting, he was too afraid of a vigorous cross. "I think," Tagliabue recalls, "that he backed off because he was really afraid of where Rothman could go. Basically, he had tried to intimidate us, but when that failed he was still very much afraid of what Frank could do to him on cross."

Davis needn't have worried. True to Alioto's promise, Davis's testimony didn't mean much. It was Trump and Cosell who held the key, and Rothman played them like a violin. Cosell, as he expected, self-destructed, and Trump's arrogance had reestablished Rozelle's credibility when the commissioner was brought back for a second shot by the defense.

And the way things went earlier on Rozelle's first trip to the stand, it needed to be reestablished. Myerson had surprised the defense team a little when he called Rozelle as his first witness and threw him off stride as only a brilliant lawyer could.

In retrospect, it is worth looking into the different styles of Myerson and Rothman to understand the ebb and flow of the entire trial. Each style scored points—Myerson with all the subtlety of a bulldozer at the start, and Rothman with something akin to death by a thousand cuts at the finish.

Myerson was up first. There were those in the legal profession who referred to him as Heavy Hitter Harvey; others called him the Agent Orange of all lawyers. Among the trappings of his lifestyle were raccoon coats, footlong Cuban cigars, a Rolls-Royce, a wife in a lavish home, and a longtime trophy blonde girlfriend on his arm.

As a litigator his delivery relied heavily on dramatic pauses and

phrases that sounded as if they had all been offered in capital letters. With Leon Hess, owner of the Jets, on the stand, for some reason he felt he was putting him on the defensive through derisive pronouncement, as in "Now, Mr. Hess." At one point during direct examination of Rozelle, he referred to him as "this monopolist." The judge sustained Rothman's objection, but Rozelle was clearly angered by the jury hearing an accusation that he knew the judge would strike from the record. In short, Myerson would come off as advertised.

He had called Rozelle to the stand as a hostile witness. And he was relentless. To quote Dan Rooney, owner of the Steelers and now ambassador to Ireland: "I was there almost every day. Rothman was very good, but I still was worried how the jury might react. You know they [Trump, Cosell, Davis] weren't telling the truth, and you had to have some faith that the truth would come out, which it did, but I have to admit I was really concerned."

Rozelle's appearance as a hostile witness was not up to his usual standard. Moyer, the NFL in-house counsel, put it this way: "As an experienced trial lawyer, Myerson did what you would expect. He made Pete responsible for just about every minute of his tenure as commissioner. Pete did not blow it, but he struggled. But when he came back on direct by Rothman, he was very, very good."

Joe Browne, then the NFL executive vice president of communications and public affairs, was at the trial almost every day. He explains Rozelle's difficulty under Myerson's original direct examination like this:

Well, during that phase his testimony was far from a 10. Myerson hammered him about the so-called New York agreement that wasn't true because Davis had never proven it. His charges were outrageous. Pete was on the stand for five days, and he was exhausted. But the big thing that upset him was that for the first time in his life as a witness, he had to play defense.

And then, as the USFL attorney . . . was hammering away about Pete's meeting with Trump, which Trump claimed was to offer him

a franchise, you could see that Pete was angry because it wasn't even true. Pete took care of that when Rothman had him later as a witness.

If you were there scoring this, Myerson et al. were winners of that first round.

Myerson was insistent about a seminar given by a Harvard professor entitled "How to Conquer the USFL," attended by several NFL officials. It was part of his plan to uncover a decisive "smoking gun." In cross-examination it would come out that Rozelle had issued a memo when he learned of it, telling the staff not to act in any way on anything that was suggested in the seminar and do anything they were told there.

Myerson demanded to know if staying in the spring was so good, why had the NFL never played in that season? Rozelle laboriously gave the reasons an established league didn't even have to consider that thought, but if a new league could get television money that way, then for them, it could work—if they properly managed costs:

MYERSON: Wasn't it your view that playing in the spring would have a minor league stamp on it?

ROZELLE: I think it was the best way to start a new league, to play in the spring and not have the college competition and the end of baseball season. When you are just starting something you can't expect to get a big television contract.

They argued over the USFL's signing of underclassmen. Billy Cannon, a Heisman winner, was the subject of the debate. He had been signed by Rozelle when Rozelle was general manager of the Rams. But of more importance was the following exchange:

MYERSON: And do you happen to recall of your own personal knowledge who it was that signed Billy Cannon to a professional contract prior to the time he graduated?

ROZELLE: I definitely do.

MYERSON: Who was that, Commissioner Rozelle? (and here he dramatically demanded) Look at the jury and tell them.

ROZELLE: I did.

MYERSON: You were the general manger of the Rams and the fact of the matter is that you signed Billy Cannon under the goal posts of the Los Angeles Coliseum prior to the time that he graduated from college, isn't that correct?

ROZELLE: No.

MYERSON: You didn't sign him under the goal posts, you did not?

ROZELLE: No.

MYERSON: You don't ever remember appearing with Billy Cannon under the goal posts?

ROZELLE: No. I didn't.

MYERSON: Weren't disciplinary proceedings commenced against the Rams by the NFL?

ROZELLE: Absolutely not.

MYERSON: And Commissioner Rozelle, if one of your owners comes into the courtroom and testifies under oath that you quashed those disciplinary proceedings as commissioner, he would be lying wouldn't he?

Can it be that Al Davis made promises to Mr. Myerson? Was he the "NFL owner" in this case? If not Davis, who else could it be? Since nobody answered that intriguing question in court, we'll never know.

Myerson was relentless. Rozelle was frustrated, and his annoyance bordered on anger. It went on this way for days. Myerson questioned him over the fact Hess had been on the board of directors of ABC, creating what the attorney implied was a conflict of interest because he owned the Jets at the same time. Rozelle said he didn't see it that way. Myerson drilled away at what he indicated was Rozelle's part in a conspiracy to keep the USFL off autumn television.

In short, he continually attacked, and Rozelle tried to fight back but grew more annoyed as the dialogue went on. As Dan Rooney had feared, the USFL jumped out to an early lead.

After Davis followed Rozelle, Donald Trump was called to the stand for the USFL.

The media billed him, along with Howard Cosell, as key witnesses. He had created this suit. He had insisted that Myerson be hired as the USFL's lead attorney. And he was the one who could recount what he insisted were his private conversations with the commissioner—all of which could not be corroborated.

Trump claimed that at a private meeting between the two at the Pierre hotel, Rozelle had offered him an NFL franchise in New York if the USFL withdrew its suit against the older league. Among other things to which he testified was his insistence that Rozelle was an old friend who had turned against him after he joined the USFL.

He also claimed that Rozelle had told him he controlled network sports television and implied that his (Trump's) inability to get a fall contract was because of that.

The NFL had set up a small headquarters near the courthouse where their lawyers and owners would meet during the lunch break. Tagliabue, Moyer, and Browne knew that Rozelle had made notes after the meeting about which Trump testified. He still had them and was prepared to bring them with him when Rothman put him back on the stand.

Browne knew all about those notes and how they contradicted everything testified to earlier by Trump. He also recalled for me their conversation during the break that day. He says he asked Rozelle, "Why would Donald Trump lie under oath about something like that?"

Then, he says, Rozelle, a chain smoker, took a long, slow drag on his cigarette, blew out a column of smoke, and replied, "Because, Joe, in some circles, some folks are said to believe that Donald Trump is a liar."

When I told that to Moyer, he said that was as close as he came during this incredibly stressful time to voicing an opinion about what he felt. "Through the litigation," Moyer continued, "I never saw him take a vindictive attitude. He put on a brave face, but you

could tell he honestly felt he didn't deserve all that Myerson put him through."

What eventually blunted Trump's testimony once Rozelle got on the stand was Trump's determination to slough off facts and, instead, interpret how he interpreted other people's thoughts because of his own intellect and business acumen. Rothman offered repeated objections that were often sustained.

He became particularly vulnerable when he explained what he insisted were Rozelle's attempts to buy him off with a merger. During Rozelle's subsequent testimony (this time as an NFL witness), Trump's version of the circumstances and the content of his one-on-one meeting with the commissioner in the Hotel Pierre were held to fire.

Trump had testified that Rozelle had told him he would never get a fall television contract because he controlled the networks:

ROTHMAN: Commissioner, did that conversation take place in the lobby of a public hotel (as Trump claimed)?

ROZELLE: That's preposterous it never took place in a hotel lobby or a hotel ballroom.

ROTHMAN: Did it take place anywhere?

ROZELLE: No.

ROTHMAN: (reads from record that Trump said he and Rozelle were good friends in 1981 and 1982 before Trump bought the Generals)

ROZELLE: No, he wasn't a friend.

ROTHMAN: (reads from record where Trump said they had multiple conversations during that time before March of 1984)

ROZELLE: Never. I did not. The only times I spoke with him were . . . a couple of charity affairs and then all I would say was hello.

ROTHMAN: (continued to read from the record that Trump testified at that meeting at The Pierre hotel Rozelle had offered him an NFL franchise)

ROZELLE: I certainly did not. That would call for 21 (owners) votes. I did not offer it, suggest it or encourage him.

Among other parts of the Trump testimony that Rozelle denied was Trump's assertion that Rozelle had called him to set up the meeting at the Pierre. It was Trump who called him, and ultimately Rozelle was not in the office at the time. He ultimately called Trump back, and Trump set up the meeting, renting a suite at the Pierre.

When Trump said he wanted a franchise, Rozelle testified that he asked him what he would do with the Generals if he managed to get one. Rozelle said Trump told him he would "sell them to some stiff."

When Rozelle left the stand the figurative scoreboard now seemed to read: Myerson, 1; Rothman, 1.

"I think after Pete's testimony rebutting so much of what Trump claimed," Moyer says, "and the way Pete rebutted it when Frank put him back on the stand, Trump sort of became a symbol of everything negative about the USFL."

All along, Rothman had been waiting to cross-examine the next witness. Howard Cosell claimed he was striking a blow for New York City and for free enterprise because the Giants and Jets had been stolen away by New Jersey. He was vociferous in self-praise as the self-anointed warrior destined to crush the NFL's professional football monopoly.

He was also the same Howard Cosell who loved the sound of his own voice so passionately he never seemed to know when it was time to shut up. The world casually sensed that was happening more and more with the retired broadcaster.

And Frank Rothman was counting on it. Rothman's plan was brilliant. While Myerson's dramatic rhetoric, accusatory stares, and bombast scored early points, in the end it was Rothman's velvet stiletto that made the difference. Myerson devoted every breath in his body and every question he asked to hitting a grand-slam home run.

Rothman, on the other hand, turned to the oldest of boxing maxims, and it brought him the knockout. Trainers put it like this: "Kill the body and the head will die."

And if Trump and Cosell had been boxers, they would have left the ring on wobbly legs. First, Rothman used Rozelle's role as an NFL witness to counterpunch to hit the body of Trump's testimony. Then he used a vocal rope-a-dope to keep Howard talking, and the more Howard talked under Rothman's seemingly gentle prodding, the more Howard blew himself out of the fight.

"With Trump," Shep Goldfein said, "you got the feeling that his impatience brought an enterprise down that might have succeeded in the spring as most of the owners wanted. He came across as a kind of impatient megalomaniac. And with Cosell, well, Frank just let him keep talking because he looked (and sounded) as though he made absolutely no sense."

Cosell's testimony degenerated into a side show once Rothman began to cross-examine him. He lectured the jury on the history of pro football in stentorian tones that were more arrogant than informative. Rothman gave him his head and let him take it all where Rothman wanted it to go.

ROTHMAN: Mr. Cosell, if I ask you a question you don't understand, you stop me, okay?

COSELL: If you ask me a question I don't understand, you'll have the biggest story of the century.

During one such dialogue, Cosell rambled on and on and on. Then he paused, and Rothman innocently asked, "Is it my turn now?"

Cosell was a counterpuncher like Rothman's ideal target.

ROTHMAN: Have you not indicated that the three great men of American television journalism would be Walter Cronkite for news, Johnny Carson for entertainment and Howard Cosell for sports?

COSELL: Words spoken with an obvious jocularity sometime contain total truth, sir and that happens to be so in this case.

Arrogance may have helped Cosell feed his ego, but beyond entertainment it did not help get the USFL message across to the jury.

ROTHMAN: Mr. Cosell, what I am trying to understand is how did they deter you when they let you (here Cosell interrupts and Rothman has to raise his voice) . . . I didn't finish the question, sir.

COSELL: I am sorry if you have difficulty with your interrogation, sir.

ROTHMAN: I do have difficulty in being interrupted. I will ask the question and only the judge will tell me when I do it wrong, not you, sir.

The more Cosell obfuscated, the closer Cosell came to committing witness hari-kari. His arrogance overrode his expertise.

ROTHMAN: Let me see if I understand that, Mr. Cosell.

COSELL: I can't understand your inability to understand.

ROTHMAN: I am not as smart as you are, sir.

COSELL: Well, we have learned that long ago.

ROTHMAN: Are you through?

COSELL: Apparently you are groping for thought.

ROTHMAN: I have a degree of civility and I am going to use it.

COSELL: Frank, you used to be my lawyer and I am sure you will use it.

ROTHMAN: And I had trouble with you then, too.

Cosell had come to testify with a battle plan. He had already retired at ABC. But Howard needed a stage, and this would be it—he thought. He would be the centerpiece that would topple Rozelle. When the Giants moved to New Jersey, Howard had railed against them and the commissioner who helped authorize it. He was "the Cosell," and he would put the NFL and its boss in their place now.

Now he, alone in his brilliance, would square all debts with the league. This, he believed, would be the valedictory that would remind the sports world he was always right. But instead of How-

ard as a superhero, his appearance played out as a requiem for Howard as Pagliacci.

When he left the stand, Cosell walked past the defense table, turned, and said to Rothman, "How could you do that to me? I thought you were my friend." He never considered the possibility that he had done it to himself.

Soon after that, with all the testimony and both lawyers' closing statements a part of history, there was nothing to do but wait.

"We did what we always did during the trial. We left our temporary office and walked the two blocks to the courthouse as we did each time the jurors' lunch break was over. I don't recall who was with me," Joe Browne says.

Further uptown, Rozelle was having lunch with Val Pinchbeck, his television guy. When he was told the jury was back, they headed down toward the courthouse.

Meanwhile, out in Kirtland, Ohio, at the Browns' preseason camp, Art Modell was telling Ernie Accorsi, his general manager, "Well, Rothman did all he could, but if we lose anything like the $1.7 billion they are asking for, well, Ernie, I could be out of business."

And then the jury was back, and the foreperson, a woman named Patricia McCabe, began to read the verdict. The verdict sheet from which she read was unusually long because there were so many charges. It took perhaps four or five minutes to get through it. Rarely have so many people gone from so many lows to so many highs in a span of just three hundred seconds. The first thing she read was guilty on the charge of antitrust violation.

Out in Kirtland Kevin Byrne, the Browns' communications director, was walking slowly toward Modell and Accorsi. His head was down. He was perhaps thirty feet away when Modell said, "Oh, my God, we lost."

Back in New York, after finishing lunch with Rozelle, Pinchbeck had turned the car radio to WINS, an all-news station, and the announcer was saying: "This just in. The jury has just found the NFL guilty." Rozelle had no desire to walk into that courtroom. He

told Pinchbeck to turn the car around and head back to the office.

"I remember," Shep Goldfein recalled, "that Donald Trump was standing in the back of the courtroom with his arms folded."

Modell ran into the Browns' trailer and called New York. Joe Browne was on the phone with Rozelle. McCabe was still reading. And then all hell broke loose.

Out in Ohio Modell dropped the telephone and began to laugh hysterically. Browne, who was on the phone to Rozelle, almost shouted, "Wait . . . wait . . . wait a minute . . . the damages are a dollar. The punitive damages triple it. The judge says with interest that comes to $3.76." Rozelle told Pinchbeck to turn the car back around and head toward the courthouse—again.

On the telephone again Modell said to Rothman, "As soon as Pete signs the check, I want to be the one who personally delivers it to Trump." Goldfein, stunned by the strange verdict, told Rothman, "I can't believe we lost," and Rothman answered, "Don't ever say that again. The only thing we lost was that the NFL has to pay their legal fees. We didn't lose. We won."

Now Rozelle was on the courthouse steps, and he kissed Rothman right there. Inside the court, meanwhile, Goldfein looked toward the back of the courtroom. Trump was gone. For Rozelle, it was a time for celebration. He had no way of knowing that it would be perilously close to serving as a last hurrah.

17

The Final Battles

It was the day before the Super Bowl in Miami, and Hugh Culverhouse and I were supposed to wrap up the new free-agent deal, so we went to Pete's suite at 8:30 in the morning. He opened the door, and he was white as a ghost. Tears were streaming down his face. He said, "I can't talk now. My stepson is dead."

—Gene Upshaw on Pete Rozelle's very private trauma

I thought, as a young woman who lived in the city would, that he was great and charming, and yet with all the pressure of the league and raising his daughter by himself, he just might be desperately alone in New York City.

—Blair Sabol on the Pete Rozelle people never saw

For almost three decades he had been all things to all men . . . a statesman holding his ground among the partisans—far more leader than czar. Rozelle fought the battles in the boardroom, in the media, and in the courtrooms. And you could see the physical marks of the toll it was taking. "I would be part of some special meetings in the league office usually around 9 a.m.," recalled Gil Brandt, who was one of the point men in the babysitting operations of the NFL-AFL war and whose scouting knowledge still kept him in the loop, "and he'd come bouncing in tanned and ready to listen and act and take on the world.

"But in the end the spring was gone from his step, and the tan was less noticeable, and, looking back, I realize now how much those battles had aged him."

"You could almost feel some of the air going out of him by this time," Paul Tagliabue recalled.

He had to cope with so much. I think it started with the Davis move to Los Angeles with those two trials and a huge verdict against us at the end.

Then Robert Irsay moves the Colts out of Baltimore in the middle of the night, and because of the Davis trials, Pete couldn't do anything about it. There were the two player strikes . . . the first the battle with Garvey and the second strike when the management council forced the replacement games on him against his intense objections, and, again, he had no authority to countermand them. There was the USFL trial and the horrible shock of his stepson's death in 1989 on the eve of the Super Bowl.

There were so many things that he just couldn't come to grips with the way they kept happening. Two pictures of him on my wall come to mind—one with me and one with George Halas. In those pictures, his usual tan is gone. He has bags under each eye. He looks like a guy who hasn't slept for two weeks. They are a reminder to me of how many battles he had to fight.

He was in California testifying off and on for a year and a half in the first Al Davis case, and the judge declared a mistrial. There was another trial, and then he was in Washington trying to get legislation passed. Then there was the USFL trial when he came under personal attack.

You would have thought that somehow, after all the years in which he had brought order out of chaos among feuding owners and replaced their self-centered passion with his logical reasoning, the post-USFL trial years would have been a walk in the park.

As far back as 1970 he engineered a plan in which his league had stolen Monday nights from America's living rooms, saloons, and PTA meetings. Just as he had handled the Great Super Bowl Mystery (Who got to televise the first one? "Hell, I'll sell it to both football networks"), he set out to merchandize a new football night in America. Rebuffed by NBC and CBS, which did not want to give up their prime-time shows, he muscled ABC by threatening to move the whole deal to the emerging outlet of cable television.

Roone Arledge, who ran ABC Sports at the time, finally agreed to Monday-night games.

And then Rozelle paused for an instant and doubted his own wisdom when Arledge told him he was putting Howard Cosell behind one of the microphones. "Why didn't you just go out and dig up Caligula?" an unhappy Rozelle told him.

But Pete, to his own reluctant delight, was totally wrong. America learned to either love or hate Cosell, and whichever it was, Howard drove the ratings higher and higher.

Asked why he originally had the idea, Rozelle replied, "There are a lot more TV sets in use on Monday night than on Sunday afternoons." The league reached a zenith in popularity. The Super Bowl became a worldwide phenomenon. NFL Films made big money and won critical acclaim. NFL Properties seemed to clothe half the nation.

But with it all, Tagliabue's and Brandt's assessments were correct. Rozelle was, indeed, fading, and, physically, it began to show.

So why was the former boy wonder's appetite for the kind of challenges that used to sustain him slipping away? For one thing, the NFL Management Council, which had been created with full authority to negotiate all labor deals, did not ignore Rozelle. Rather, led by Culverhouse, its point man, and abetted by Schramm, who ironically was Rozelle's longtime friend, the council did not even consult him.

Tagliabue, as his closest legal counselor and a close friend, saw it happening to the detriment of the league, which is why he would not agree to become Rozelle's successor without a written understanding that he would have legal control of the management council in all its negotiations.

In that sense Pete Rozelle was no longer the total decision maker in football's 100-yard Garden of Eden. He had won so many wars for the owners at a terrific emotional cost to himself, but as new owners arrived, that didn't matter. Some of them decided that the members of the old guard, upon whom Rozelle relied for critical support for years, were now simply becoming just old guys no

longer in the forefront of management—especially in relation to how it handled labor.

They did not pause to measure what all these battles on behalf of their league had sapped from the commissioner. Inevitably, Rozelle now began quietly to count up that emotional cost. It was at this juncture that he privately began to speculate on his future beyond football.

He had not lost his passion for the game itself, and he never would. But the battles swirling around his continued role as commissioner had now become totally personal.

Now he had to look at its impact on the personal things that mattered most to him. He had always had this "other life" . . . the one in which he was his daughter's loving father, teacher, protector, and best friend . . . the one in which his first marriage had collapsed . . . the one in which he had for so long been basically a man's man with a select few but fiercely loyal friends . . . the one in which he would meet, marry, and love Carrie Cooke Rozelle.

To understand why, for the first time, he had begun silently to think of retirement, you have to forget football for a moment and think about the people in that "other world."

Rozelle married his first wife, an artist named Jane Coupe, in 1949. He had met her in Chicago when he was on leave from the navy and married her during those salad days in San Francisco. Their daughter, Anne Marie, was born nine years later at halftime of the Rams' season opener in 1958.

Apparently, they had tried for some time to have a child, but the prior attempts had resulted in several miscarriages. "She was an alcoholic," the daughter, Anne Marie Bratton, said, "and she kept saying it would change . . . everything would be all right if she had a child . . . something of her own to love . . . but you know that's never all there is to something like this. She was shy and had no self-confidence, and she probably felt inferior. She was an alcoholic, but she became violent when she drank, and then there were psychological issues that made it far worse."

They had married while Myron De Long and Rozelle were work-

ing for USF, and De Long, as one of his closest friends, was then very much aware of the start of Jane's problems. When describing his close friendship with Rozelle during that time, he would only say of her, "Yes, I was there when he married her," and then he immediately changed the subject.

The drinking had become more intense when Rozelle joined Ken Macker's public relations firm before he became the general manager of the Rams. This led to evenings alone for her while he entertained clients at dinner, and the relationship worsened. He admitted to De Long that the worse it got, the later he chose to stay out working.

"In that PR lifestyle," Anne Marie explained with a knowledge as painful as it was accurate, "all business got done in restaurants and bars at all hours of the night. I think I know how it was for him, and it went on long after he came back to football. He worried about what he would find when he opened the door or what he would find when he came back from a business trip."

After he became commissioner, he still managed to keep her problem more or less a secret. But those closest to him knew, as social engagement after social engagement came and went without her attendance.

He was desperately trying to keep his balance while walking a gossamer tightrope between keeping the NFL on course during some of its most difficult times and battling to protect his daughter.

The former was extremely difficult. The latter at times became a nightmarish proposition.

"It was terrifying," Anne Marie said in total candor. "As a child I grew up with that. I remember days hiding behind chairs in the dark, waiting for my dad to come home, and I would run and jump into his arms and whisper our prearranged code words for what happened. It was 'She had a lousy day.' I don't know how he did it. I wouldn't want to come home to that night after night."

The one constant for Anne Marie besides her father was Thelma Elkjer, the secretary who had worked for Pete with the Rams and

came to New York when he became commissioner. Thelma was her refuge, her safe haven, her best friend. They would make paper-clip jewelry in her father's office. She would often spend weekends with Thelma. She would play with Thelma's cats. Thelma, who never married, was there for her so many times when her father could not be.

"She took me shopping for clothes . . . did so many thing mothers generally do. She had turned over one of her closets to this dollhouse we were making. She would buy fabric, and I would come over there, and we would cut out little swatches to make wallpaper. I think she was there from the time I could walk and talk."

Meanwhile, Jane became even more violent. She was hospitalized several times. She tried rehab and failed.

Separation and then divorce were inevitable. For Rozelle, the custody fight was intense. Jane vigorously contested the divorce, but at a time when only a handful of fathers anywhere in the country ever won such a battle, Pete Rozelle was granted legal custody of his daughter before the divorce was final in 1967.

Once the split was permanent, Rozelle dated often. He had become, after all, one of New York's most eligible bachelors, although there appeared to be nothing serious because raising Anne Marie had remained his top priority.

The one woman he apparently saw the most was an actress named Caroline McWilliams, who at the time was featured on the soap opera *Guiding Light*. Blair Sabol, the daughter of NFL Films founder Ed Sabol, remembers her well.

"I met her when my boyfriend and my dad and I went to the Copa with them. I saw her a number of times, and I recall thinking that she was safe for him. She was very guarded about their relationship because, after all, he was the commissioner. She was protective of him, and he dated her for a long time."

He had always been what is known as a man's man, with that

kind of small but closely knit inner circle: Frank Gifford; Jack Landry from Philip Morris; Bill MacPhail, the sports director at CBS (which had the first television contract with Rozelle's NFL); Pat Summerall, the old Giants placekicker and by then a radio sportscaster in New York; Don Klosterman; Ed Sabol; Herb Siegel, venture capitalist and Sabol's brother-in-law; Dave Mahoney, chairman of Norton-Simon Corp.; and Bob Tisch.

Philip Morris was a huge NFL sponsor, and Landry and Rozelle shared a love of the racetrack, a love of lunch at 21 (along with several others among them), and a love of practical jokes. One day Landry called Pete with a luncheon request. He told him he had a cousin he would like to join the group at lunch. She was a nun, and it was her first trip to New York. After Pete said sure, Landry said, "Well, we'll all have to watch our language."

So they met at noon, and Pete was his usual charming self. "How do you like New York, Sister?" he asked, and she said it was all very exciting, and they continued to talk. Then, Rozelle felt something brush his leg, and it was moving up, and as he spoke he realized it was her hand.

"Dad didn't know what to think," Anne Marie said when she told the story. "The hand moved higher, and then they all laughed. Obviously, she was not a nun, and Landry was the one behind the joke."

In some ways Gifford was his closest friend in that there was apparently almost nothing they didn't share with each other about their lives.

Klosterman was the oldest friend, dating back to when he played quarterback for Loyola of Los Angeles and Rozelle promoted the football fortunes of USF. Their friendship stood the test of time but occasionally suffered from geographical distance.

Landry, Siegel, Mahoney, and Tisch were his closest Manhattan friends. A love of competitive weekend tennis held most of all the above together.

And then there was Sabol, the Philadelphian who had gone from unhappy overcoat salesman to brilliant filmmaker. Like the others, he played tennis. But unlike them, he and Rozelle shared

an intense love of deep-sea fishing. As a sport that pastime has all the qualities of rhubarb. Either you love it or you hate it. There is no middle ground. "He loved tennis," Ed Sabol said.

> He was a good competitor but a lousy player. My brother-in-law Herb [Siegel] got him on the board of Chris-Craft, and Pete got a boat. He loved that boat. He liked to take his friends out on it, but that really wasn't for fishing.
>
> Fishing was different. For us, fishing was serious business. We didn't talk football; we fished. He needed it to empty his mind. He needed that with the pressures he constantly faced.
>
> Sometime we'd go alone. If the purpose was serious fishing, there would never be more than a few others on board. We went to Bimini when there was nothing there . . . no place to eat but one restaurant and conch fritters, conch stew, conch everything.

Those trips were vital to him. The closest he ever came to a serious commitment to a female during that period was probably Caroline McWilliams. But between the league and single parenting, he could not bring himself to do it, and he had yet to meet Carrie.

Clearly, there was a side to him that only a chosen few knew. Beyond the urbane, witty, articulate statesman reflected in his public face and the concerned, loving father that Anne Marie saw each day, there was yet a third Pete Rozelle.

Blair Sabol recalls a night at what was then named the Alvin Theater on West Fifty-Second Street. This was in 1970, when she and her father and Rozelle had tickets to see *Company*, Stephen Sondheim's Tony-winning musical. The three often attended Broadway shows together, and while none of them knew the plot in advance, they did know that *Company* was a "hot ticket" attraction. The show's lead character was a single man named Bobby who was unable to commit to a steady relationship, let alone marriage.

The plot revolves around his thirty-fifth birthday, with five married couples who are his best friends and three girlfriends. Essentially, Bobby is the one they count on, as in "Don't worry,

Bob will fix it" or "Bob will know what to do" or "Have I got a girl for you, Bob."

He walks out on the party, and when he returns, in front of the cakes whose candles are still lit, he sings a song called "Being alive": "Make me confused, mock me with praise, let me be used, vary my days, but alone is alone, not alive."

"He had such a quick wit, and he loved the theater so much that usually he would whisper to me during a show and make me or my dad laugh," Blair Sabol said.

> But this night, he never said a word . . . not during the second act and not as we left the theater. I felt something was going on here, so I said to him, "Pete, you were really into that," and suddenly it occurred to me that he had so identified with the main character. He thought for a moment and then shook his head about that last song, and then he said, "That guy up there was so much like me."
>
> I never heard him speak that way, nor had my dad, and I remember I thought, as a young woman who lived in the city would, that he was great and charming, and yet with all the pressure of the league and raising his daughter by himself, he just might be desperately alone in New York City.

When I repeated this story for Anne Marie during our interview and asked her if she agreed with Blair, she said, "I never heard about this before, but, yes, I can understand how my dad must have felt that way."

That happened in the summer of 1970, after he had just concluded a pressure-packed, emotionally draining negotiation with the NFL Players Association on a new four-year contract. Small wonder he confided how deeply Bobby's final song in *Company* affected him, and small wonder how intensely personal was the time he spent as a total man's man with his friends.

But in 1973 his world changed forever. It happened in the bar at the Hotel Bel-Air in Los Angeles. He was sitting with Landry and Summerall on the eve of Super Bowl VII when he first saw Carrie Cooke. She was, indeed, a room stopper.

Anne Marie heard of that first meeting in the Bel-Air from Landry. "She lit up the room when she walked in," she recalled Landry telling her, "and he knew the second they met that Dad was smitten. She offered to play tennis with him the next morning."

From that moment the romance flourished. Rozelle had made up his mind. But in the euphoria of his newfound love, he did not handle her introduction to Anne Marie all that well. He was in California, and she was there visiting her mother. He called and said he was coming to get her.

"He almost never came to her house to get me. They would meet halfway, but now he was coming there, and I was thinking I must have done something terrible for him to drive all the way there.

"He took me back to his suite at the Beverly Hills, and we had room service for dinner. He had two scotches and he still didn't explain, and I thought, 'Oh, my God, what did I do? It must be something awful.'"

Finally, without any warning, he told her, "I've met someone I want to marry. You'll like her. Her name is Carrie Cooke. She has three sons and a daughter. I've bought a house in Westchester, and you'll meet them all tomorrow."

I went to bed thinking, "What are those kids going to be like?" Until now my world had been so small. I don't know how to take this. In the morning they came in all at once. The kids were running around and calling my dad "Petey," and I can't believe what is happening. This whole family knew, and I knew nothing. I'm mad. It's a done deal, and nobody had bothered to discuss it with me.

But when she first walked into the room, I thought she was the most glamorous woman I had ever seen. She was so confident. She had been a nurse, a model, a race car driver, and had been married to the son of Jack Kent Cooke, who owned the Lakers, the Redskins, and the LA Forum. She was incredibly bright and well traveled. She appeared to be the ideal female person, and that was intimidating.

They were married within a year at Herb Siegel's Manhattan apartment.

"In the beginning," Anne Marie says, "he was so happy."

He had always been around great people, but she was bringing him into a slice of her world, which was pretty high on the glamour side in which he had never been involved. On the plus side, she had a lot of wonderful qualities.

But I think she thought I was insignificant and should not be around so much. It was easier if I let them have their family. I decided that's what I'd do. But Dad managed to make it a point to have dinner with me once a week. I do think he was happy in the beginning, but, you know, things did change for him. He couldn't see his friends the way he used to see them. After the glamour wore off, it wasn't the perfect marriage.

"I think she was good for him," Joe Browne says, "in that she personally added positives to his life. But she came with baggage, as most people do. He went from a nice Manhattan apartment with his daughter to a house in Westchester with four kids who had some problems."

The unexpected baggage was real. At least two of the three boys were dyslexic. Rozelle had always wanted a son, and now he had three. He had always managed to solve his daughter's problems, but this was too much. He tried, but he solved almost none.

According to Anne Marie, they were in and out of schools— sometimes for academic reasons and sometimes for social reasons. They flunked out or were thrown out. The biggest favor he asked for them was help in getting Philip into Cornell Law, and Rozelle told him, "Please, don't let me down."

"But Philip," she said, "was there for a very short time, and then he quit suddenly without even telling anyone. And Jack (the oldest) had far more serious problems."

Anne Marie said he had drug problems, and she believes they were at least a partial cause of his death. There was that and the fact that he was an alcoholic. At Super Bowl XXII in 1988 in San Diego, he showed up at the commissioner's party and demanded to see his mother. His condition was such that security removed him.

Those who knew him best cited his severe learning disability and overwhelming sense of failure as the likely root causes of his alcohol and drug problems. He was the grandson of Jack Kent Cooke and bore his name, and his friends felt that he was forever a disappointment to his grandfather (and perhaps to himself) when measured against his grandfather's expectations. All of this had led Carrie Rozelle to establish what is now the National Center for Learning Disabilities—a group that she and Pete continued to work hard to support until they died.

A year after Jack's brush with security at the Super Bowl party, Carrie, Pete, and Anne Marie were together at the next championship game. Because Pete had a lot of serious labor business to conduct, they did not stay at the league headquarters in Miami. Instead, they were at the Doral Hotel in Miami Beach.

The official commissioner's party is always held on Friday. When they returned to the hotel that night, the message light in the Rozelles' room was blinking. The horrendous news on the voice mail said that Jack had been found dead that night alone in his apartment in Glendale, eight miles north of Los Angeles. The coroner would later say he had been dead for three days. He was twenty-six years old.

"I was there with my dad," Anne Marie recalled. "I saw Dad cry. My father had tried so hard to solve all the kids' problems. But he couldn't. I am sure he felt Jack's death was a failure for him."

The next morning Hugh Culverhouse, representing the NFL Management Council, and Gene Upshaw, the NFL Players Association executive director, had an 8:30 appointment with the commissioner to finalize a new four-year collective bargaining agreement.

When Rozelle opened the door to the suite, both men recoiled in shock. "He was as pale as a ghost," Upshaw would later tell Tagliabue. "Tears were streaming down his face. All he said was, 'I can't talk. My stepson is dead.'"

The Super Bowl was just a day away. Carrie flew back to Los Angeles. Nothing was announced. That night Joe Montana drove the 49ers ninety-two yards in three minutes to beat the Bengals.

Rozelle presented the postgame trophy. The millions watching on television and the Niners' players, coaches, and front-office personnel had no idea of the pain he had gone through since Friday night.

There was little joy left in being commissioner for him. Paul Tagliabue, his eventual successor, recalls having dinner with Carrie and Pete and Tagliabue's wife, Chan:

> It was 1986 or '87, and all of a sudden he said, "You did a hell of a job over the years. There is no way we would be where we are today without you. I want you to know I appreciate it." And then he turned to Chan and he added, "I know you had hell to pay as much as he was away working, and you trying to raise a few kids. Believe me, I know that's tough."
>
> Then Carrie inserted herself into our conversation. She said, "I tell Pete many times that you did so much, you should have his position when the time comes," and Pete says, "We didn't come here to talk about this, but what Carrie said has a lot of truth to it."
>
> I don't know whether she put the idea in his head, but on a couple of occasions later he said right after his retirement that he hoped this [selecting the new commissioner] would work out the way he wanted it to work out.
>
> I'm telling you this because I believe with all he had been through, he was now thinking about retirement, and Carrie, who wanted that, seemed to be telling him, "The guy is sitting right here, so why are you waiting?"

It was just before a regular league meeting in March 1989 in Palm Desert, California, that the commissioner finally acted on a decision that had been percolating in the back roads of his mind since October. He had already spoken about it with Wellington Mara and Leon Hess and given them a heads-up after pledging them to secrecy. Now he told Tagliabue. "I am going to announce my retirement today," he said as they were prepping for the formal league meeting. "I don't want this repeated until I do it, but I want to be sure you are there because I want someone there taking clear notes as to what I am going to say."

He had already written a memo to his staff, but would not release it until after the meeting. The memo was typical of him. It was an apology for keeping them in the dark all those months, but he explained that he did not want a full season as a lame-duck commissioner because there were things that had to be done. "I wanted everything solved on a high note with no outstanding litigation," he would say. "But eventually I just realized this job cannot be like that anymore. There is always going to be something."

He had closed as many loose ends as he could while never even hinting at retirement to anyone on his staff. Nobody even suspected. He would announce his decision in March and stay until a successor had been found in October.

He and Carrie had already decided that when the time came, they would move to California. The key reason was their friendship with Gene Klein and his wife, Joyce. Klein, who owned the San Diego Chargers, also shared a love of horse racing with the commissioner in transit. His brilliant filly Winning Colors had won the Kentucky Derby. He was instrumental in the building of Rancho Santa Fe, home to the wealthiest home owners in San Diego County.

Klein sold him a choice lot for what was said to be seven hundred thousand dollars, overlooking his thoroughbred training center. Carrie would drive to California, move into rental property, and have the new house built to her specs. Carrie headed for Rancho Santa Fe in July 1989, and Pete, with a new commissioner in the job, would join her in November.

After the home was built, the plan was to travel extensively with the Kleins, who had become their best friends. But a year after the move, as the two couples were preparing to vacation on a Pacific island, Klein died of a heart attack. Now a widow, Joyce would move away.

The very reason they had chosen their retirement locale had disappeared. Some (including Rozelle's friend Bob Tisch) said that from a health standpoint, Rozelle would have done better staying in the East. But all of that was in the future.

Now, at the meeting in March 1989, the most powerful people in all of pro football sat in stunned disbelief while the man who had risen from "commissioner by accident" to the role of "lord high innovator and problem solver" delivered his totally unexpected valedictory. The best way to describe their reaction was a kind of shock and awe—shock that the moment had actually arrived and awe at their realization of what his stewardship had meant.

The brief announcement rocked the room. His tears as he exited were real. As he made his way toward the exit, he received a standing ovation. The owners generally sat in the same seats at each league meeting. Davis always sat in the back on the left-hand side.

Pete left through the door on the left. There are varied accounts of the instant when he walked past Davis. There are those who talk about Davis's rush to embrace him.

This is what actually happened, according to Joe Browne, who was there. "He did leave on the side where Davis, Mike Brown [Bengals], and Tom Benson [Saints] sat. They all shook his hand as he passed by. He was crying. Davis did not embrace him."

The emotionally bloody, pressure-filled battles were over. Soon, the owners would decide between Tagliabue, the trusted legal counselor, and Jim Finks, the former player and general manager, as the new commissioner. Rozelle would settle into his new role as consultant. There were no more wars to fight. Or so he thought.

Before the year ended, he would take yet another emotional hit that would jolt him to the core. It would come from the man who had been one of his best friends . . . the man who hired him as a kid at Compton Junior College to put out the Rams' preseason programs . . . the man whom he helped get the general manager's job at the newly minted Dallas Cowboys . . . the man who had been his presenter when he was inducted into the Pro Football Hall of Fame.

This least expected last battle was joined shortly after Jerry Jones, the new owner, had fired Tom Landry as coach and was about to do the same to Tex Schramm, the Dallas Cowboys' general manager. "Ever since we had won the USFL trial," Tagliabue

recalled, "Pete had been thinking about whether the USFL would have been viable had it stayed in the spring. He told me, 'I'm not all that hot on the idea, but some smart people say spring football could survive on the right scale. Maybe we should do it as a kind of development league.'"

A month before Jones was about to fire Schramm, Rozelle offered him a job as the president and commissioner of a development league that would be called the World League of American Football. Some of its franchises would be in Europe and one in Canada; others would be in those American cities he could test as potential NFL franchises of the future. Since he was going to launch the league in any event, it would give Schramm a face-saving job at a reasonable salary.

Pete saw it as a venture wholly owned by the NFL with Schramm in charge, and the former Cowboy general manager accepted on those terms. But then Pete got a strange telephone call from him. "I've got a little different plan than we discussed," Schramm said. "It's better for everyone. You are going to love it. Come on down to Washington and meet me."

"I don't think I like what I'm smelling here," Rozelle told Tagliabue. "I want you to fly down there with me."

They met at 5:30 p.m. in the bar of the Willard Hotel. Sitting next to Tex was a venture capitalist from Austin, Texas, named Richard Rainwater, who had his own plan.

"This is great," Tex said. "Rainwater puts up all the money and sells off thirty teams at ten million each, and I get 15 percent equity, and the NFL puts up the players and no money and becomes a minority owner . . . no money down by the NFL . . . a great deal for everybody. Am I right or am I right?"

The more Tex talked, the hotter Rozelle got. After an hour Rozelle was steaming, but he kept his poker face, and he told Schramm, "I'd like to sleep on this. Let's say you come to my suite tomorrow at 8:00 a.m. for breakfast, and we'll talk it over. And, Tex, you come alone."

The next morning Tex walked into the suite, and he was rub-

bing his hands together, and he said, "Hell of an idea, Pete. What do you think?"

And Rozelle, who rarely cursed, let loose a barrage for the ages: "You fuckin' son of a bitch. Who the fuck do you think you are? You're a fuckin' idiot! For twenty-five years you and I are working for this league, and you work out a deal where you are going to make millions, and this Texas asshole is going to own the thing and the league gets minority interest, and you expect me to go back and tell that to twenty-eight owners who are going to put up all the players? You go down to that bar and tell your Texas friend there's no deal."

And when Rozelle finally took a breath, Schramm shot back, "You don't want to do it? Fine. We don't need you. We'll do it on our own."

Rozelle was livid. He was yelling now and told Schramm, "No you won't. Just the fact that you can bring the NFL this fucked-up deal and then look me in the eye and tell me you will do it on your own . . . well . . . here's what you are really going to do on your own. You are going down to that bar, and you will tell your friend he's out. Forty years together in the trenches, and you dare to pull this crap on me."

To save his new job, Schramm went down to the bar and told Richard Rainwater that the deal was dead. But it was only a temporary reprieve. In Rozelle's eyes, Schramm had betrayed him. He said as much later to Dan Rooney, one of the owners who would oversee the new league. Rooney waited until Pete left for California, and then he fired Schramm, replacing him with Mike Lynn, a vice president of the Minnesota Vikings.

Indicative of how furious Rozelle was, Joe Browne, who saw him just about every day after Joe was promoted out of the mailroom, said he could recall only two times in all those years when he heard Pete raise his voice in rage. He and Schramm made up before Rozelle's death, but it was never quite the same between them. As Anne Marie said when she heard the story, "You can make up, but deep down in your heart you don't forget something like that."

So now the days until departure time were dwindling to a precious few. One of those who wanted to say good-bye and thanks was a man in a similar position. His name was David Stern, and, as commissioner of the NBA, he had learned from Rozelle's example. With that model, Stern had saved his league from being consigned forever to the limbo of cable television. Stern said:

He is held up as the paragon of what a commissioner must be in the modern world, and I think those who say that are absolutely right. He taught us how to use television and how to get the most out of sponsors. NFL Properties led the way for NBA Properties, and both of us led the way for the other sports.

He had the experience, and I had the legal background, and we constantly shared views. I wanted him to know how much I appreciated him, so I took him out for a farewell lunch.

I told him that one day I would be planning my own exit, and I wanted to know exactly how he felt. And now that the time had come for him, I asked him how badly he wanted to leave.

"I can answer that," he said, "with a joke I once heard. It pretty well sums it up for me. There was this girl who always wanted to play comedy in the movies, and she met this producer who told her he could help if she slept with him. So she did, and the next day he called back to her that now she had to sleep with the director. So she did that too and got the job.

"Then she went on location to a little village outside of Calcutta, and the guy in charge of the trailers told her he only had one with air conditioning, but she could have it if she slept with him. So she did.

"That night she had dinner in the filthiest place in which she had ever eaten. As she lay on her bed in the violent throes of ptomaine poisoning, she called her agent back in Los Angeles and weakly croaked into the telephone, 'Now who do I have to sleep with to get the hell out of here?'"

Pete laughed and then he said: "That's exactly how I feel."

Clearly, it was movin' time.

18

Death Be Not Proud

A man's real life is that accorded to him in the thoughts of other men by reason and respect.
—Joseph Conrad

Reputation is what people think you are, and your character is what you really are.
—Pete Rozelle, recalling what one of his high school coaches taught him and he never forgot

On November 5, 1989, Paul Tagliabue took over as commissioner of the National Football League. As promised, Pete Rozelle had stayed on in New York during the selection process that had narrowed down to Jim Finks and Tagliabue and was privately pleased with the choice.

His respect for Tagliabue had been heightened three years earlier, just before the start of the USFL trial. He had always respected the lawyer's intellectual and legal abilities. Now he had an important personal reason to admire Tagliabue's willingness to fight for a principle—one that influenced his own conviction that Tagliabue should be his successor.

Rozelle's integrity had been personally challenged by the pretrial ramblings of Howard Cosell and Donald Trump. To him, those charges had crossed the line, and now he was more than ready to fight. But not everyone else was.

Shortly before the annual spring meeting that year (1986), Jay Moyer, Rozelle's in-house counsel, had taken Bob Fiske to dinner. Fiske, a respected New York lawyer, had been hired specifically

for the USFL case, and he shocked Moyer (in Moyer's own words) when he suggested that the NFL should settle and not go to trial.

"I couldn't blame Bob," Moyer said, "because he was doing what he thought was best to protect Wellington Mara and people like that. He thought they could be destroyed if the trial went badly. But Pete and Paul and I did not agree with him.

"We had an owners' meeting, and Norman Braman [Eagles] asked Bob what he thought we should do, and when he said we should consider settling, I elbowed Paul and said he better speak up right now, and that's what he did."

Tagliabue said he told Braman that "the USFL suit was full of holes and that a jury was very likely to see through their claim, and, therefore, it was far too early to settle."

But afterward, in private, he told Rozelle what he really thought. He said that he "would have to be crazy to settle; that personally, he wouldn't settle on any basis whatsoever."

You could make a strong case that in that moment Rozelle, who had begun to think of retiring, knew exactly who it was that should succeed him. Three years later, when a selection committee chose Tagliabue, Rozelle was delighted. He was convinced he was leaving the league's unfinished business to someone he trusted to finish the job the way he would have wanted it done.

When Pete left in November Carrie was already in California, planning the new home. She was spending a lot of time with the Kleins, who had become their closest friends in Southern California. Beyond their friendship Klein had been Rozelle's constant ally in his consistently abrasive relationship with Al Davis. Klein himself had his own high-profile battles with Davis.

At one point he actually sued Davis, claiming that the Raiders' owner's inclusion of him in a suit against the league was vindictive, without merit, and triggered his first heart attack. Incredibly, he actually won that case initially but lost it on appeal.

Klein, whose initial income came from a highly successful used-car dealership, had become Rozelle's racetrack buddy. As president and chairman of the board, he turned National General Corpora-

tion into a major financial player. An avid sports fan, he headed the group that brought the NBA to Seattle and bought the San Diego Chargers from Barron Hilton.

His shared passion with Rozelle for race horses was what brought them together socially. After he sold the Chargers in 1984, he hired Hall of Fame trainer D. Wayne Lukas, and together they won the Preakness, the Kentucky Derby, and seven Breeders' Cup championships.

Rozelle had been a fan of the racetracks for a long time. When Jack Landry, perhaps his closest friend, had put together the proposal for a New York stakes race to be called the Marlboro Cup, he and Rozelle visited Penny Chenery Tweedy at her summer home up in Saratoga to try to convince her to turn the first one into a match race between her two great horses, Riva Ridge and Secretariat.

Rozelle loved to tell the story of the day Secretariat ran the greatest Belmont Stakes in history: "As he turned for home, I knew I was looking at greatness. I was totally focused on him. I was yelling and jumping up and down, and I felt a hand on my leg. I looked down and realized it was someone trying to steady me because in my excitement I had jumped on top of a table."

"To this day," he later told the writer Bill Nack, "I have absolutely no recollection how I got there."

The retirement home of Pete and Carrie Rozelle was on a choice piece of property at Rancho Santa Fe, overlooking the Del Mar Training Center that Klein had built.

"They had built a kind of kitchen area facing the track," Lukas told me, "and I could look up there and see him watching the horses during their morning works."

He had an office on our grounds. Sometimes he would walk down the hill, and we would talk.

He was an interesting guy. Usually when an outsider comes up to you, he will ask you something like, "Who do you like in the third race at Delmar?" but not Pete. He never once did that. I don't recall

him as any kind of bettor at all. Instead, he wanted to know how you decide where to place a horse . . . why you move him up from six furlongs to, say, a mile. . . . What was the theory when you stretched him out? He had a very analytical mind, and he was intellectually curious. He was a hell of a guy.

With all their common interests, the Rozelles and the Kleins shared an active social life. They were, in fact, planning a trip to the South Pacific when Klein suffered his third heart attack and died in the spring of 1990, just four months after Pete had joined Carrie at Rancho Santa Fe.

And then Pete and Carrie were diagnosed with brain tumors almost simultaneously. They were told that hers was malignant and his benign, prompting him to say in an interview, "I look at her, and I love her so much I wish mine were the one that is malignant."

"After his initial surgery," Moyer said, "he came back to New York to visit, and I couldn't believe my eyes. The tumor was benign. He was tanned. The bags under his eyes were gone. I thought, 'My God, he has turned back the clock fifteen years.' Ironically, although her tumor had been diagnosed as malignant, she would outlive him by a number of years."

Meanwhile, back in New York, Thelma Elkjer was still running a kind of "Rozelle-in-exile command post." There was a permanent office waiting for her on the West Coast at the edge of the Delmar Training Center, but her dog was too sick to travel, and she would not leave him. She continued to handle all of Rozelle's correspondence and appointments. There was plenty to do. He had invested in a housing project in Coeur d'Alene, Idaho, with the man who had built the Rancho Santa Fe home, and he often consulted on league matters with Tagliabue.

Her job had not diminished. Neither had her influence.

Back when Tagliabue and Jim Finks were competing for Rozelle's job, Thelma was no fan of Finks. When he called to speak to Rozelle, the guardian of access to the commissioner would invariably transfer him to Don Weiss, an aide de camp. In his book *The*

Making of the Super Bowl, Weiss tells of one such time when Finks didn't even bother to identify himself when he heard Weiss's voice. He simply said, "I guess the damned dog is still alive."

Nor did the newly minted successor to Rozelle have much more success with her. "I had this idea," Tagliabue explained, "that I wanted to decorate the hall with pictures of the league's founding fathers and patriarchs—you know, Halas . . . Thorpe . . . Rooney . . . Mara, but Thelma stopped the guy from doing it."

The man who had now risen to the most powerful position in the NFL, and possibly all of sports, explained to the secretary of the man who was no longer even in the building, "Well, these are the pioneers, Thelma. They are the men that made the league happen."

She simply replied, "Not a good idea. If you want to do it," said the lady who had refused to let Rozelle put his own stuffed fish on her office wall, "then so will someone else."

Tagliabue laughed when he told the story and then said with a hint of awe, "I actually had to wait until she moved to California."

In the early days of his retirement, Rozelle remained active. He also never lost his sense of concern for others. During a hospital visit he was introduced to an octogenarian and asked him, "Do you know who I am?" The fellow responded, "Of course I do. You are Paul Tagliabue, commissioner of the National Football League." Rozelle immediately grinned and said, "That's right."

When a doctor tried to correct the man, Rozelle shook him off.

Eventually, the time finally came when Thelma prepared to join her old boss. She had a fear of flying, so Anne Marie was recruited to serve as her companion on a chartered flight along with Elkjer's cats. Once in Rancho Santa Fe, she bought a car, found an apartment nearby, and set up shop in Rozelle's little office.

Rozelle's condition had worsened even as Carrie's had improved. He was diagnosed with another brain tumor. This one was malignant. By January 1996 he had begun to fail.

The Super Bowl that year would be played in Tempe, Arizona. At that time there remained six writers and five photographers who had covered every one. It was Weiss's idea to set up a confer-

ence call between them and Rozelle. For all of them it would be a chance to offer their final farewells. We were at kickoff minus forty-eight hours when Rozelle's voice came over the speaker.

It was weaker than we remembered but stronger than we expected. He spoke to us one at a time, and as he was told a name it would trigger a flood of memories for him. With each of us, he would bring a shared moment for which the common denominator was laughter. Each anecdote was laced with the intense power of affection.

We had come to the time expecting to console an old friend, but just as he had always seemed to do during the tough debates with us in more vibrant times, he had turned the situation completely around.

It was the way he wanted it. He knew that while the telephone conversation would limit us to audio, it also afforded us the gift of supplying our own video, enabling each of us to remember him as tanned and still boyish, with a look in his eyes that reminded you his ubiquitous laughter was always just a beat away.

The image of that evening remains evergreen even today. It gave each of us a small but significant victory over death's obscene technique. The last thing he said was, "I wish I could be there with you guys tonight. Don't forget to have a drink on me."

There was total silence after the connection was broken, and then somebody symbolically raised his glass and the others followed. We knew we would probably never hear his voice again, but to these friends and writers who knew him better than anybody else in this business, the message was clear: "Raise the glass. Sing no sad songs for me. We had us some times, didn't we?"

As summer stretched out toward autumn and the end of his fight grew more obvious, Thelma became the traffic cop for the steady stream of old friends who made the trip to see him one last time. Myer recalled:

I had spoken to him on the telephone in September, and he was slurring his words so badly. He was saying the right things, but he was

having great difficulty articulating them. I was so shocked that I called Thelma and asked to know what was happening here. She told me the cancer had come back, and it was multiplying rapidly.

The next time she called she said, "I know you want to see him, and he wants to see you, so you better get to it soon." That same day we made arrangements to fly to San Diego. We spent a day there with him. He was fine cognitively, but physically he was gone. He couldn't walk by himself. He was speaking in a whisper and slurring his words. But everything he said made perfect sense.

The last thing he said was, "We had a hell of a run, didn't we?" and I said, "Yeah, Pete, but it was your run, and we were just there to help." And then he looked at me, and he said, "Remember, the best things in life are family and friends. Please take care of [your wife] Terry."

For Joe Browne, it was much the same:

I was in Los Angeles, and I had to go to San Francisco next, but Paul [Tagliabue] said you better not wait. So I drove down there the next day. He was in his den. Three TVs were going with football, and there was an ashtray with a cigarette burning in front of each of them the way he had always done.

I knew the end was close, so I did most of the talking, and he'd say, "Is that right? Is that right?"

He did a lot of nodding. He looked very pale and bloated from the medicine. He recognized me, but he had nothing to say. I was there for about an hour.

For Tagliabue, the last visit held no surprises.

I had lunch with him a few times that year and dinner at least once, and we had seen him back in January when we talked about the league. My wife and Carrie talked about personal stuff, but Pete and I talked about football.

The last time I saw him was in California not long before he died. He was so sick. I remember that afterward I made some notes because I wanted always to remember the visit, and then I went back over them and changed the word "said" to "whispered." He could barely speak.

Time was rapidly melting away, but Anne Marie will always remember those final months for two surprising but dramatically poignant moments. The first would link her even closer to Thelma Elkjer.

There had been a moment more than two decades earlier when her father decided to take Anne Marie with him to a league meeting in Miami Beach. This was not uncommon for him, and in the past various owners' wives would share the role of babysitter. But as she recalled, this was going to be a particularly sensitive meeting, and he didn't want to involve them with her.

He asked Thelma to make the trip and look out for his teenage daughter.

"For her," Anne Marie said, "this was a huge, huge deal."

I remember that she asked me if I would go shopping with her. We were staying at the Kenilworth Hotel in Miami Beach, and we went across the street to the Bal Harbour mall, and she bought her first-ever bathing suit—a yellow one-piece.

We had this gigantic suite with three separate bedrooms for us, and every night we would change into our pajamas and bathrobes, and we'd have a nightcap and then go to bed.

I remember that one night I was coming out of my room to join them, and they were on the terrace. She was wearing this long peignoir. They had a drink in their hands, and they were looking at the view and talking, and I looked at Thelma and saw her face, and I suddenly was struck with the thought, "Wow, she has a romantic interest in him!"

We had always wondered why she never had a boyfriend or a husband. My dad's theory was that maybe she had been married and he had been killed in the war.

I believe that time in Miami Beach was one of the best weekends she ever had in her life. I know she took one vacation when she went to Denmark, where her family originally came from, but I think that was the only vacation she ever had.

She worked five days a week for my dad in New York, sometimes

as late as nine at night, and then I was there in her apartment so many weekends as a kid. She always seemed to be there for me from the time I was born.

I think about when she moved here. She was seventy years old, and she never drove a car in her entire life, but she bought one and got her driver's license, and they worked in that office at the bottom of the hill.

When Rozelle became bedridden in the final month of his life, Thelma came up the hill from the office and to the house regularly. Anne Marie, who like her father had worked in public relations, was now married with her own family in Fort Worth, Texas. But Thelma told her it was time to come. Anne Marie knew that if Thelma said it, she would be on her way.

"I slept on the floor next to his bed until the end," Anne Marie said. "His mind was so strong and his body was so weak, and I remember I thought that, because of that, it was so unfair for him to be watching himself die."

During those final months, Carrie and Thelma were not in the same room very often. They did not like each other much. Anne Marie thought it might have been because Carrie suspected that Thelma was in love with him.

"Thelma was there every day now," Anne Marie said, "and she'd give him reports like, 'I know you'd want to know that so-and-so called today,' or 'Mr. Tagliabue wants you to know such-and-such.'"

He could barely speak by then, and then one day she came in and walked upstairs to where Dad and I were, and she said to me, "I really have to speak to your father in private, and I don't want other people coming in," and I told her I understood, and I started to back out and close the door. But she said, "No, don't go. I want you to hear this."

I can't recall it exactly word for word, but while I stood there she told him how important he was to her. She said something like he was a great man and meant so much to her, and then I clearly remember she added: "I have given you more than forty years of my life, and I have always really loved you."

He tried to speak, and his voice was barely audible, and, very weakly, he said, "Thelma . . . Thelma . . . Thelma."

And I thought how hard it must have been for this woman to endure all the women he dated. I thought how she came here to him at seventy in the middle of nowhere and how hard it must have been for her, and she did it all for him. Even after that, I can't ever remember her calling him anything but Mr. Rozelle.

Time was rapidly running out for him, and he knew it. So did his stepson Philip, who was on a mission of his own. He had designated himself to protect the interests of his mother, his surviving brother, and his sister.

He sent a barrage of e-mails to Pete, Anne Marie said, and he dropped by to visit him. He wanted him to turn over power of attorney. Rozelle did not answer his e-mails. He ignored the requests on the visit. He never forgot the Cornell failure. Philip had disappointed him terribly in life. He wasn't going to give him the opportunity to fail him again, this time when he was near death.

"The hospice people say that sometimes the body is ready to die, but something they feel they need to do keeps them alive until they get it done," Anne Marie said. She is convinced that it was that way with her father:

Philip came downstairs one day, and he said, "You won't believe it. It's almost like your father is coming back to life."

So I go upstairs and Dad is very agitated. He locks his eyes on me and he is staring very hard, and I ask what is it, and then he turns his head and locks them in on Philip, who is standing next to me. Then he does the whole thing all over again—twice more—and I understand he is trying to tell me something about Philip. The side of his hospital bed is up, and he grips it and with tremendous effort pulls himself until he's almost sitting up.

Then he stares at me again and turns back to Philip and gives him the finger, and I understand what he's doing. He is saying, "Don't trust this man."

He died within twenty-four hours, on December 6. And he was right, of course, because Philip engineered a family suit over the will. It held the estate settlement up for a long time.

He had left Thelma some money, but the case was tied up for so long that she died before it was settled, and the money went to her brother and sister.

The funeral, as Rozelle requested, was private, with burial in El Camino Park, San Diego. He also made two other requests that were typical of him. Because he knew there were so many on the East Coast who would want to be there, he requested the family hold two separate memorials so as not to put a travel burden on them. He also asked that they be held after Christmas so as not interfere with the plans of his friends' families.

The first was held more than a month after his death in a hotel ballroom in Beverly Hills, California. The East Coast memorial was the following week at the Fifth Avenue Presbyterian Church in Manhattan. The Loyola University choir sang his favorite song, "Try to Remember," at the West Coast memorial, whose speakers included Frank Gifford, Jack Kemp, Don Klosterman, and lifelong friend John Lehman. At the East Coast memorial, the speakers were Wellington Mara, Roone Arledge, Joe Browne, Herb Siegel, Frank Gifford, and Paul Tagliabue. Anne Marie Rozelle Bratton spoke at both.

Her speeches were a kind of genetic reflection of the man they had come to honor, turning the mourners into celebrants on both occasions. She spoke of how her father—a single dad for almost all of her youth—rode with her eleven straight times on the "Small, Small World" ride, how he danced with her "on two left feet," how they hid the food her nanny cooked because they didn't want to hurt her feelings and then sneaked out for hamburgers.

"He never missed a father-daughter dance, a birthday, or a graduation," she told them, "and he never broke a promise."

Perhaps her best anecdote was about Talking Barbie, the doll she wanted for Christmas. Every store was sold out. "Then Dad went to every black market source he could find, and on Christ-

mas morning, there it was under the tree. I ran to it and pulled the string, and it said, 'Buenos dias. Donde esta Ken?'"

It broke up the audience.

"After I finished my eulogy at the Beverly Hills memorial," Anne Marie recalled,

I was momentarily blinded by flashbulbs, and I could feel someone was grabbing my hand. There were photographers everywhere, and then my vision cleared, and I looked down and Al Davis was gripping it. He looked up at me and said, "I revered your father."

I can't believe this is happening at my dad's memorial. There are cameras everywhere, and here I am with my father's nemesis, and he is making it a photo op. I was upset, but then I took a deep breath and I did exactly what I thought my dad would have wanted.

I looked at him and put a smile on my face.

She was, in that instant, every inch the commissioner's daughter.

List of Interviews

Ernie Accorsi, employee of Rozelle, Rosenbloom, and Modell
Ron Borges, sportswriter and former Oakland beat writer
Gil Brandt, Cowboys scout, personnel man, and key NFL "babysitter" in the war between leagues
Anne Marie (Rozelle) Bratton, Pete Rozelle's daughter
Joe Browne, former NFL communications chief and current government affairs specialist for the NFL
Bill Cunningham, on Lynwood memories of Rozelle's youth
Al Davis
Myron De Long
David Dixon, helped build Superdome and bring NFL to New Orleans
Marc Duncan, early Rozelle hire as NFL supervisor of officials
Thelma Elkjer, Rozelle secretary
Larry Felzer
Pete Finney, New Orleans columnist
Larry Fleisher
Jim Gallagher, former Eagles GM
Frank Gifford, Giants player and friend of Rozelle
Shep Goldfein, lawyer in USFL case
Dr. Bob Goldman, author and internationally recognized expert on illegal use of steroids in sports
Bill Granholm, Rams equipment man and NFL employee
Jerry Greene, *Detroit News* writer, covered every Super Bowl
Peter Hadhazy, former Rozelle and USFL employee
George Halas, owner of the Chicago Bears
Jim Hamilton
Doug Hart
Mickey Herskowitz, Houston columnist and former AFL and NFL employee
Paul Hornung, Green Bay Packer all-pro
Jim Lee Howell
Lamar Hunt, AFL founder and Kansas City Chiefs owner
Jim Kensil, NFL publicist and New York Jets president
Gene Kilroy, former Philadelphia Eagles marketing director

Don Klosterman, boyhood friend of Rozelle, Loyola-SF rival, pro football exec

Vince Lombardi

D. Wayne Lukas, thoroughbred horse trainer and friend of Pete Rozelle

Jerry Magee, former San Diego Chargers beat writer

John Mara, co-owner of the New York Football Giants

Tim Mara, Wellington's nephew and co-owner of the Giants

Wellington Mara, Giants owner and Rozelle ally

Art Modell, owner of the Browns, then Ravens

Jay Moyer, Rozelle's in-house counselor

Dave Newhouse, retired *Oakland Tribune* columnist

Murray Olderman, sportswriter, author, and cartoonist

Jose Ortiz, on Lynwood and Compton

Bernie Parrish

Edwin Pope, *Miami Herald* writer, covered every Super Bowl

Eddie Robinson

Dan Rooney, former Steelers president and ambassador to Ireland

Carroll Rosenbloom, owner of the Colts and Rams

Harold Rosenthal

Pete Rozelle, interviewed regularly and often privately over thirty-five years

Ray Rozelle, Pete's father

Blair Sabol, daughter of Ed, NFL Films founder

Ed Sabol, founder of NFL Films

Steve Sabol, president of NFL Films

George Sauer Sr.

Tex Schramm

Blackie Sherrod

Herb Siegel, Rozelle's close personal friend for years

Mo Siegel

Seymour Siwoff

David Stern

Scotty Stirling, former Raiders GM

Pat Sumerall, player, TV announcer, and close friend to Rozelle

Paul Tagliabue, former NFL commissioner and Rozelle's close friend

John Unitas

Wayne Valley

Pete Waldmeir, former *Detroit News* columnist

Lloyd Wells

Sonny Werblin

Buddy Young

George Young, installed as Giants GM during Mara-versus-Mara feud

Gertrude Young

Notes

33 **"We went to preseason camp":** Interview with Granholm.

34 **"I do wonder what really might have":** Interview with Rozelle.

35 **"I wasn't all that serious":** Interview with De Long.

35 **"It was," Rozelle confirmed:** Interview with Rozelle.

36 **"I think it was on a Monday":** Interview with Ray Rozelle.

37 **"I don't think I would ever tell him":** Interview with Ray Rozelle.

39 **"You can laugh if you want":** Interview with Mark Duncan.

40 **"But Gilman had a friend":** Interview with Granholm.

41 **When Rozelle ignored the request:** Interview with Rozelle.

41 **"I think in a way":** Interview with Granholm.

42 **"Everything he did really prepared him":** Interview with De Long.

3. THE ACCIDENTAL CORONATION

47 **There are two schools of thought:** Interview with Ernie Accorsi.

47 **On the twentieth ballot:** Interview with Accorsi.

48 **"I know him":** Interview with Rozelle.

48 **"This will never end":** Interview with Wellington Mara.

49 **Mara, eager to end this marathon:** Interview with Dan Rooney.

49 **"It was a mistake":** Interview with Carroll Rosenbloom.

49 **But back then Rosenbloom was eager:** Interview with Rosenbloom.

50 **Reassured by Reeves's promise of neutrality:** Interview with Rozelle.

50 **"I heard it on the radio":** Interview with De Long.

51 **"I'm going to move the league":** Interview with Rozelle.

51 **On the day he moved the operation:** Interview with Rozelle.

4. THE BOY WONDER TAKES CENTER STAGE

52 **Yet, ironically, at the end of the 1959 season:** Events confirmed by *Sports Illustrated* profile of Walter Wolfner, April 4, 1960.

54 **"Hail to the Redskins":** Interview with Mo Siegel.

55 **"No son of a bitch who steals":** Interview with Rozelle.

55 **Their reluctant choice of commissioner:** Interview with Rosenbloom.

59 **At one point every league official:** Interview with Accorsi.

59 **"He had an ability to attract good people":** Interview with Accorsi.

60 **It was, indeed, an interview:** Interview with Jim Kensil.

61 **He conceived of a package:** Interview with Mara.

5. HOW DO YOU TELL VINCE?

63 **In addition, his television contacts:** Interview with Sonny Werblin.

64 **"You are made to feel special":** Jerry Izenberg, *The Rivals* (New York: Simon and Flynn, 1968).

65 **Alvin Paris, a man who left no other:** Interview with Mara.

66 **Shortly after three on that Saturday:** Interview with Mara.

67 **When Unitas was challenged:** Told to reporters in the postgame dressing room and verified by former Colts GM Ernie Accorsi.

67 **On January 3, 1961:** Halas's request told to me in a background interview in Rozelle's office.

68 **In 1956 Hornung, a Notre Dame senior:** Interview with Paul Hornung.

68 **By the summer of 1959:** Interview with Jim Hamilton.

69 **His public relations instincts told him:** Interview with Rozelle.

70 **"I knew the Packers were not":** Interview with Rozelle.

71 **But more important, the Karras issue:** Interview with Pete Waldmeir.

71 **"They would walk across an alley":** Interview with Waldmeir.

74 **"I remember," Rozelle said, "that I watched him read it":** Interview with Rozelle.

75 **"I felt the first thing I wanted to do":** Interview with Rozelle.

76 **After he called Hornung and Karris:** Interview with Rozelle.

77 **the keys on the office TWX machine:** Interview with Mara.

78 **But I have another theory:** Interview with Jerry Greene.

79 **Karras remained as volatile as ever:** Interview with Waldmeir.

80 **"Mr. Karras," the referee said:** Interview with Waldmeir.

80 **The week that his hiring was announced:** Interview with Jim Hamilton.

6. HEADS THEY WIN, TAILS HE LOSES

83 **In Cleveland, Browns owner Art Modell:** Interview with Art Modell.

84 **Salinger seemed to speak:** Interview with Rozelle.

84 **The emotions and the events of the day:** Interview with Modell.

85 **Modell said that in Cleveland:** Interview with Modell.

86 **It was on that day and still is:** Interview with Frank Gifford.

87 **"It was odd that we never":** Interview with John Mara.

88 **"In 1989 when he was leaving":** Interview with Joe Browne.

7. THE 100-YARD ARMAGEDDON

90 **As an aside Tim Mara:** Interview with Mara.

91 **The teenage Wellington replied:** Interview with Mara.

92 **"There probably wouldn't have been":** Sam Corovano, first league meeting, June 1944.

92 **Dan Topping, owner of the NFL Yankees:** *Scrapbook History of Pro Football* (Indianapolis: Bobbs-Merrill, 1976).

93 **Before it was over:** *New York Times*, December 9, 1949.

94 **Davey O'Brien, who had been:** Ed Gruver, *The American Football League: A Year by Year History*, 1960-69 (Jefferson NC: McFarland, 1997).

94 **Hunt believed that demographics:** Interview with Lamar Hunt.

94 **Hunt went home and began calling:** Interview with Hunt.

95 **"There is no longer cause to worry":** Gruver, *American Football League*.

95 **Ralph Wilson, a wealthy insurance man:** Interview with Larry Felzer.

95 **"Those meetings were nothing like":** Interview with Rozelle.

100 **"I wasn't sure how the case was going":** Interview with Jim Lee Howell.

104 **"I think the Flowers signing":** Interview with Rozelle.

8. SEX, LIES, AND BRINGING UP BABY

131 **Scotty Stirling, who had replaced Davis:** Interview with Scotty Stirling.

132 **I knew this last because:** Interview with Stirling.

132 **"I know Al was upset":** Interview with Rozelle.

132 **"No," Rozelle insisted, "because here":** Interview with Rozelle.

133 **"Listen," Schramm said:** Interview with Tex Schramm.

135 **"It was bad luck for Al":** Interview with Herskowitz.

135 **At three on the morning of June 7:** Interview with Rozelle.

136 **Schramm and Rozelle met at what was then:** Interview with Rozelle.

137 **In midafternoon Herskowitz called me:** Telephone conversation with Herskowitz.

139 **"I was in the next office":** Interview with Herskowitz.

139 **Above the raucous voices:** Interview with Herskowitz.

139 **"Mickey, I hope someday, someplace":** Interview with Herskowitz.

10. BRINGING IN THE SHEAVES

141 **"When I was a junior":** *Pro Football's Shotgun Wedding* (ABC Television Network, 1969).

144 **"This would allow us to implement":** Rozelle press conference.

145 **"I didn't know him, and I didn't expect":** Interview with David Dixon.

145 **Dixon had been active:** Interview with Finney.

146 **The deal was simple:** Interview with Rozelle.

146 **"I invited Rozelle to my apartment":** Senator Russell Long (D-LA), interview with the *New Orleans Times-Picayune*.

146 **"I spent quite a lot of time":** Interview with Rozelle.

146 **"They are simply poor negotiators":** Representative Emanuel Celler, press conference after NFL hearings.

147 **"I believe it word for word":** Interview with Dixon and David Klack's report to Dixon.

147 **not a single club owner knew about the deal:** Interview with Rozelle.

147 **It began when Celler demanded:** Interview with Finney.

148 **On November 1, 1966:** Interview with Kensil.

149 **The first telephone call:** Interview with Kensil.

149 **And Rozelle ignored both of them:** Interview with Rozelle.

150 **"As long as I am commissioner":** Interview with Rozelle.

151 **But he was—constantly:** Interview with Mara.

152 **Told of Vince's intention:** Interview with Rozelle.

152 **"This is how well organized Pete was":** Interview with Herskowitz.

153 **"In no time we were out of everything":** Interview with Seymour Siwoff.

153 **"I can still recall the way I felt":** Interview with Rozelle.

155 **"It was hard to surprise him":** Interview with Accorsi.

155 **"If there hadn't been a merger":** Interview with Wayne Valley.

156 **"There are certain areas of difficulty":** Interview with Modell.

157 **"If you take three teams":** Interview with Herskowitz.

158 **"I was thinking when we adjourned":** Interview with Rozelle.

158 **That night, on the eve of the final session:** Interview with Modell.

159 **"I told Rooney that morning":** Interview with Mara.

159 **"I know Rosenbloom likes to tell":** Interview with Modell.

160 **And then Pete Rozelle:** Interview with Rozelle.

160 **"Here's the deal," the commissioner said:** Interview with Rozelle.

11. THE FAILED COUPS

163 **"I should like to thank Mr. Rozelle":** Statement issued by the Department of the Interior in announcing the agreement with George Preston Marshall.

164 **"Edward Bennett Williams, who once owned":** John Kole, *Milwaukee Journal*.

165 **"Frankly," Accorsi said, "I don't think you":** Interview with Accorsi.

165 **A case in point was his vitriolic feud:** Interview with Accorsi.

166 **Returning to Baltimore:** Interview with Accorsi.

167 **One person with whom he socialized:** Interview with Herb Siegel.

167 **In the rear there was gambling:** Atlantic City newsletter by Archie Black.

168 **In truth, Wellington Mara once logically speculated:** Interview with Mara.

169 **Because of the growing sensitivity:** Interview with Accorsi.

171 **"There was this squawk box":** Interview with Accorsi.

173 **The owners called for a voice vote:** Interview with Jay Moyer.

173 **"I knew it was going to be a big thing":** Interview with Modell.

173 **"Then he gave this long, rambling speech":** Interview with Mara.

175 **The attorney read aloud:** Interview with Moyer.

12. POWER TO THE TACKLES

177 **In 1947 the Pittsburgh Steelers:** Jerry Izenberg, *Newark Star-Ledger* column.

178 **Eight years later players representing:** Izenberg, *Newark Star-Ledger* column.

178 **The very same year:** Interview with Rosenthal.

178 **And a fellow named Larry Fleisher:** Interview with Larry Fleisher.

179 **no discrimination against players because of:** The Gordy letter.

179 **Moreover, the owners were far ahead:** Interview with Bernie Parrish.

180 **This is what he told me:** Interview with Doug Hart.

181 **For the view from the other end:** Interview with John Unitas.

184 **"They [the owners] got the message":** Ed Garvey in the Associated Press.

187 **Rosenbloom, for example, who would have blamed:** Interview with Rosenbloom.

188 **Meanwhile, Garvey was not idle:** *Washington Post*.

188 **"Who is Pete Rozelle?":** *Sports Illustrated*.

188 **"Is he the neutral guardian":** Interview with Garvey.

188 **But when I asked him about that:** Interview with Rozelle.

189 **It was obvious that there was:** Garvey interview in the *Washington Star*.

189 **Recalling that, Paul Tagliabue:** Interview with Paul Tagliabue.

191 **Then Anderson made a courageous move:** Interview with Dan Rooney.

13. ANOTHER DAY, ANOTHER DRAGON TO SLAY

197 **no less an authority than Vince:** Interview with Lombardi.

198 **Among them was John William DiGiovanni:** Report given by Jack Danahy, NFL security, to Rozelle.

199 **"They're going to knock over":** Anonymous by request.

199 **What Philbin had no way of knowing:** Interview with Rozelle.

200 **They were told that law enforcement people:** Interview with Danahy.

202 **"He came to my apartment":** Interview with Rozelle.

202 **"This is interesting," he told Sabol:** Interview with Steve Sabol.

204 **It was becoming the kind of nightmare:** Interview with Rozelle.

204 **Rozelle called Tim and told him:** Interview with Rozelle.

205 **Back at league headquarters:** Interview with Rozelle.

206 **But there was a time:** Interview with Gifford.

206 **The league's limited licensing procedures:** Interview with Rozelle.

208 **When the owners agreed:** Interview with Ed Sabol.

209 **"He understood even better than we did":** Interview with Ed Sabol.

14. AT WAR WITH THE COUNTERCULTURE

212 **"I was so much younger":** Interview with Blair Sabol.

214 **"It's tough when you're supposed to be the guardian":** Interview with the National Academy of Achievement.

214 **"Read the damned thing":** Interview with George Young.

215 **a man named Houston Ridge:** The 1969 lawsuit against the San Diego Chargers.

216 **A man who was, however, was named Dr. John Ziegler:** Interview with Dr. Bob Goldman.

217 **First, there were doctors out there:** Interview with Goldman.

217 **"I wish to God now":** Interview with Goldman.

218 **swept the playing field:** ESPN, *Outside the Lines*.

218 **"I still remember what the bottle said":** Ron Mix, *Sports Illustrated* interview.

219 **"Upshaw was very good on steroids":** Interview with Moyer.

220 **"We tried to educate the players":** *New York Times* interview.

221 **"I think the league decided":** *San Diego Union-Tribune* interview with Mike Ariey.

221 **"We did pretty well":** Interview with George Young.

223 **Incredibly, he would actually testify:** Trial record, USFL V. NFL, 84 civ. 7484 (1986).

223 **"each man lost a lot":** Interview with Gifford.

223 **"Al Davis . . . don't ask":** Interview with Modell.

223 **"There was a reason":** Interview with John Mara.

223 **"There was no mystery":** Interview with Tagliabue.

224 **"an old-school, tough construction guy":** Interview with Dave Newhouse.

225 **"Well, around that time Pete and I":** Interview with Moyer.

225 **One of those stockholders:** Interview with Newhouse.

226 **"He was told it was imperative":** Interview with Newhouse.

226 **The father was said to have had:** Interview with Moyer.

227 **It was Joe Thomas:** "Lords of the Realm," by John Helyar.

227 **It is interesting to note here:** Interview with Newhouse.

228 **"There was a league meeting":** Interview with Newhouse.

229 **I well remember a night:** Conversation between Davis Rosenbloom, halftime at the Ram-Raiders game in 1979.

230 **"He never would have thought":** Interview with Newhouse.

231 **"I really think that if Al":** Interview with Borges.

235 **"Dooley feigned innocence":** Gordon Forbes in *USA Today* in 1983.

235 **"There are two types":** Joe Stein, ESPN.com.

239 **"Donald was always about Donald":** Carl Peterson quoted in *The USFL: The League the NFL Didn't Respect but Feared.*

240 **"It was around July 4":** Interview with Shep Goldfein.

242 **"We won't do much":** Interview with Goldfein.

243 **"During a brief recess":** Bob Ley, *Outside the Lines,* ESPN.

243 **"I think," Tagliabue recalls:** Interview with Tagliabue.

245 **"Wasn't it your view":** Start and continuation of exchange between Myerson and Rozelle in trial transcript.

247 **Trump claimed that at a private meeting:** Direct examination of Donald Trump, in trial record, binder no. 6, 4051–52.

247 **Browne knew all about those notes:** Interview with Browne.

248 **Trump had testified that Rozelle:** Direct testimony by Rozelle in trial record.

249 **"I think after Pete's testimony":** Interview with Moyer.

250 **"With Trump," Shep Goldfein said:** Interview with Goldfein.

250 **"Mr. Cosell, if I ask you a question":** Cross-examination of Cosell, in trial record, 4483–537.

252 **When he left the stand:** Interview with Goldfein.

252 **"We did what we always did":** Interview with Browne.

252 **Meanwhile, out in Kirtland, Ohio:** Interview with Accorsi.

17. THE FINAL BATTLES

254 "I would be part of some special meetings": Interview with Brandt.

254 "You could almost feel": Interview with Tagliabue.

256 "Why didn't you just go out and dig up Caligula?": Dave Kindred in *Sound and Fury* (New York: Free Press, 2006), 148.

257 "She was an alcoholic": Interview with Anne Marie Rozelle Bratton.

258 "In that PR lifestyle": Interview with Bratton.

258 "It was terrifying": Interview with Bratton.

259 "I met her when my boyfriend": Interview with Blair Sabol.

260 "Philip Morris was a huge": Interview with Bratton.

261 "He loved tennis": Interview with Ed Sabol.

262 "He had such a quick wit": Interview with Blair Sabol.

263 "She lit up the room": Interview with Bratton.

263 "He almost never came to her house": Interview with Bratton.

264 "In the beginning": Interview with Bratton.

265 "I was there with my dad": Interview with Bratton.

265 The next morning Hugh Culverhouse: Interview with Tagliabue.

266 "It was 1986 or '87": Interview with Tagliabue.

266 "I am going to announce": Interview with Tagliabue.

268 "He did leave on the side": Interview with Browne.

268 "Ever since we had won": Interview with Tagliabue.

269 "I don't think I like what I'm smelling": Interview with Tagliabue.

269 "This is great," Tex said: Interview with Tagliabue.

269 The next morning Tex: Interview with Tagliabue.

271 "He is held up as": Interview with David Stern.

18. DEATH BE NOT PROUD

272 Shortly before the annual spring meeting: Interview with Moyer.

273 Tagliabue says he told: Interview with Tagliabue.

274 Rozelle loved to tell the story: Interview with Rozelle.

274 "They had built a kind of kitchen area": Interview with D. Wayne Lukas.

275 "After his initial surgery": Interview with Moyer.

275 Back when Tagliabue and Jim Finks: Don Weiss, *The Making of the Super Bowl* (New York: Contemporary Books, 2003), 329.

276 "I had this idea": Interview with Tagliabue.

277 "I had spoken to him": Interview with Moyer.

278 "I was in Los Angeles": Interview with Browne.

278 "I had lunch with him": Interview with Tagliabue.

279 "For her," Anne Marie said: Interview with Bratton.

280 "I slept on the floor": Interview with Bratton.

280 "Thelma was there every day": Interview with Bratton.

281 "The hospice people say": Interview with Bratton.

282 Perhaps her best anecdote: Interview with Bratton.

Index

lege players, 110, 114–15; relationship between Rozelle and, 164; and Rozelle's retirement, 267; and sale of 49ers to Eddie DeBartolos, 226–28; steals Raiders from Wayne Valley, 224–25; and USFL antitrust lawsuit against NFL, 238–43
Davis, Ernie, 163
DeBartolo, Eddie Jr., 226–28
DeBartolo, Eddie Sr., 226
deep-sea fishing, 261
De Long, Myron: attends Compton Junior College, 17–19; on confidant of Rozelle, 7; enlists in navy, 13; on growing up in Lynwood, California, 8–10; interview with, 5; on Jane Coupe, 258; leaves University of San Francisco, 29; on life following military service, 16; moves to University of San Francisco, 19–20, 21; on playing hearts, 27; on preparation of Rozelle to become commissioner, 42; promotes Qantas Airlines, 35; on promoting USF, 24; on Rozelle's election as NFL commissioner, 50
Depression, 10–12
Dianabol, 216–17, 218
DiGiovanni, John William, 198
District of Columbia Stadium, 163
Dixon, Dave, 144–45, 147, 234–35
Donlan, Jack, 190, 195
Dons, 22, 24–26, 28–29
Dooley, Vince, 235
Dotson, Al, 108
drugs, 163–64, 210–21
drug testing, 212–14, 220–21
Duncan, J. Walter, 235
Duncan, Mark, 39, 59, 153

Eagles, 177
Ehrhart, Steve, 235
Elkjer, Thelma: as constant for Anne Marie Bratton, 258–59; and final days of Rozelle, 279–81; fish trophy and, 175; responsibilities of, 160–61; and retirement of Rozelle, 275–76; Rozelle hires, 58–59

Farr, Mel, 141–42

Feinsinger, Nate, 185
50-50-50 plan, 130–31
Filchock, Frank, 66–67
film rights, for NFL, 207–9
Finks, Jim, 275–76
Finney, Peter, 100
fishing, 261
Fiske, Bob, 272–73
Fleisher, Larry, 178–79
Flowers, Charlie, 100, 104
Forbes, Gordon, 235
Ford, William Sr., 78
Fordham University, 24–25
49ers: AFL-NFL merger and, 134–35; sale of, to Eddie DeBartolos, 225–28
Foss, Joe, 116, 117–18
freedom issues, in standard player contracts, 182–84
Fulton County Stadium, 116–17
Fusia, Vic, 108

Gabriel, Roman, 132
Gallagher, Jack, 118, 119
gambling: during military service, 15; as part of American culture, 63–64; Rozelle takes action against, 67–80; rumors surrounding Carroll Rosenbloom and, 168; scandal regarding, 65–66; as threat to NFL, 64–65
Gardoqui, 14–15
Garvey, Ed, 177, 182, 184, 185, 188–93
Gehrke, Fred, 39
Generals, Donald Trump buys, 236–37
Giants: AFL-NFL merger and, 134–35; coach for, 203–6; court battle between Chargers and, 100; and creation of AFL, 90–91; gambling scandal involving, 65–67; 1958 championship game between Colts and, 56, 67, 168; owners' feud over, 203–4; Pete Gogolak signed to, 121–24; Tim Mara buys, 203
Gibbons, Harold, 179
Gifford, Frank: on criticism of Rozelle following Kennedy assassination, 81, 86; as friend of Rozelle, 260; on Rozelle as negotiator, 206; on Rozelle-Davis feud, 223

for NFL under Bell, 57; for NFL under Rozelle, 57–58; and plan for sale of television rights, 60–61; for Rams, 17; Rozelle works in, 34–35. *See also* journalism

Pyle, C. C., 90–91

Qantas Airlines, 35

Radovich, William, 182
Raiders: Al Davis as coach of, 120; Al Davis moves, to Los Angeles Coliseum, 229–33; Al Davis steals, from Wayne Valley, 224–25; joins AFL, 97; realignment and, 155–56
Rainwater, Richard, 269, 270
Rams: Carroll Rosenbloom swaps Colts for, 165; corporate structure of, 30–31; helmets of, 39–40; move to Los Angeles, 16–17; Robert Irsay buys, 228–29; Rozelle as general manager of, 36–37, 40–41, 95; Rozelle hired by, 29–30; Rozelle resigns from, 33; Rozelle's hires to, 38–39; team picture for, 32–33
realignment, 154–61
recruitment. *See* college players
Redskins, 45, 54–55, 162–63
Reed, Wallace, 109, 110
Reeves, Dan: advice of, regarding New York, 51; and election of NFL commissioner, 48, 50; learning under, 30; moves Rams to California, 16; as Rams owner, 31; as Rams' spokesman, 95; Rozelle meets, 17; tensions between Ed Pauley and, 36, 37
Reinsch, Leonard, 116–17
retirement, of Pete Rozelle, 257, 266–68, 271, 273–76
Rickey, Branch, 5
Ridge, Houston, 215, 218
Robinson, John, 120
Rockets, 30
Rodgers, Don, 210–11
Rooney, Art, 49, 158–59
Rooney, Dan, 244, 270
Rose, Bert, 38, 58, 106–7
Rosenbloom, Carroll: AFL-NFL merger and, 123–24; Al Davis and, 228; and

election of NFL commissioner, 46–48, 49; on expansion into Dallas, 55; gambling rumors surrounding, 67; on Kapp lawsuit, 187; leads coup against Rozelle, 165, 168–76; mind and personality of, 165–68; Pete Rozelle on, 162; realignment and, 160; on saving of NFL, 162; on voting for Rozelle, 43
Rosenthal, Harold, 25, 116
Ross, George, 228
Rothman, Frank, 240, 242, 243–45, 248–53
Roy, Alvin, 218
Rozelle, Anne Marie. *See* Bratton, Anne Marie Rozelle
Rozelle, Carrie Cooke, 262–66, 267, 275, 280
Rozelle, Dick, 11
Rozelle, Hazel Healey, 11
Rozelle, Jane Coupe, 257–58, 259
Rozelle, Pete: competitiveness of, 9–10, 27, 88–89; at Compton Junior College, 16–19; death of, 282; early years of, 8–13; failing health of, 276–81; as father, 282–83; impact of, 1–2, 6; military service of, 14–15; retirement of, 257, 266–68, 271, 273–76; at University of San Francisco, 19–27; as visionary, 60–61
Rozelle, Ray: on Depression, 11–12; influence of, on Pete Rozelle, 10–11; on Rozelle returning to Rams, 37; on Rozelle's enlistment in navy, 14; on Rozelle's sabbatical during high school, 13
Rozelle Rule, 168, 183–85, 187, 191
Ruby, Jack, 84

sabbatical, during high school, 12–13
Sabol, Blair, 211–12, 254, 259, 261–62
Sabol, Ed, 207–8, 209, 260–61
Sabol, Steve, 202, 208–9
Saints, 148
Salinger, Pierre, 61, 83–84
Sarnoff, Robert, 113
Sauer, George Jr., 112
Schliebaum, Bill, 8
Schmidt, Joe, 77
Schramka, Paul, 18–19

Other works by Jerry Izenberg

Through My Eyes: A Sports Writer's 58-Year Journey

No Medals for Trying: A Week in the Life of a Pro Football Team

New York Giants: Seventy-Five Years

The Jerry Izenberg Collection

How Many Miles to Camelot? The All-American Sport Myth

The Rivals

The Greatest Game Ever Played

Great Latin Sports Figures: The Proud People

Championship: The Complete NFL *Title Story*